THE LOEB CLASSICAL LIBRARY

FOUNDED BY JAMES LOEB

EDITED BY

G. P. GOOLD

HORACE

ODES AND EPODES

LCL 33

297 (XIII.69)
CICERO TO SERVILIUS ISAURICUS

Rome, 46–44

From Cicero to his colleague[1] P. Servilius best greetings.

C. Curtius Mithres is, as you know, the freedman of my very good friend Postumus, but he pays as much respect and attention to me as to his own ex-master. At Ephesus, whenever I was there, I stayed in his house as though it was my home, and many incidents arose to give me proof of his good will and loyalty to me. If I or someone close to me want anything done in Asia I am in the habit of writing to Mithres and of using his faithful service, and even his house and purse, as though they were my own.

I have told you this at some length to let you understand that I am not writing conventionally or from a self-regarding motive, but on behalf of a really intimate personal connection. Accordingly may I request you, as a compliment to me, to accommodate Mithres in the dispute he has on hand with a certain citizen of Colophon concerning a rural property, and in all other matters, so far as your conscience will permit and so far as you conveniently can—though from my knowledge of him he has too much sense of propriety to be burdensome to you in any respect. If my recommendation and his own worth win him your good opinion, he will feel that he has gained every purpose. So I do particularly ask you to take him under your wing and include him in your circle.

I shall give my most careful and devoted attention to anything that I think you would like or that appears to concern you.

298 (XIII.70)

Scr. Romae an. 46–44

M. CICERO P. SERVILIO COLLEGAE S. P.

Quia non est obscura tua in me benevolentia, sic fit ut multi per me tibi velint commendari. ego autem tribuo nonnumquam in vulgus, sed plerumque necessariis, ut[1] hoc tempore. nam cum T. Ampio Balbo mihi summa familiaritas necessitudoque est. eius libertum, T. Ampium Menandrum, hominem frugi et modestum et patrono et nobis vehementer probatum, tibi commendo maiorem in modum. vehementer mihi gratum feceris si, quibuscumque rebus sine tua molestia poteris, ei commodaris. quod ut facias te vehementer etiam atque etiam rogo.

299 (XIII.71)

Scr. Romae an. 46–44

M. CICERO S. D. P. SERVILIO COLLEGAE

Multos tibi commendem necesse est, quoniam omnibus nota nostra necessitudo est tuaque erga me benevolentia. sed tamen, etsi omnium causa quos commendo velle debeo, tamen cum omnibus non eadem mihi causa est.

T. Agusius et comes meus fuit illo miserrimo tempore et omnium itinerum, navigationum, laborum, periculo-

---

[1] in

298 (XIII.70)
CICERO TO SERVILIUS ISAURICUS

Rome, 46–44

From M. Cicero to his colleague P. Servilius best greetings.

Your good will towards me is no secret, and so it happens that many persons want to be recommended to you by me. Sometimes I comply without much discrimination, but mostly for my friends, as in the present instance; for with T. Ampius Balbus I have the closest friendship and connection. His freedman, T. Ampius Menander, is a worthy, modest person, of whom both his former master and I have an excellent opinion. I specially recommend him to you. You will particularly oblige me if you will accommodate him as and when you can without trouble to yourself; and I beg you so to do as a special favour.

299 (XIII.71)
CICERO TO SERVILIUS ISAURICUS

Rome, 46–44

From M. Cicero to his colleague P. Servilius best greetings.

I cannot help recommending a good many people to you, since our friendship and the good will you have for me is common knowledge. Still, though I am bound to wish well to all those I recommend, they do not all have the same claim on me.

T. Agusius was my companion in my time of tribulation. He shared all my journeys by land and water, all my

43

rum meorum socius; neque hoc tempore discessisset a me nisi ego ei permisissem. qua re sic tibi eum commendo ut unum de meis domesticis et maxime necessariis. pergratum mihi feceris si eum ita tractaris ut intellegat hanc commendationem sibi magno usu atque adiumento fuisse.

300 (XIII.72)

Scr. Romae an. 46–44

M. CICERO P. SERVILIO COLLEGAE S.

1   Caerelliae, necessariae meae, rem, nomina, possessiones Asiaticas commendavi tibi praesens in hortis tuis quam potui diligentissime, tuque mihi pro tua consuetudine proque tuis in me perpetuis maximisque officiis omnia te facturum liberalissime recepisti. meminisse te id spero; scio enim solere. sed tamen Caerelliae procuratores scripserunt te propter magnitudinem provinciae multitudinemque negotiorum etiam atque etiam esse commonefaciendum.

2   Peto igitur ut memineris te omnia quae tua fides pateretur mihi cumulate recepisse. equidem existimo habere te magnam facultatem (sed hoc tui est consili et iudici) ex eo senatus consulto quod in heredes C. Vennoni factum est Caerelliae commodandi. id senatus consultum tu interpretabere pro tua sapientia; scio enim eius ordinis auctoritatem semper apud te magni fuisse. quod reliquum est, sic

fatigues and dangers. He would not have left my side now, if I had not given him leave. Accordingly I recommend him to you as a member of my domestic circle with whom I have the most intimate connection. You will oblige me very much indeed if you treat him so as to let him understand that this recommendation has been to his no small help and advantage.

300 (XIII.72)
CICERO TO SERVILIUS ISAURICUS

Rome, 46–44

From M. Cicero to his colleague P. Servilius greetings.

I recommended the financial interests of my friend Caerellia—her investments and property in Asia—to you when we were together at your place in the suburbs, as warmly as I was able; and you, conformably to your habit and the constant flow of your signal services to me, undertook most handsomely to do all I asked. I expect you ro member—I know you rarely forget. However, Caerellia's agents write that, because of the size of your province and the quantity of business, you should be frequently reminded.

May I request you therefore to bear in mind the ample undertaking you gave me to do all that your conscience would permit? I believe (but it is for you to consider and judge) that you have a great opportunity to accommodate Caerellia, arising out of the Senate's decree in respect of C. Vennonius' heirs. You will interpret that decree in the light of your own wisdom—I know you have always held the au-

velim existimes, quibuscumque rebus Caerelliae benigne feceris, mihi te gratissimum esse facturum.

301 (XIII.30)

Scr. Romae an. 46

CICERO ACILIO PRO COS.[1] S.

1   L. Manlius est Sosis. is fuit Catinensis, sed est una cum reliquis Neapolitanis civis Romanus factus decurioque Neapoli; erat enim adscriptus in id municipium ante civitatem sociis et Latinis datam. eius frater Catinae nuper mortuus est. nullam omnino arbitramur de ea hereditate controversiam eum habiturum, et est hodie in bonis. sed quoniam habet praeterea negotia vetera in Sicilia sua, et hanc hereditatem fraternam et omnia eius tibi commendo, in primisque ipsum, virum optimum mihique familiarissimum, iis studiis litterarum doctrinaeque praeditum[2] quibus ego maxime delector.

2   Peto igitur abs te ut eum, sive aderit sive non venerit in Siciliam, in meis intimis maximeque necessariis scias esse itaque tractes ut intellegat meam sibi commendationem magno adiumento fuisse.

   [1] proconsuli *(SB, et itidem in sequentibus epp.)*
   [2] deditum *Lamb*

thority of the House in high regard. For the rest, please take it that any kindness you may do Caerellia will greatly oblige me.

301 (XIII.30)
CICERO TO ACILIUS

Rome, 46

From Cicero to Acilius, Proconsul,[1] greetings.

L. Manlius Sosis was formerly a citizen of Catina, but became a Roman citizen along with the rest of the Neapolitan community and a town councillor at Naples, having been enrolled as a citizen of that municipality before the franchise was granted to the allies and the Latins.[2] His brother recently died at Catina. We do not expect any dispute to arise as to his title to the estate, and he is in possession of it at the present time. However, since he also has some old affairs of business in his part of Sicily, I beg to recommend to your notice this matter of his brother's estate and all other concerns of his, above all the man himself. He is an excellent person, a familiar friend of mine, conversant with the literary and scholarly pursuits in which I chiefly delight.

Let me then ask you (whether or not he goes to Sicily) to be aware that he is one of my closest and most intimate friends, and to let him understand by the way you treat him that my recommendation has been of substantial assistance to him.

[1] In Sicily.
[2] In 90.

302 (XIII.31)

Scr. Romae an. 46

CICERO ACILIO PRO COS. S.

1   C. Flavio, honesto et ornato equite Romano, utor valde familiariter; fuit enim generi mei, C. Pisonis, pernecessarius meque diligentissime observant et ipse et L. Flavius, frater eius. quapropter velim honoris mei causa, quibus rebus honeste et pro tua dignitate poteris, quam honorificentissime et quam liberalissime C. Flavium tractes. id
2   mihi sic erit gratum ut gratius esse nihil possit. sed praeterea tibi adfirmo (neque id ambitione adductus facio sed cum familiaritate et necessitudine tum etiam veritate) te ex C. Flavi officio et observantia et praeterea splendore atque inter suos gratia magnam voluptatem esse capturum.

Vale.

303 (XIII.32)

Scr. Romae an. 46

CICERO ACILIO PRO COS. S.

1   In Halaesina[1] civitate tam lauta tamque nobili coniunctissimos habeo et hospitio et familiaritate M. et C. Clodios[2] Archagathum et Philonem. sed vereor ne, quia compluris tibi praecipue commendo, exaequare videar ambitione

---

[1] hales- *(R. Klotz)*   [2] clodius MV: -um DH *(Man.)*

302 (XIII.31)
CICERO TO ACILIUS

Rome, 46

From Cicero to Acilius, Proconsul, greetings.

I am on very familiar terms with C. Flavius, a respected and distinguished Roman Knight. He was a great friend of my son-in-law, C. Piso, and both he and his brother L. Flavius are sedulous in their attentions to me. I hope therefore that as a compliment to me you will treat C. Flavius in the most handsome and flattering fashion in all respects consistent with your honour and dignity. Nothing could oblige me more. But furthermore I assure you (and I do so, not from any interested motive, but out of friendship and attachment, also because it is the truth) that C. Flavius' sense of obligation and attentive courtesy, together with his eminence and the influence he enjoys among men of his own rank, will be a source of much gratification to yourself.

Good-bye.

303 (XIII.32)
CICERO TO ACILIUS

Rome, 46

From Cicero to Acilius, Proconsul, greetings.

In the rich and famous community of Halaesa I have the closest ties of hospitality and friendship with two persons, M. Clodius Archagathus and C. Clodius Philo. But I feel some uneasiness in recommending so many people to you in special terms in case I may appear to be placing all

quadam commendationes meas; quamquam a te quidem
cumulate satis fit et mihi et meis omnibus.

2   Sed velim sic existimes, hanc familiam et hos mihi
maxime esse coniunctos vetustate, officiis, benevolentia.
quam ob rem peto a te in maiorem modum ut iis omnibus
in rebus, quantum tua fides dignitasque patietur, commodes. id si feceris, erit mihi vehementissime gratum.

304 (XIII.33)

Scr. Romae an. 46

‹CICERO ACILIO PRO COS. S.›

Cn. Otacilio Nasone utor familiarissime, ita prorsus ut
illius ordinis nullo familiarius; nam et humanitate eius et
probitate in consuetudine cottidiana magno opere delector. nihil iam opus est exspectare te quibus eum verbis tibi
commendem quo sic utar ut scripsi. habet is in provincia
tua negotia quae procurant liberti, Hilarus, Antigonus,
Demostratus; quos tibi negotiaque omnia Nasonis non se-
cus commendo ac si mea essent. gratissimum mihi feceris
si intellexero hanc commendationem magnum apud te
pondus habuisse.

Vale.

my recommendations on a level from a self-regarding motive—not but that your response is more than gratifying both to myself and to all connected with me.

Anyhow, please take it that the family to which I refer, and these members of it especially, are bound to me by length of acquaintance, good offices, and good will. Therefore I particularly ask you to accommodate them in all respects, so far as your conscience and dignity will allow. I shall be very sincerely beholden if you do.

304 (XIII.33)
CICERO TO ACILIUS

Rome, 46

From Cicero to Acilius, Proconsul, greetings.

I am on a very familiar footing with Cn. Otacilius Naso, as familiar in fact as with any gentleman of his rank. His attractive manners and worth of character make my daily contacts with him very agreeable. You will not need to wait and see what words I use to recommend one with whom I am on such terms. He has affairs of business in your province, to which his freedmen Hilarus, Antigonus, and Demostratus are attending. I recommend to you these persons and all Naso's affairs exactly as though they were my own. You will oblige me deeply if I find that this recommendation has carried much weight with you.

Good-bye.

305 (XIII.34)

Scr. Romae an. 46

‹CICERO ACILIO PRO COS. S.›

Avitum mihi hospitium est cum Lysone, Lysonis filio, Lilybitano,[1] valdeque ab eo observor cognovique dignum et patre et avo; est enim nobilissima familia. quapropter commendo tibi maiorem in modum rem domumque eius magnoque opere abs te peto cures ut is intellegat meam commendationem maximo sibi apud te et adiumento et ornamento fuisse.

306 (XIII.35)

Scr. Romae an. 46

CICERO ACILIO PRO COS. S.

1   C. Avian‹i›us Philoxenus antiquus est hospes meus et praeter hospitium valde etiam familiaris. quem Caesar meo beneficio in Novocomensis rettulit; nomen autem Aviani secutus est quod homine nullo plus est usus quam Flacco Avianio, meo, quem ad modum te scire arbitror, familiarissimo. quae ego omnia collegi ut intellegeres non vulgarem esse commendationem hanc meam.

[1] -toni *(Vict.)*

---

[1] Nothing to do with Lyso of Patrae.
[1] Caesar had enrolled five hundred distinguished Greeks in

305 (XIII.34)
CICERO TO ACILIUS

Rome, 46

From Cicero to Acilius, Proconsul, greetings.

My relations of hospitality with Lyso,[1] son of Lyso, of Lilybaeum, go back to his grandfather. He is most attentive to me, and I find him worthy of his grandfather and father—it is a very distinguished family. Therefore I particularly recommend his property and domestic circle to your notice, and earnestly request you to make him realize that my recommendation has tended to his great honour and advantage in your eyes.

306 (XIII.35)
CICERO TO ACILIUS

Rome, 46

From Cicero to Acilius, Proconsul, greetings.

C. Avianius Philoxenus is an old host of mine and, apart from relations of hospitality, my very good friend. Caesar through my good offices entered him as a citizen of Novum Comum.[1] He took the name of Avianius because of his especially close relations with Flaccus Avianius, a very good friend of mine, as I think you know. I have put all these facts together to let you understand that this recommendation of mine is outside the ordinary.

his colony of Novum Comum under a law passed during his Consulship, though they did not settle there. Their Roman citizenship was now, of course, established.

53

2   Peto igitur abs te ut omnibus rebus, quod sine molestia
tua facere possis, ei commodes habeasque in numero tuorum perficiasque ut intellegat has litteras meas magno sibi
usui fuisse. erit id mihi maiorem in modum gratum.

307 (XIII.36)

Scr. Romae post m. Sept. an. 46

< CICERO ACILIO PRO COS. S. >

1   Cum Demetrio Mega mihi vetus hospitium est, familiaritas autem tanta quanta cum Siculo nullo. ei Dolabella
rogatu meo civitatem a Caesare impetravit, qua in re ego
interfui; itaque nunc P. Cornelius vocatur. cumque propter
quosdam sordidos homines, qui Caesaris beneficia ven-
debant, tabulam in qua nomina civitate donatorum incisa
essent revelli iussisset, eidem Dolabellae me audiente
Caesar dixit nihil esse quod de Mega vereretur; beneficium suum in eo manere.

2   Hoc te scire volui ut eum in civium Romanorum numero haberes, ceterisque in rebus tibi eum ita commendo ut
maiore studio neminem commendarim. gratissimum mihi
feceris si eum ita tractaris ut intellegat meam commendationem magno sibi ornamento fuisse.

May I therefore request you to accommodate him in all respects, so far as you can do so without trouble to yourself, and to admit him to your circle? Let him understand that this letter of mine has been very useful to him. I shall be greatly beholden.

307 (XIII.36)
CICERO TO ACILIUS

Rome, after September 46

From Cicero to Acilius, Proconsul, greetings.

I have old ties of hospitality with Demetrius Megas, and no native of Sicily is on such familiar terms with me. At my request Dolabella obtained the franchise for him from Caesar—I was involved. So now his name is P. Cornelius. And when Caesar, on account of certain mercenary fellows who were selling his favours, gave orders for the removal of the plaque on which the names of grantees of citizenship had been engraved, he told the same Dolabella in my presence that he need not worry about Megas. In his case the favour held good.

I wanted you to know this, so that you should regard him as a Roman citizen, and in all other respects I recommend him as warmly as I have ever recommended anyone. I shall be very much beholden to you if you deal with him so as to let him understand that my recommendation has been a great asset to him.

308 (XIII.37)

Scr. Romae an. 46

⟨CICERO ACILIO PRO COS. S.⟩

Hippiam, Philoxeni filium, Calactinum, hospitem et necessarium meum, tibi commendo in maiorem modum. eius bona, quem ad modum ad me delata res est, publice possidentur alieno nomine contra leges Calactinorum. id si ita est, etiam sine mea commendatione ab aequitate tua res ipsa impetrare debet ut ei subvenias. quoquo modo autem se res habet, peto a te ut honoris mei causa eum expedias, tantumque ei commodes et in hac re et in ceteris quantum tua fides dignitasque patietur. id mihi vehementer gratum erit.

309 (XIII.38)

Scr. Romae an. 46

⟨CICERO ACILIO PRO COS. S.⟩

L. Bruttius, eques Romanus, adulescens omnibus rebus ornatus, in meis familiarissimis ⟨est⟩ meque observat diligentissime; cuius cum patre magna mihi fuit amicitia iam inde a quaestura mea Siciliensi. omnino nunc ipse Bruttius Romae mecum est. sed tamen domum eius et rem familiarem et procuratores tibi sic commendo ut maiore studio commendare non possim. gratissimum mihi feceris si curaris ut intellegat Bruttius, id quod ei recepi, hanc meam commendationem sibi magno adiumento fuisse.

308 (XIII.37)
CICERO TO ACILIUS

Rome, 46

From Cicero to Acilius, Proconsul, greetings.

Let me particularly recommend to you my host and friend Hippias, son of Philoxenus, of Calacte. As the matter has been represented to me, his property is being held by the state under a different name in violation of the laws of Calacte. If that is true, the nature of the case entitles him to your assistance as a just magistrate even without any recommendation of mine. But whatever the position, allow me to request you, as a compliment to me, to extricate him from his difficulty, and to accommodate him in this and other matters as far as your conscience and dignity will allow. I shall be truly beholden.

309 (XIII.38)
CICERO TO ACILIUS

Rome, 46

From Cicero to Acilius, Proconsul, greetings.

L. Bruttius, a young Roman Knight of quality in every sense of the word, is one of my most familiar friends and most sedulous in his attentions to me. I was a great friend of his father's from the time when I was Quaestor in Sicily. Bruttius himself is now with me in Rome, but I beg to recommend to you his domestic circle, property, and agents with all possible warmth. I shall be very much beholden if you will let Bruttius understand that my recommendation has been of great assistance to him, as I undertook that it would be.

310 (XIII.39)

Scr. Romae an. 46

<CICERO ACILIO PRO COS. S.>

Cum familia Titurnia necessitudo mihi intercedit vetus; ex qua reliquus est M. Titurnius Rufus, qui mihi omni diligentia atque officio est tuendus. est igitur in tua potestate ut ille in me satis sibi praesidi putet esse. quapropter eum tibi commendo in maiorem modum et abs te peto efficias ut is commendationem hanc intellegat sibi magno adiumento fuisse. erit mihi vehementer gratum.

311 (IX.13)

Scr. Romae c. Kal. Febr. an. 45

CICERO DOLABELLAE S.

1   C. Subernius Calenus et meus est familiaris et Leptae, nostri familiarissimi, pernecessarius. is, cum vitandi belli causa profectus esset in Hispaniam cum M. Varrone ante bellum et[1] in ea provincia esset in qua nemo nostrum post Afranium superatum bellum ullum fore putaret, incidit in ea ipsa mala quae summo studio vitaverat. oppressus est enim bello repentino, quod bellum commotum a Scapula ita postea confirmatum est a Pompeio ut nulla ratione ab

    [1] ut *(SB)*

310 (XIII.39)
CICERO TO ACILIUS

Rome, 46

From Cicero to Acilius, Proconsul, greetings.

There is an old connection between myself and the Titurnius family. Its only surviving representative is M. Titurnius Rufus, whom I am in duty bound to protect and assist to the best of my ability. It rests with you therefore to let him feel that he has in me a sufficiently powerful patron. Accordingly I recommend him to you warmly and request you to let him understand that this recommendation has been greatly to his advantage. I shall be truly beholden.

311 (IX.13)
CICERO TO DOLABELLA

Rome, ca. 1 February 45

From Cicero to Dolabella greetings.

C. Subernius of Cales is a friend of mine and very closely attached to my intimate friend Lepta. In order to escape the war he went to Spain with M. Varro before its outbreak, and was living in a province where, after Afranius' defeat, none of us supposed there would be any fighting; but, as luck would have it, he found himself in the very trouble which he had tried so hard to avoid. The war which suddenly flared up caught him unawares; started by Scapula, it later gained such momentum under Pompey[1] that he could not possibly extricate himself from this

---

[1] Cn. Pompeius the Younger.

2   illa miseria se eripere posset. eadem causa fere est M. Plani Heredis, qui est item Calenus, Leptae nostri familiarissimus.

Hosce igitur ambos tibi sic commendo ut maiore cura, studio, sollicitudine animi commendare non possim. volo ipsorum causa meque in eo vehementer et amicitia movet et humanitas. Lepta vero cum ita laboret ut eius fortunae videantur in discrimen venire, non possum ego non aut proxime atque ille aut etiam aeque laborare. quapropter, etsi saepe expertus sum quantum me amares, tamen sic velim tibi persuadeas, id me in hac re maxime iudicaturum.

3   Peto igitur a te, vel, si pateris, oro, ut homines miseros et Fortuna, quam vitare nemo potest, magis quam culpa calamitosos conserves incolumis velisque per te me hoc muneris cum ipsis amicis hominibus, cum municipio Caleno, quocum mihi magna necessitudo est, tum Leptae, quem omnibus antepono, dare.

4   Quod dicturus sum puto equidem non valde ad rem pertinere, sed tamen nihil obest dicere. res familiaris alteri eorum valde exigua est, alteri vix equestris. quapropter, quoniam iis Caesar vitam sua liberalitate concessit nec est quod iis praeterea magno opere possit adimi, reditum, si me tantum amas quantum certe amas, hominibus confice. in quo nihil est praeter viam longum;[2] quam idcirco non fugiunt ut et vivant cum suis et moriantur domi. quod ut enitare contendasque, vel potius ut perficias (posse enim te mihi persuasi), vehementer te etiam atque etiam rogo.

---

2 longam (*SB, qui etiam* longi *coni.*)

wretched environment. The case of M. Planius Heres, also of Cales and a close friend of Lepta's, is almost identical.

I recommend both these persons to you, and I could not do so with a greater measure of sincere concern and anxiety. I am interested for their own sake; friendship and humanity alike move me strongly on their behalf. But when Lepta is so profoundly concerned (his fortunes seem to be at stake), my concern must approach, or even equal, his. Therefore I should like you to persuade yourself that, often as I have experienced the warmth of your affection for me, I shall judge of it particularly in this affair.

Accordingly I request you, or beg you if you will allow me, to save these unhappy persons, whose calamities are due to Fortune, whom there is no evading, rather than to any fault of their own, and to make it your wish that through you, I may confer this favour not only upon the principals, friends of mine as they are, but upon the town of Cales, with which I have a close connection, and upon Lepta, who matters to me most of all.

What I am about to say is probably not very relevant to the matter at issue, but still it can do no harm to mention it. One of the two has very little money, the other hardly up to Knight's qualification. Since, then, Caesar has generously granted them their lives and there is nothing much else which can be taken from them, get them permission (if you love me as much as I am sure you do) to return to Italy. There is nothing in that which need take up much time, except the journey; and this they are ready to undertake in order to live with their families and die at home. Once again I earnestly ask you to try your utmost, or rather to *do* it, for I am satisfied that you have the power.

312 (XIII.52)

Scr. Romae post m. Apr. an. 46

CICERO REGI S.

A. Licinius Aristoteles Melitensis antiquissimus est hospes meus et praeterea coniunctus magno usu familiaritatis. haec cum ita sint, non dubito quin tibi satis commendatus sit; etenim ex multis cognosco meam commendationem plurimum apud te valere. hunc ego a Caesare liberavi; frequens enim fuerat nobiscum atque etiam diutius in causa est quam nos commoratus; quo melius te de eo existimaturum arbitror.

Fac igitur, mi Rex, ut intellegat has sibi litteras plurimum profuisse.

313 (XIII.49)

Scr. Romae an. incerto

CICERO CURIO PRO COS.

Q. Pompeius Sex. f. multis et veteribus causis necessitudinis mihi coniunctus est. is, cum antea meis commendationibus et rem et gratiam et auctoritatem suam tueri consuerit, nunc profecto te provinciam obtinente meis litteris adsequi debet ut nemini se intellegat commendatiorem umquam fuisse. quam ob rem a te maiorem in

---

[1] Presumably in an official position in Sicily. On his provenance see my Commentary.   [1] Nothing is known of Curius or his province or the person recommended.

312 (XIII.52)
CICERO TO REX

Rome, after April 46

From Cicero to Rex[1] greetings.

A. Licinius Aristoteles of Malta has a very old-established tie of hospitality with me, and is furthermore attached to me by much familiar personal contact. That being so, I don't doubt that he is sufficiently recommended to your favour. Indeed I am told on all hands that a recommendation from me counts for a great deal with you. I obtained his pardon from Caesar—he had been much with me, and actually stayed in the cause longer than I did, which I imagine will make you think all the better of him.

So make him understand, my dear Rex, that this letter has tended greatly to his advantage.

313 (XIII.49)
CICERO TO CURIUS

Rome, date uncertain

From Cicero to Curius,[1] Proconsul.

Many ties of long standing go to form my connection with Q. Pompeius, son of Sextus. He has been in the habit of protecting his financial interests, personal influence, and prestige by means of my recommendations; and now that you are in charge of the province, a letter from me should surely gain him enough to let him feel that he has never been better recommended to any governor. Therefore I particularly request you, bound as you are in virtue

modum peto ut, cum omnis meos aeque ac tuos observare
pro necessitudine nostra debeas, hunc in primis ita in tuam
fidem recipias ut ipse intellegat nullam rem sibi maiori
usui aut ornamento quam meam commendationem esse
potuisse.

Vale.

314 (XIII.2)

Scr. Romae an. incerto

CICERO MEMMIO S.

C. Avianio Evandro, qui habitat in tuo sacrario, et ipso
multum utor et patrono eius M. Aemilio familiarissime.
peto igitur a te in maiorem modum, quod sine tua molestia
fiat, ut ei de habitatione accommodes.[1] nam propter opera
instituta multa multorum subitum est ei remigrare[2] Kal.
Quint. impedior verecundia ne te pluribus verbis rogem;
neque tamen dubito quin, si tua nihil aut non multum in-
tersit, eo sis animo quo ego essem si quid tu me rogares.
mihi certe gratissimum feceris.

[1] commodes *Benedict*
[2] demig- *Corr.*

of our connection to pay as much regard to my friends as to your own, to take Pompeius under your especial patronage, so that he himself realizes that nothing could have been more to his advantage and distinction than my recommendation.

Good-bye.

314 (XIII.2)
CICERO TO MEMMIUS

Rome, year uncertain

From Cicero to Memmius[1] greetings.

C. Avianius Evander, who is residing in your family chapel, is a person with whom I have a good deal to do and I am on very friendly terms with his former master, M. Aemilius. May I therefore particularly request you to accommodate him in the matter of his residence as far as you can without inconveniencing yourself? It is rather sudden for him to move back on the Kalends of July, because he has a number of commissions on hand for various patrons. Modesty forbids me to ask you at much length, but I am sure that if the matter is of no consequence to you, or not much, you will feel as I should feel if you made any request of me. I shall certainly be most grateful.

---

[1] Possibly son of the recipient of Letter 63.

315 (XIII.3)

Scr. Romae an. incerto

CICERO MEMMIO S.

A. Fufium, unum ex meis intimis, observantissimum studiosissimumque nostri, eruditum hominem et summa humanitate tuaque amicitia dignissimum, velim ita tractes ut mihi coram recepisti. tam gratum mihi id erit quam quod gratissimum. ipsum praeterea summo officio et summa observantia tibi in perpetuum devinxeris.

316 (XIII.16)

Scr. Romae ex. an. 46 vel in. an. 45, ut vid.

CICERO CAESARI S.

1   P. Crassum ex omni nobilitate adulescentem dilexi plurimum et ex eo cum ab ineunte eius aetate bene speravissem, tum optime[1] existimare coepi [ex] iis[2] iudiciis quae de eo feceras[3] cognitis. eius libertum Apollonium iam tum equidem cum ille viveret et magni faciebam et probabam. erat enim et studiosus Crassi et ad eius optima studia vehe-
2   menter aptus; itaque ab eo admodum diligebatur. post mortem autem Crassi eo mihi etiam dignior visus est quem in fidem atque amicitiam meam reciperem quod eos a se observandos et colendos putabat quos ille dilexisset et quibus carus fuisset. itaque et ad me in Ciliciam venit mul-

---

[1] per me *(Man.)*   [2] ex hi(i)s *(Ern.)*
[3] feceram *(Madvig)*

315 (XIII.3)
CICERO TO MEMMIUS

Rome, date uncertain

From Cicero to Memmius greetings.

A. Fufius is one of my inner circle, most attentive and devoted to me. He is a learned, highly cultivated person, thoroughly worthy to be your friend. I hope you will treat him in accordance with the promise you made me orally. I shall take it most kindly. Furthermore you will permanently attach to yourself a very serviceable and punctilious gentleman.

316 (XIII.16)
CICERO TO CAESAR

Rome, December 46 or January 45 (?)

From Cicero to Caesar greetings.

Young P. Crassus was my favourite among the whole range of our aristocracy. From his earliest youth I had good hopes of him, but he rose really high in my estimation when I saw how well you thought of him. Even during his lifetime I had a great regard and liking for his freedman Apollonius. He was warmly attached to Crassus, and admirably fitted to join him in his liberal interests, so naturally Crassus was very fond of him. After Crassus' death I thought him all the worthier of admission to my patronage and friendship because he felt it proper to pay respect and attention to those whom Crassus had loved and who had loved him in return. Accordingly he joined me in Cilicia,

tisque in rebus mihi magno usui fuit et fides eius et prudentia et, ut opinor, tibi in Alexandrino bello, quantum
studio et fidelitate consequi potuit, non defuit.

3   Quod cum speraret te quoque ita existimare, in Hispaniam ad te maxime ille quidem suo consilio sed etiam me
auctore est profectus. cui ego commendationem non sum
pollicitus, non quin eam valituram apud te arbitrarer, sed
neque egere mihi commendatione videbatur, qui et in
bello tecum fuisset et propter memoriam Crassi de tuis
unus esset, et, si uti commendationibus vellet, etiam per
alios eum videbam id consequi posse; testimonium mei[4]
de eo iudici, quod et ipse magni aestimabat et ego apud te
valere eram expertus, ei libenter dedi.

4   Doctum igitur hominem cognovi et studiis optimis
deditum, idque a puero. nam domi meae cum Diodoto
Stoico, homine meo iudicio eruditissimo, multum a puero
fuit. nunc autem incensus studio rerum tuarum eas litteris
Graecis mandare cupiebat. posse arbitror; valet ingenio,
habet usum, iam pridem in eo genere studi litterarumque
versatur, satis facere immortalitati laudum tuarum mirabiliter cupit.

Habes opinionis meae testimonium, sed tu hoc facilius
multo pro tua singulari prudentia iudicabis. et tamen,
quod negaveram, commendo tibi eum. quicquid ei com-
modaveris, erit id mihi maiorem in modum gratum.

[4] meum *(C. Stephanus)*

where his loyalty and good sense proved very useful to me in many connections. And I believe that in the Alexandrian War such service as his zeal and fidelity could render you was not lacking.

Hoping that you are of the same opinion, he is leaving to join you in Spain, mainly on his own initiative, but not without encouragement from me. I did not promise him a recommendation, not that I did not think it would carry weight with you, but because a man who had seen military service at your side and whom Crassus' memory made one of your circle did not seem to me to need one. And if he did wish to make use of recommendations, I knew he could obtain them elsewhere. But I am glad to give him a testimonial of what I think of him, since he makes a point of it and my experience has shown me that you pay attention to such.

I know him to be a scholar, devoted to liberal studies from boyhood. For he was much in my house from an early age with Diodotus the Stoic, a most erudite person in my opinion. Now his imagination has been captured by your career, and he wants to write an account of it in Greek. I think he can do it. He has a strong natural talent cultivated by practice, and has for a long time been engaged in this type of literary work. To do justice to your immortal fame is his passionate ambition.

Well, there you have my considered testimony, but your own keen discernment will provide you with a much easier means of assessing the matter. And after all, I do recommend him to you, having said I should do no such thing. Any kindness you do him will particularly oblige me.

317 (XIII.15)

Scr. in Tusculano (?) m. Mai. vel Iun. an. 45 (?)
CICERO CAESARI IMP. S.

⟨P.⟩[1] Precilium tibi commendo unice, tui necessari, mei familiarissimi, viri optimi, filium. quem cum adulescentem ipsum propter eius modestiam, humanitatem, animum et amorem erga me singularem mirifice diligo tum patrem eius re doctus intellexi et didici mihi fuisse semper amicissimum. em hic ille[2] est de illis maxime qui irridere atque obiurgare me solitus est quod me non tecum, praesertim cum abs te honorificentissime invitarer, coniungerem.

ἀλλ' ἐμὸν οὔ ποτε θυμὸν ἐνὶ στήθεσσιν ἔπειθεν.

audiebam enim nostros proceres clamitantis

ἄλκιμος ἔσσ', ἵνα τίς σε καὶ ὀψιγόνων εὖ εἴπῃ.
ὣς φάτο, τὸν δ' ἄχεος νεφέλη ἐκάλυψε μέλαινα.

Sed tamen idem me consolatur etiam. hominem ⟨enim⟩[3] perustum etiamnum gloria volunt incendere atque ita loquuntur:

μὴ μὰν ἀσπουδί γε καὶ ἀκλειῶς ἀπολοίμην,
ἀλλὰ μέγα ῥέξας τι καὶ ἐσσομένοισι πυθέσθαι.

sed me minus iam movent, ut vides. itaque ab Homeri magniloquentia confero me ad vera praecepta Εὐριπίδου:

[1] *(Kleyn*)*
[2] hic *vel* ille *delendum coni.* SB
[3] *(SB)*

317 (XIII.15)
CICERO TO CAESAR

Tusculum (?), May or June 45 (?)

From Cicero to Caesar, Imperator, greetings.

I recommend P. Precilius to you with peculiar warmth, the son of a very worthy gentleman who is connected with you and intimate with me. I have an extraordinary regard for the young man himself because of his modesty, amiability, and notably affectionate disposition towards me; and experience has taught me to appreciate his father's unfaltering good will. For, mark you, he is the one man above all others who used to jeer and gird at me because I would not join you despite your most flattering invitations. But 'the heart within my breast he ne'er did sway.'[1] For I used to hear our men of light and leading clamouring

Be bold, and earn the praise of men unborn.[2]
He spake; but grief's dark mist the other cloaked.[3]

But he comforts me too. Burned child as I am, they are still trying to kindle the fire of ambition in my heart:

No sluggard's fate, ingloriously to die,
But daring that which men to be shall learn.[4]

That is the way they talk. But, as you see, I am not so responsive nowadays. So I turn from Homer's magniloquence to the sound precepts of Euripides:

[1] *Odyssey* 7.258 = 9.33 (Calypso and Circe could not persuade Ulysses).   [2] *Odyssey* 1.302 (Athene to Telemachus).
[3] *Odyssey* 24.315 (of Laertes).
[4] *Iliad* 22.304 f. (Hector is speaking).

71

μισῶ σοφιστήν, ὅστις οὐχ αὑτῷ σοφός.

quem versum senex Precilius laudat egregie et ait posse eundem et 'ἅμα πρόσσω καὶ ὀπίσσω' videre et tamen nihilo minus

αἰὲν ἀριστεύειν καὶ ὑπείροχον ἔμμεναι ἄλλων.

Sed ut redeam ad id unde coepi, vehementer mihi gratum feceris si hunc adulescentem humanitate tua, quae est singularis, comprehenderis et ad id quod ipsorum Preciliorum causa te velle arbitror addideris cumulum commendationis meae. genere novo sum litterarum ad te usus ut intellegeres non vulgarem esse commendationem.

318 (XIII.4)

Scr. Romae fort. inter m. Nov. an. 46 et Sept. an. 45

M. CICERO S. D. Q. VALERIO Q. F. ORCAE LEGATO PRO PR.

1   Cum municipibus Volaterranis mihi summa necessitudo est. magno enim meo beneficio adfecti cumulatissime mihi gratiam rettulerunt; nam nec in honoribus meis nec laboribus umquam defuerunt. cum quibus si mihi nulla causa intercederet, tamen, quod te vehementissime diligo

---

5 Cf. Letter 27.2.

6 *Iliad* 1.343 = *Odyssey* 24.452.

7 *Iliad* 6.208 = 11.784. This had been Cicero's watchword in his early days; cf. *Letters to Quintus* 25 (III.5).4.

8 See my Commentary suggesting that the underlying purpose of this unconventional epistle of recommendation was to plead

Who for himself's not wise, his wisdom scorn,[5]

a verse which old Precilius extols in fine style, and says that a man may look 'both to front and rear,'[6] and yet at the same time 'e'er be the first, o'ertopping all the rest.'[7]

But to go back to my starting point: I shall be truly grateful if you will take the young fellow under your wing with the kindness which is so conspicuous a trait of yours, and add my recommendation to crown the good will which I suppose you to bear the Precilii for their own sakes. I have written you an unconventional sort of letter to let you understand that this is no ordinary recommendation.[8]

318 (XIII.4)

CICERO TO VALERIUS ORCA

Rome, between November 46 and September 45 (?)

M. Cicero to Q. Valerius Orca, son of Quintus, Legate *pro praetore*, greetings.[1]

I have a very close connection with the people of Volaterrae. Having received an important favour at my hands, they repaid me most amply, never stinting their support either in my advancements or in my tribulations. But even if there was nothing between me and them, I should advise and urge you out of my warm affection for you and my con-

---

not guilty of clandestine anti-Caesarian activity in rebuttal of Q. Cicero junior's calumnies. The latter was at Caesar's headquarters in Spain, busy maligning his uncle.

[1] Cf. Letter 57. Orca was now apparently in charge of the assignment of land in Etruria to Caesar's veterans.

quodque me a te plurimi fieri sentio, et monerem te et hortarer ut eorum fortunis consuleres, praesertim cum prope praecipuam causam haberent ad ius obtinendum, primum quod Sullani temporis acerbitatem deorum immortalium benignitate subterfugerunt, deinde quod summo studio
2 populi Romani a me in consulatu meo defensi sunt. cum ⟨enim⟩[1] tribuni pl. legem iniquissimam de eorum agris promulgavissent, facile senatui populoque Romano persuasi ut eos civis quibus Fortuna pepercisset, salvos esse vellent. hanc actionem meam C. Caesar primo suo consulatu lege agraria comprobavit agrumque Volaterranum et oppidum omni periculo in perpetuum liberavit, ut mihi dubium non sit quin is qui novas necessitudines adiungat vetera sua beneficia conservari velit. quam ob rem est tuae prudentiae aut sequi eius auctoritatem cuius sectam atque imperium summa cum tua dignitate secutus es aut certe illi integram omnem causam reservare. illud vero dubitare non debes quin tam grave, tam firmum, tam honestum municipium tibi tuo summo beneficio in perpetuum obligari velis.
3 Sed haec quae supra scripta sunt eo spectant ut te horter et suadeam. reliqua sunt quae pertinent ad rogandum, ut non solum tua causa tibi consilium me dare putes sed etiam quod mihi opus sit me a te petere et rogare. gratissimum igitur mihi feceris si Volaterranos omnibus rebus

[1] *(Man.)*

---

[2] Sulla had passed a law depriving the Volaterrans of Roman citizenship and confiscating their land in punishment for their long resistance to his army. But the law seems to have remained

sciousness of your high regard for me to consider their
financial welfare—especially as they have an almost pecu-
liarly strong claim to maintain their rights. By the grace
of the Immortal Gods they escaped the harshness of the
Sullan period;[2] and they were defended by me during my
Consulship with the enthusiastic support of the People of
Rome. When the Tribunes of the Plebs brought forward a
highly iniquitous bill concerning their lands, I had no difficulty in persuading the Senate and People of Rome to decree the preservation of Roman citizens to whom Fortune
had been merciful. During his first Consulship C. Caesar
approved my action in his agrarian bill, and gave the town
and district of Volaterrae permanent security from any
such threat. So I cannot doubt, when I see him acquiring
new connections, that he wishes his old benefactions to
stand. Accordingly your good sense will instruct you either
to take your cue from the leader in whose wake and under
whose command you have gained such high preferment,
or at least to leave the whole case open for him to determine. Moreover, you ought surely to feel no doubt about
the desirability of placing so important, well-established,
and respectable a community under a lasting obligation to
yourself by conferring a signal favour.

What I have written so far is in the nature of exhortation
and counsel. What follows is petitionary. I would not have
you think that I am merely advising you in your own interests, and not also asking you for a favour which I personally
need. Well then, I shall be greatly beholden if you decide
to preserve the people of Volaterrae in complete safety

inoperative as to the first and only partially operative as to the
second.

integros incolumisque esse volueris. eorum ego domicilia, sedes, rem, fortunas, quae et a dis immortalibus et a praestantissimis in nostra re publica civibus summo senatus populique Romani studio conservatae sunt, tuae fidei, iustitiae, bonitatique commendo.

4   Si pro meis pristinis opibus facultatem mihi res hoc tempore daret ut ita defendere possem Volaterranos quem ad modum consuevi tueri meos, nullum officium, nullum denique certamen, in quo illis prodesse possem, praetermitterem. sed quoniam apud te nihilo minus hoc tempore valere me confido quam valuerim semper apud ⟨bonos⟩[2] omnis, pro nostra summa necessitudine parique inter nos et mutua benevolentia abs te peto ut ita de Volaterranis mereare ut existiment eum quasi divino consilio isti negotio praepositum esse apud quem unum nos eorum perpetui defensores plurimum valere possemus.

319 (XIII.5)

Scr. Romae aliquanto post ep. superiorem, ut vid.

CICERO S. D. Q. VALERIO LEG. PRO PR.

1   Non moleste fero eam necessitudinem quae mihi tecum est notam esse quam plurimis, neque tamen ob eam causam (quod tu optime existimare potes) te impedi⟨i⟩ quo minus susceptum negotium pro tua fide et diligentia

[2] *(Or.)*

and integrity. To your honour, justice, and benevolence I commend their dwellings, abodes, property, and fortunes, which the Immortal Gods and the leading men in our commonwealth have maintained intact with the wholehearted approbation of the Senate and People of Rome.

If the conditions of today permitted me to defend the people of Volaterrae as it has been my habit to support those with whom I have connections, conformably to the resources which used to be at my command, I should not fail to engage in every service, every contest indeed, in which I might possibly be of use to them. But I am confident that with yourself my voice is at the present time no less powerful than it always was with all honest men. Therefore let me request you, in the name of the close connection and reciprocally equal good will that exists between us, to deserve well of the people of Volaterrae. Let them think that a divine providence has placed this business in charge of the man with whom of all others I, their constant champion, might exercise most influence.

319 (XIII.5)
CICERO TO VALERIUS ORCA

Rome, some time after the foregoing (?)

From Cicero to Q. Valerius Orca, Legate *pro praetore*, greetings.

That my friendship with you should be as widely known as possible is not disagreeable to me. At the same time I have not on that account (as you are in the best possible position to judge) stood in the way of your carrying out the task you have undertaken loyally and conscientiously in

ex voluntate Caesaris, qui tibi rem magnam difficilemque commisit, gerere possis. nam cum multi a me petant multa, quod de tua erga me voluntate non dubitent, non committo ut ambitione mea conturbem officium tuum.

2   C. Curtio ab ineunte aetate familiarissime sum usus. eius et Sullani temporis iniustissima calamitate dolui et, cum iis qui similem iniuriam acceperant amissis omnibus fortunis reditus tamen in patriam voluntate omnium concedi videretur, adiutor incolumitatis fui. is habet in Volaterrano possessionem, cum in eam tamquam a naufragio reliquias contulisset. hoc autem tempore eum Caesar in senatum legit; quem ordinem ille ista possessione amissa tueri vix potest. gravissimum autem est, cum superior factus sit ordine, inferiorem esse fortuna, minimeque convenit ex eo agro qui Caesaris iussu dividatur eum moveri qui Caesaris beneficio senator sit. sed mihi minus libet multa de aequitate rei scribere ne causa potius apud te valuisse videar quam gratia. quam ob rem te in maiorem modum rogo ut C. Curti rem meam putes esse; quicquid mea causa faceres, ut, id C. Curti causa cum feceris, existimes quod ille per me habuerit id me habere abs te. hoc te vehementer etiam atque etiam rogo.

accordance with the will of Caesar, who has entrusted you with so important and difficult a commission. Although I receive many requests from many people in their confidence of your friendly disposition towards me, I take good care not to embarrass you in the execution of your duty by solicitations of mine.

I have been on intimate terms with C. Curtius[1] since early youth. His iniquitous deprivation in Sulla's time was a grief to me; and when it appeared that persons who had suffered a similar injustice were allowed to return to their country, though with the loss of their entire fortunes, a concession which was universally welcomed, I lent my assistance in his rehabilitation. He owns a property in the district of Volaterrae into which he put what remained from the wreck of his estate. Caesar has now appointed him a member of the Senate, a rank which he can scarcely support if he loses this property. It is very hard that, having been raised in station, he should be at a disadvantage in fortune; and it is highly incongruous that a Senator by Caesar's favour should be evicted from land which is under distribution by Caesar's orders. However, I do not care to dwell on the rights of the matter, or I might seem to have prevailed with you in virtue of a strong case rather than by my personal influence. So let me particularly request you to regard C. Curtius' estate as mine, to do for C. Curtius' sake whatever you would do for mine, and, having done it, to consider that whatever comes to him through my intervention is a gift from you to me. This I most earnestly beg of you.

[1] Known only from this letter.

320 (XIII.7)

Scr., Romae inter m. Nov. an. 46 et Sept., ut vid., an. 45
CICERO CLUVIO[1] S.

1   Cum in Galliam proficiscens pro nostra necessitudine tuaque summa in me observantia ad me domum venisses, locutus sum tecum de agro vectigali municipi Atellani qui esset in Gallia, quantoque opere eius municipi causa laborarem tibi ostendi. post tuam autem profectionem cum et maxima res municipi honestissimi mihique coniunctissimi et summum meum officium ageretur, pro tuo animo in me singulari existimavi me oportere ad te accuratius scribere, etsi non sum nescius et quae temporum ratio et quae tua potestas sit tibique negotium datum esse a C. Caesare, non iudicium, praeclare intellego. qua re a te tantum peto quantum et te facere posse et libenter mea causa facturum esse arbitror.

2   Et primum velim existimes, quod res est, municipi fortunas omnis in isto vectigali consistere, his autem temporibus hoc municipium maximis oneribus pressum summis adfectum esse difficultatibus. hoc etsi commune videtur esse cum multis, tamen mihi crede singularis huic municipio calamitates accidisse; quas idcirco non commemoro ne de miseriis meorum necessariorum conquerens homines 3 quos nolo videar offendere. itaque, nisi magnam spem

[1] *anne* CLOVIO *(vide comm.)?*

---

[1] Or Clovius (see my Commentary); evidently in charge of land assignments in Cisalpine Gaul.

320 (XIII.7)
CICERO TO C. CLUVIUS

Rome, between November 46 and September 45 (?)

From Cicero to Cluvius[1] greetings.

When you called upon me at my house just before you left for Gaul (a token of our friendship and an example of your unfailing attentiveness to me), I spoke to you about the leased land in Gaul belonging to the town of Atella, and made my deep concern for the town plain to you. Bearing in mind your particularly friendly disposition towards myself, I think it incumbent upon me to write to you after your departure in greater detail, since the matter involves both a major financial interest of a highly respected township with which I have close ties, and an imperative obligation on my side—although I am not unaware of the nature of the present situation and the extent of your powers, and perfectly understand that C. Caesar has assigned you a piece of business, not asked you to exercise your discretion. I am therefore requesting of you only so much as I think you can perform, and will gladly perform for my sake.

And first I would ask you to believe, what is the fact, that the finances of the municipality depend entirely on this rent, and that in these days it is labouring under very heavy burdens and involved in serious difficulties. Many others seem to be in a similar situation, but I do assure you that this particular town has been exceptionally unfortunate. I do not go into details for fear I might seem to be casting aspersions on persons whom I have no wish to offend when I complain of the distresses of those connected with me. If I was not very hopeful that we shall establish

haberem C. Caesari nos causam municipi probaturos, non
erat causa cur a te hoc tempore aliquid contenderem; sed
quia confido mihique persuasi illum et dignitatis municipi
et aequitatis et etiam voluntatis erga se habiturum esse rationem, ideo a te non dubitavi contendere ut hanc causam
illi integram conservares.

4 　　Quod etsi nihilo minus a te peterem si nihil audivissem
te tale fecisse, tamen maiorem spem impetrandi nactus
sum postea quam mihi dictum est hoc idem a te Regiensis
impetravisse; qui etsi te aliqua necessitudine attingunt,
tamen tuus amor in me sperare me cogit te, quod tuis necessariis tribueris, idem esse tributurum meis, praesertim
cum ego pro his unis petam, habeam autem qui simili
causa laborent compluris necessarios. hoc me non sine
causa facere neque aliqua levi ambitione commotum a te
contendere etsi te existimare arbitror, tamen mihi [arbi-
tranti] adfirmanti credas velim me huic municipio debere
plurimum; nullum umquam fuisse tempus neque honorum nec laborum meorum in quo non huius municipi
studium in me exstiterit singulare.

5 　　Quapropter a te etiam atque etiam pro nostra summa
coniunctione proque tua in me perpetua et maxima benevolentia maiorem in modum peto atque contendo ut, cum
fortunas agi eius municipi intellegas quod sit mihi necessitudine, officiis, benevolentia coniunctissimum, id mihi
des; quod erit huius modi ut, si a Caesare quod speramus
impetrarimus, tuo beneficio nos id consecutos esse iudice-
mus, sin minus, pro eo tamen id habeamus, quoniam a te
data sit opera ut impetraremus. hoc cum mihi gratissimum

the town's case to C. Caesar's satisfaction, there would be no reason for me to trouble you at present. But I am confidently persuaded that he will take into account the high standing of the community, the equity of their cause, and also their disposition towards himself. Therefore I do not hesitate to urge you to leave the case open for him to determine.

I should make this appeal to you even if I had not heard that you had so acted in another case, but I became more hopeful of your granting it after I was told that you had made the same concession to the people of Regium. Even though they have a certain connection with you, your affection for me constrains me to hope that what you do for your own connections you will do for mine—especially as I am asking this only for Atella, though several communities connected with me are in similar trouble. I do not think you will suspect me of so proceeding without good reason, or of soliciting you from a trivial desire to increase my popularity. Still, I hope you will believe me when I give you my word that I am under a great debt to this municipality. In my advancements as in my tribulations their devotion towards me has on every occasion been quite outstanding.

Accordingly, let me beg you most earnestly, in virtue of the intimate bond between us and your signal and unfailing good will towards me, to grant what I ask, realizing that the finances of a municipality with which I am closely linked by mutual relations, services, and good will are here at stake. You may take it that, if we get what we hope from Caesar, we shall regard ourselves as owing it to your kindness; and if not, that we shall take the will for the deed, considering that you will have done your best to get it for us. I myself shall be deeply grateful, and an excellent and

feceris tum viros optimos, homines honestissimos eos-
demque gratissimos et tua necessitudine dignissimos summo beneficio in perpetuum tibi tuisque devinxeris.

321 (XIII.8)

Scr. Romae inter m. Nov. an. 46 et Sept. an. 45, ut vid.

M. CICERO M. RUTILIO S.

1   Cum et mihi conscius essem quanti te facerem et tuam
erga me benevolentiam expertus essem, non dubitavi a te
petere quod mihi petendum esset.

P. Sestium quanti faciam ipse optime scio; quanti autem facere debeam et tu et omnes homines sciunt. is cum
ex aliis te mei studiosissimum esse cognosset, petivit a me
ut ad te quam accuratissime scriberem de re C. Albani[1]
senatoris, cuius ex f[am]ilia[2] natus est L. Sestius, optimus
adulescens, filius P. Sesti. hoc idcirco scripsi ut intellegeres
non solum me pro P. Sestio laborare debere sed Sestium
etiam pro Albanio.

2   Res autem est haec: a M. Laberio C. Albanius praedia
in aestimationem accepit, quae praedia Laberius emerat a
Caesare de bonis Plotianis. ea si dicam non esse a re publica dividi, docere te videar, non rogare. sed tamen, cum
Caesar Sullanas venditiones et adsignationes ratas esse

---

[1] albinii *(SB)*   [2] *(Man.)*

---

[1] Evidently another land commissioner. The area in which he
operated is unknown. He may well be Caesar's former Legate, M.
Sempronius Rutilus (*Gallic War* 7.90.4), as suggested by Syme.

highly respected body, one too that well knows the meaning of gratitude and is thoroughly worthy to be connected with you, will be bound to you and yours for all time by a signal benefaction.

321 (XIII.8)
CICERO TO M. RUTILIUS

Rome, between November 46 and September 45 (?)

From M. Cicero to M. Rutilius[1] greetings.

Conscious of my regard for you and aware by experience of your good will towards myself, I do not hesitate to lay before you the request I have to make.

How highly I regard P. Sestius is best known to myself; how highly I ought to regard him is known to you and all the world. Learning from other sources of your eagerness to be of service to me, he has requested me to write to you most particularly about a matter concerning Senator C. Albanius, whose daughter was the mother of that excellent young man L. Sestius, P. Sestius' son. I mention this to let you know that, besides my obligation to concern myself on Sestius' behalf, Sestius has a like obligation towards Albanius.

The affair in question is as follows: C. Albanius received certain properties at valuation from M. Laberius, which properties had been purchased by Laberius from Caesar out of Plotius' estate. If I were to say that it is contrary to public interest that those properties should be brought under assignment, it would look as though I were not asking a favour but giving you instruction. All the same, I may point out that Caesar wishes the Sullan sales and assign-

velit quo firmiores existimentur suae, si ea praedia divi-
dentur quae ipse Caesar vendidit, quae tandem in eius
venditionibus esse poterit auctoritas?

3   Sed hoc quale sit tu pro tua prudentia considerabis. ego
te plane rogo, atque ita ut maiore studio, iustiore de causa,
magis ex animo rogare nihil possim, ut Albanio parcas,
praedia Laberiana ne attingas. magna me adfeceris non
modo laetitia sed etiam quodam modo gloria si P. Sestius
homini maxime necessario satis fecerit per me, ut ego illi
uni plurimum debeo.[3] quod ut facias te vehementer etiam
atque etiam rogo; maius mihi dare beneficium nullum
potes. id mihi intelleges esse gratissimum.

322 (VI.15)

Scr. Romae an. incerto

CICERO BASILO[1] S.

Tibi gratulor, mihi gaudeo. te amo, tua tueor. a te amari
et quid agas quidque agatur certior fieri volo.

[3] debeam (*Ern.*)
[1] Basilio (*Lamb.*)

ments to be valid in order that his own may be thought more secure. If properties sold by Caesar himself are to be brought under assignment, what sort of title will his sales carry in future?

But you in your wisdom will consider that aspect of the matter. I am simply making a request of you (and I could make none with more earnestness and sincerity, or in a juster cause) to spare Albanius and not to touch the properties formerly belonging to Laberius. You will make me not only very happy but also rather proud to have been the means of enabling P. Sestius to meet the needs of a close connection, owing him as I do more than any other man. Allow me to ask you most pressingly so to do. You can confer upon me no higher favour, and you will find me most grateful.

322 (VI.15)
CICERO TO MINUCIUS BASILUS

Rome, date uncertain[1]

From Cicero to Basilus greetings.

Congratulations. I am delighted on my own account. Be sure of my affection and active concern for your interests. I hope I have your affection, and want to hear what you are doing and what is going on.

---

[1] There are serious objections to the tempting view that this evidently hasty note refers to Caesar's assassination.

323 (VI.16)

Scr. in Sicilia fort. ex. m. Mart. an. 44

BITHYNICUS CICERONI S.

Si mihi tecum non et multae et iustae causae amicitiae privatim essent, repeterem initia amicitiae ex parentibus nostris, quod faciendum iis existimo qui paternam amicitiam nullis ipsi officiis prosecuti sunt. itaque contentus ero nostra ipsorum amicitia, cuius fiducia peto a te ut absentem me, quibuscumque in rebus opus fuerit, tueare, si nullum officium tuum apud me intermoriturum existimas.

Vale.

324 (VI.17)

Scr. Romae fort. m. Mai. an. 44

CICERO BITHYNICO

1   Cum ceterarum rerum causa cupio esse aliquando rem publicam constitutam tum velim mihi credas accedere, id etiam quo magis expetam, promissum tuum quo in litteris

2   uteris. scribis enim, si ita sit, te mecum esse victurum. gratissima mihi tua voluntas est, facisque nihil alienum necessitudine nostra iudiciisque patris tui de me, summi viri. nam sic habeto, beneficiorum magnitudine eos qui tempo-

---

[1] Propraetor in Sicily.

[1] This is evidently not a reply to the preceding, though it probably belongs to the same period.

88

323 (VI.16)
POMPEIUS BITHYNICUS TO CICERO

Sicily, ca. end of March (?) 44

From Bithynicus[1] to Cicero greetings.

If my friendship with you did not rest on many good grounds peculiar to ourselves, I should go back to its origins and speak of our parents. But that I take to be appropriate when family friendship has not been followed up by personal good offices. Therefore I shall be content with our personal friendship, and relying thereupon would ask you to defend my interests during my absence, wherever there may be need, in the persuasion, I hope, that no service you render will ever lose its freshness in my memory.

Good-bye.

324 (VI.17)
CICERO TO POMPEIUS BITHYNICUS[1]

Rome, May 44 (?)

From Cicero to Bithynicus greetings.

There are all manner of reasons why I am anxious to see the commonwealth settled at long last, but, believe me, the promise you make in your letter adds one to their number, causing me to long for that event yet the more. For you write that, if it comes about, you will be much in my society. Your wish is most gratifying to me, and you express it in the spirit of our friendship and of the opinion which that fine man, your father, held of me. You may be assured that, although those whom events made, or make, powerful are

ribus valuerunt <a>ut vale[a]nt[1] coniunctiores tecum esse quam me, necessitudine neminem. quam ob rem grata mihi est et memoria tua nostrae coniunctionis et eius etiam augendae voluntas.

325 (XI.1)

Scr. Romae c. xi Kal. Apr., ut vid., an. 44

D. BRUTUS BRUTO SUO ET CASSIO S.

1   Quo in statu simus cognoscite. heri vesperi apud me Hirtius fuit; qua mente esset Antonius demonstravit, pessima scilicet et infidelissima. nam se neque mihi provinciam dare posse aiebat neque arbitrari tuto in urbe esse quemquam nostrum; adeo esse militum concitatos animos et plebis. quod utrumque esse falsum puto vos animadvertere atque illud esse verum quod Hirtius demonstrabat, timere eum ne, si mediocre auxilium dignitatis nostrae habuissemus, nullae partes iis in re publica relinquerentur.

2   Cum in his angustiis versarer, placitum est mihi ut postularem legationem liberam mihi reliquisque nostris, ut aliqua causa proficiscendi honesta quaereretur. haec se impetraturum pollicitus est, nec tamen impetraturum confido; tanta est hominum insolentia et nostri insectatio.

---

[1] *(Graevius)*

---

[1] At least a half dozen dates have been assigned to this letter, of which Cicero no doubt received a copy from the recipients. I accept the view that it was written soon after the disturbances that followed Caesar's funeral on 20 March.

more closely attached to you than I in respect of the magnitude of what they have conferred upon you, none stands nearer in friendship. I am therefore gratified by your mindfulness of our connection and your wish to strengthen it still further.

325 (XI.1)
D. BRUTUS TO M. BRUTUS AND CASSIUS

Rome, ca. 22 (?) March 44[1]

From D. Brutus to his friend Brutus and to Cassius greetings.

Let me tell you how we stand. Yesterday evening Hirtius was at my house. He made Antony's disposition clear—as bad and treacherous as can be. Antony says he is unable to give me my province,[2] and that he thinks none of us is safe in Rome with the soldiers and populace in their present agitated state of mind. I expect you observe the falsehood of both contentions, the truth being, as Hirtius made evident, that he is afraid lest, if our position were enhanced even to a moderate extent, these people would have no further part to play in public affairs.

Finding myself in so difficult a predicament, I thought it best to ask for a Free Commission[3] for myself and the rest of our friends, so as to get a fair excuse for going away. Hirtius promised to get this agreed to, but I have no confidence that he will, in view of the general insolence and

[2] Cisalpine Gaul according to Caesar's assignment.
[3] See Glossary under Legate.

ac si dederint quod petimus, tamen paulo post futurum
puto ut hostes iudicemur aut aqua et igni nobis inter-
dicatur.

3   'Quid ergo est' inquis 'tui consili?' dandus est locus
Fortunae, cedendum ex Italia, migrandum Rhodum aut
aliquo terrarum arbitror. si melior casus fuerit, revertemur
Romam; si mediocris, in exsilio vivemus; si pessimus, ad
4   novissima auxilia descendemus. succurret fortasse hoc
loco alicui vestrum cur novissimum tempus exspectemus
potius quam nunc aliquid moliamur. quia ubi consistamus
non habemus praeter Sex. Pompeium et Bassum Cae-
‹ci›lium; qui mihi videntur hoc nuntio de Caesare adlato
firmiores futuri. satis tempore ad eos accedemus ubi quid
valeant scierimus. pro Cassio et te si quid me velitis recipere, recipiam; postulat enim hoc Hirtius ut faciam.

5   Rogo vos quam primum mihi rescribatis; nam non
dubito quin de his rebus ante horam quartam Hirtius
certiorem me sit facturus. quem in locum convenire possimus, quo me velitis venire, rescribite.

6   Post novissimum Hirti sermonem placitum est mihi
postulare ut liceret nobis Romae esse publico praesidio.
quod illos nobis concessuros non puto; magnam enim invi-
diam[1] iis faciemus. nihil tamen non postulandum putavi
quod aequum esse statuerem.

[1] umquam

vilification of us. And even if they give us what we ask, I think it won't be long before we are branded as public enemies or placed under interdict.

You may ask what I advise. We must give way to Fortune, leave Italy, go to live in Rhodes or anywhere under the sun. If things go better, we shall return to Rome. If so-so, we shall live in exile. If the worst happens, we shall take any and every means to help ourselves. Perhaps one of you will wonder at this point why we should wait till the last moment instead of setting something on foot now. Because we have nowhere to base ourselves, except for Sex. Pompeius[4] and Bassus Caecilius—I imagine their hands will be strengthened when this news about Caesar gets through. It will be time enough for us to join them when we know what their power amounts to. I shall give any undertaking you and Cassius wish on your behalf. Hirtius demands that I do this.

Please let me have your reply as soon as possible. I don't doubt that Hirtius will inform me on these points before ten o'clock. Let me know where we can meet, where you wish me to come.

After Hirtius' latest talk I have thought it right to demand that we be allowed to stay in Rome with a public bodyguard. I don't suppose they will agree—we shall be putting them in a very invidious light. However, I think I ought not to refrain from demanding anything that I consider fair.[5]

[4] Pompey's younger son, still fighting in Spain.
[5] This paragraph is probably not, as generally supposed, a postscript added after Hirtius' return, since it does not say what answer Hirtius brought back.

326 (IX.14)

Scr. in Pompeiano v Non. Mai. an. 44

CICERO DOLABELLAE COS. SUO SAL.

1   Etsi contentus eram, mi Dolabella, tua gloria satisque ex ea magnam laetitiam voluptatemque capiebam, tamen non possum non confiteri cumulari me maximo gaudio quod vulgo hominum opinio socium me adscribat tuis laudibus. neminem conveni (convenio autem cottidie plurimos; sunt enim permulti optimi viri qui valetudinis causa in haec loca veniant, praeterea ex municipiis frequentes necessarii mei) quin omnes, cum te summis laudibus ad caelum extulerunt, mihi continuo maximas gratias agant. negant enim se dubitare quin tu meis praeceptis et consiliis obtemperans praestantissimum te civem et singularem consulem praebeas.

2   Quibus ego, quamquam verissime possum respondere te quae facias tuo iudicio et tua sponte facere nec cuiusquam egere consilio, tamen neque plane adsentior, ne imminuam tuam laudem si omnis a meis consiliis profecta videatur, neque valde nego; sum enim avidior etiam quam satis est gloriae. et tamen non alienum est dignitate tua, quod ipsi Agamemnoni, regum regi, fuit honestum, habere aliquem in consiliis capiendis Nestorem, mihi vero gloriosum te iuvenem consulem florere laudibus quasi alumnum disciplinae meae.

3   L. quidem Caesar, cum ad eum aegrotum Neapolim

---

[1] This letter is also found in the Atticus series, 371A (XIV.17A). Dolabella, who became Consul after Caesar's death, had drastically repressed some pro-Caesarian demonstrations in Rome.

326 (IX.14)
CICERO TO DOLABELLA[1]

Pompeii, 3 May 44

From Cicero to his friend Dolabella, Consul, greetings.

Content as I am, my dear Dolabella, with *your* glory, and finding as I do sufficient cause in that for delight and rejoicing, yet I cannot but confess that my cup of happiness is filled to overflowing by the popular opinion which makes me a sharer in your laurels. Every single person I have met (and I meet a great many every day, for a large number of the best people come hereabouts for their health, and I have many visits in addition from friends in the neighbouring towns) has first praised you sky high in the most glowing terms and then in the same breath expressed deep gratitude to me, not doubting, so they say, that it is in conformity with my precepts and advice that you are showing yourself so admirable a citizen and so outstanding a Consul.

I can reply with perfect truth that what you do you do by your own judgement and volition, needing nobody's advice. In fact, however, I neither give a direct assent, in case I might detract from your credit by letting it appear to have proceeded entirely from my counsels, nor yet a very vigorous disclaimer, for I am fond, perhaps too fond, of glory. And yet it detracts nothing from your prestige to have a Nestor to consult, as did the King of Kings, Agamemnon himself, without any loss of dignity. As for me, it is a proud thing that a young Consul should win such laurels as, so to speak, a pupil from my school.

I visited L. Caesar on his sick bed at Naples. His whole

venissem, quamquam erat oppressus totius corporis dolo-
ribus, tamen, ante quam me plane salutavit, 'o mi Cicero'
inquit, 'gratulor tibi cum tantum vales apud Dolabellam
quantum si ego apud sororis filium valerem, iam salvi esse
possemus. Dolabellae vero tuo et gratulor et gratias ago,
quem quidem post te consulem solum possumus vere consulem dicere.' deinde multa de facto ac de re gesta tua;[1]
nihil magnificentius, nihil praeclarius actum umquam,
nihil rei publicae salutarius. atque haec una vox omnium
est.

4   A te autem peto ut me hanc quasi falsam hereditatem
alienae gloriae sinas cernere meque aliqua ex parte in
societatem tuarum laudum venire patiare. quamquam, mi
Dolabella (haec enim iocatus sum), libentius omnis meas,
si modo sunt aliquae meae, laudes ad te transfuderim
quam aliquam partem exhauserim ex tuis. nam cum te
semper tantum dilexerim quantum tu intellegere potuisti,
tum his tuis factis sic incensus sum ut nihil umquam in
amore fuerit ardentius. nihil est enim, mihi crede, virtute
5   formosius, nihil pulchrius, nihil amabilius. semper amavi,
ut scis, M. Brutum propter eius summum ingenium, sua-
vissimos mores, singularem probitatem atque constantiam; tamen Idibus Martiis tantum accessit ad amorem ut
mirarer locum fuisse augendi in eo quod mihi iam pridem
cumulatum etiam videbatur. quis erat qui putaret ad eum
amorem quem erga te habebam posse aliquid accedere?
tantum accessit ut mihi nunc denique amare videar, antea
dilexisse.

[1] tum *(Wes.)*

body racked with pain though it was, he had scarcely greeted me before he exclaimed 'Oh my dear Cicero, congratulations! If I had as much influence with my nephew[2] as you have with Dolabella, we might now be out of our troubles. As for your Dolabella, I congratulate him and thank him. He is the first Consul since yourself who deserves the name.' Then he went on to speak at large of your action and achievement, which he called as magnificent, distinguished, and publicly salutary as any in history. And this is the sentiment expressed by all.

Now please allow me to accept this counterfeit inheritance, so to speak, of an acclaim which does not belong to me, and admit me to some small partnership in your triumph. Not but what, my dear Dolabella—for I have written the above only in jest—I would sooner transfer to you all the credit for my own achievements, if any such there be, than divert any part of yours. You cannot but know how deep my regard for you has always been; but your recent exploits have kindled in me such enthusiasm that no affection was ever more ardent. Nothing, believe me, is more beautiful, fair, and lovable than manly virtue. As you are aware, I have always loved M. Brutus for his fine intellect, the charm of his manners, and his outstanding uprightness and reliability. Yet the Ides of March added so much to my love for him that I was astonished to find room for increase where I had long believed all was full to overflowing. Who would have thought that the love I bore you admitted of any accession? Yet the accession is such that it seems to me as though I only now feel love where formerly I felt affectionate regard.

[2] Mark Antony, the other Consul.

97

6   Qua re quid est quod ego te horter ut dignitati et gloriae
servias? proponam tibi claros viros, quod facere solent qui
hortantur? neminem habeo clariorem quam te ipsum. te
imitere oportet, tecum ipse certes. ne licet quidem tibi iam
7   tantis rebus gestis non tui similem esse. quod cum ita sit,
hortatio non est necessaria, gratulatione magis utendum
est. contigit enim tibi, quod haud scio an nemini, ut summa
severitas animadversionis non modo non invidiosa sed
etiam popularis esset et cum bonis omnibus tum infimo
cuique gratissima. hoc si tibi fortuna quadam contigisset,
gratularer felicitati tuae; sed contigit magnitudine cum
animi tum etiam ingeni atque consili. legi enim contionem
tuam. nihil illa sapientius; ita pedetemptim et gradatim
tum accessus a te ad causam facti, tum recessus, ut res ipsa
maturitatem tibi animadvertendi omnium concessu daret.
8   Liberasti igitur et urbem periculo et civitatem metu
neque solum ad tempus maximam utilitatem attulisti sed
etiam ad exemplum. quo facto intellegere debes in te posi-
tam esse rem publicam tibique non modo tuendos sed
etiam ornandos esse illos viros a quibus initium libertatis
profectum est. sed his de rebus coram plura, propediem ut
spero. tu, quoniam rem publicam nosque conservas, fac ut
diligentissime te ipsum, mi Dolabella, custodias.

There is no need for me to urge you to cherish the high standing and glory you have won. Why should I, in hortatory fashion, remind you of famous names? I can quote none more famous than your own. You yourself should be your model, it is yourself you have to emulate. After such exploits you no longer have the *right* to fall below your own standard. Exhortation is therefore superfluous, felicitation rather is called for. In your case, and I dare say in yours only, the extreme of penal rigour has brought not merely no odium but actual popularity, delighting the lower orders as well as all honest folk. If this had come to you by a stroke of luck, I should congratulate you on your good fortune; but you owe it to your generous courage and, no less, to your ability and sound judgement. I have read your speech, an excellently conceived performance. How cautiously you felt your way towards the issue, now approaching, now drawing back, so that by common consent the simple facts of the case showed the time to be ripe for your punitive action!

So you have rescued Rome from danger and her inhabitants from fear. You have done a vast deal of good, not only for the present occasion, but as a precedent for the future. Having done that, you should understand that the commonwealth rests upon your shoulders, and that those men from whose initiative freedom has sprung are deserving, not only of your protection, but of your favour. But on these matters more when we meet; soon, I hope. Lastly, my dear Dolabella, as the commonwealth's guardian and mine, see that you take the utmost care for your own safety.

Scr. in Pompeiano v Non. Mai. an. 44

CICERO CASSIO S.

1   Finem nullam facio, mihi crede, Cassi, de te et Bruto
nostro, id est de tota re publica, cogitandi, cuius omnis
spes in vobis est et in D. Bruto; quam quidem iam habeo
ipse meliorem re publica a Dolabella meo praeclarissime
gesta. manabat enim illud malum urbanum et ita corrobo-
rabatur cottidie ut ego quidem et urbi et otio diffiderem
urbano, sed ita compressum est ut mihi videamur omne
iam ad tempus ab illo dumtaxat sordidissimo periculo tuti
futuri.

    Reliqua magna sunt ac multa, sed posita omnia in vobis.
quamquam primum quidque explicemus. nam ut adhuc
quidem actum est, non regno sed rege liberati videmur.
interfecto enim rege regios omnis nutus tuemur, neque
vero id solum, sed etiam quae ipse ille, si viveret, non faceret, ea nos quasi cogitata ab illo probamus. nec eius quidem rei finem video. tabulae figuntur, immunitates dantur,
pecuniae maximae discribuntur, exsules reducuntur, senatus consulta falsa referuntur, ut tantum modo odium illud
hominis impuri et servitutis dolor depulsus esse videatur,
res publica iaceat in iis perturbationibus in quas eam ille
coniecit.

2   Haec omnia vobis sunt expedienda, nec hoc cogitan-
dum, satis iam habere rem publicam a vobis. habet illa

---

1 With what follows cf. *Letters to Atticus* 368 (XIV.14).2.

327 (XII.1)
CICERO TO CASSIUS

Pompeii, 3 May 44

Cicero to Cassius greetings.

Believe me, Cassius, I never stop thinking about you and our friend Brutus, that is to say about the whole country, whose only hope lies in you both and in D. Brutus. I myself now feel more optimistic after the splendid performance of my dear Dolabella. The rot in Rome was spreading and getting more virulent every day, so that I for one was alarmed for the city and for public order inside it. But this has been so effectually suppressed that I think we may now reasonably consider ourselves safe for all time to come from that most squalid of threats at any rate.

The tasks that remain are many and serious, but all depends on you three. However, let us solve each problem as it arises.[1] As things have gone so far, it appears that we are free of the despot, but not of the despotism. Our king has been killed, but we are upholding the validity of his every regal nod. And not only that, but we sanction measures which he himself would not be taking if he were alive on the pretext that he had them in mind. I see no end to the business. Laws are posted up, exemptions granted, large sums of money assigned, exiles brought home, decrees of the Senate forged—it seems we are merely rid of the disgust we felt for an abominable individual and of the mortification of slavery, while the state still lies in the chaotic condition into which he flung it.

You and your friends must straighten out the whole tangle. You must not think that you have done enough for your country already. She has indeed had more from you

quidem tantum quantum numquam mihi in mentem venit optare; sed contenta non est et pro magnitudine et animi et benefici vestri a vobis magna desiderat. adhuc ulta suas iniurias est per vos interitu tyranni, nihil amplius. ornamenta vero sua quae reciperavit? an quod ei mortuo paret quem vivum ferre non poterat? cuius aera refigere debebamus, eius etiam chirographa defendimus? at enim ita decrevimus. fecimus id quidem temporibus cedentes, quae valent in re publica plurimum; sed immoderate quidam et ingrate nostra facilitate abutuntur.

Verum haec propediem et multa alia coram. interim velim sic tibi persuadeas, mihi cum rei publicae, quam semper habui carissimam, tum amoris nostri causa maximae curae esse tuam dignitatem. da operam ut valeas.

Vale.

328 (XII.16)

Scr. Athenis VIII *Kal. Iun. an. 44*

TREBONIUS CICERONI S.

1   S. v. b.

Athenas veni a. d. XI Kal. Iun. atque ibi, quod maxime optabam, vidi filium tuum deditum optimis studiis summaque modestiae fama. qua ex re quantam voluptatem ceperim scire potes etiam me tacente. non enim nescis

---

[2] In the temple of Tellus on 17 March, when the Senate confirmed Caesar's 'acts.'

[1] Trebonius was on his way to take over the province of Asia.

than it ever entered my mind to hope, but she is not satisfied; she wants great things from you, proportionate to
the greatness of your hearts and service. So far she has
avenged her injuries by the death of the tyrant at your
hands, nothing more. What of her dignities? Which of
them has she recovered? The right to obey a dead man,
whom she could not tolerate alive? Are we defending the
paper memoranda of one whose laws graven on bronze we
ought to annul? Oh yes, we have so decreed.[2] When we did
that, we bowed to circumstances, which in politics count
for a great deal. But some people are abusing our facility
without restraint or gratitude.

But of this and much else when we meet, soon. Meanwhile, please believe that I have your public standing very
much at heart, both for the sake of the commonwealth,
which has always been dearer to me than anything else in
the world, and for that of our mutual affection. Take care
of your health.

Good-bye.

328 (XII.16)
TREBONIUS TO CICERO

Athens, 25 May 44

From Trebonius to Cicero greetings.

I trust you are well.

I arrived in Athens on 22 May,[1] and there saw what I
most desired to see, your son devoting himself to liberal
studies and bearing an exemplary character. How much
pleasure this gave me you can appreciate even without my
telling you. You are not unaware how much I think of you

quanti te faciam et quam pro nostro veterrimo verissi-
moque amore omnibus tuis etiam minimis commodis, non
modo tanto bono, gaudeam. noli putare, mi Cicero, me hoc
auribus tuis dare. nihil adulescente tuo atque adeo nostro
(nihil enim tibi a me[1] potest esse seiunctum) aut amabilius
omnibus his qui Athenis sunt est aut studiosius earum ar-
tium quas tu maxime amas, hoc est optimarum. itaque tibi,
quod vere facere possum, libenter quoque gratulor nec
minus etiam nobis, quod eum quem necesse erat diligere
qualiscumque esset talem habemus ut libenter quoque
diligamus.

2   Qui cum mihi in sermone iniecisset se velle Asiam
visere, non modo invitatus sed etiam rogatus est a me ut id
potissimum nobis obtinentibus provinciam faceret. cui nos
et caritate et amore tuum officium praestaturos non debes
dubitare. illud quoque erit nobis curae ut Cratippus una
cum eo sit, ne putes in Asia feriatum illum ab iis studiis in
quae tua cohortatione incitatur futurum. nam illum paratum, ut video, et ingressum pleno gradu cohortari non
intermittemus, quo in dies longius discendo exercendoque
se procedat.

3   Vos quid ageretis in re publica, cum has litteras dabam,
non sciebam. audiebam quaedam turbulenta, quae scilicet
cupio esse falsa, ut aliquando otiosa libertate fruamur;
quod vel minime mihi adhuc contigit. ego tamen nactus in
navigatione nostra pusillum laxamenti concinnavi tibi mu-
nusculum ex instituto meo et dictum cum magno nostro
honore a te dictum conclusi et tibi infra subscripsi. in qui-

[1] mihi a te (*SB*)

and how warmly I welcome any gratification that comes your way, even the most trifling, let alone such a blessing as this. Such is the longstanding and sincere affection between us. Do not suppose, my dear Cicero, that I tell you this because it is what you want to hear. This young man of yours (or rather ours, for you can have nothing I do not share) could not be more popular with everybody here in Athens, nor more enthusiastically attached to the studies for which you care most, that is to say, the highest. And so I am delighted to congratulate you, as I can sincerely do, and myself no less, upon the fact that in him we have a young man for whom it is a delight to care, since care for him we must however he had turned out.

When he let fall in conversation with me that he would like to visit Asia, I not only invited but requested him to do so during my term as governor of the province. You should have no doubt that I shall stand towards him in your stead with a father's care and affection. I shall also see that Cratippus comes with him, so you need not think that in Asia he will be taking a vacation from the studies to which he is spurred by your encouragement. He is evidently a willing student, advancing at the double. I shall be continually encouraging him to further progress through daily study and practice.

As I write this letter, I do not know how you at home are faring politically. I hear some reports of unrest. Naturally I hope they are untrue, and that we can at last enjoy freedom in peace and quiet. To date I have been very far from that good fortune. However, I got a modicum of relaxation during the voyage, and have fitted together a little present for you after my fashion—I have cast a bon mot of yours, one very complimentary to myself, into verse, and written it

105

bus versiculis si tibi quibusdam verbis εὐθυρρημονέστε-
ρος videbor, turpitudo personae eius in quam liberius in-
vehimur nos vindicabit. ignosces etiam iracundiae nostrae,
quae iusta est in eius modi et homines et civis. deinde qui
magis hoc Lucilio licuerit adsumere libertatis quam nobis?
cum, etiam si odio par[2] fuerit in eos quos laesit, tamen
certe non magis dignos habuerit in quos tanta libertate
verborum incurreret.

4   Tu, sicut mihi pollicitus es, adiunges me quam primum
ad tuos sermones; namque illud non dubito quin, si quid
de interitu Caesaris scribas, non patiaris me minimam
partem et rei et amoris tui ferre.

Vale, et matrem meosque tibi commendatos habe.

D. VIII Kal. Iun. Athenis.

329 (XI.2)

Scr. Lanuvii ex. m. Mai. an. 44

BRUTUS ET CASSIUS PRAETORES M. ANTONIO COS.

1   De tua fide et benevolentia in nos nisi persuasum esset
nobis, non scripsissemus haec tibi; quae profecto, quoniam istum animum habes, in optimam partem accipies.

Scribitur nobis magnam veteranorum multitudinem
Romam convenisse iam et ad Kal. Iun. futuram multo

---

[2] pari *Man.*

---

[2] Probably Antony.
[1] For which date Antony had summoned a meeting of the
Senate.

down for you below. If you think certain words in this little piece rather risqués, the turpitude of the figure[2] I am somewhat freely assailing will be my excuse. You will also make allowance for my irascibility, which is justified against persons and citizens of this type. And then, why should I not be allowed as much licence as Lucilius? Even granted that he hated his targets as much as I, it certainly cannot be claimed that the people he attacked with such licence of language deserved it more.

As you have promised me, you will give me a place in your conversation pieces as soon as possible. I am sure that, if you write anything on Caesar's death, you will not let me take the smallest share of the event, and of your affection.

Good-bye, and consider my mother and family as commended to your care.

Dispatched 25 May, from Athens.

329 (XI.2)
M. BRUTUS AND CASSIUS TO ANTONY

Lanuvium, May (end) 44

From Brutus and Cassius, Praetors, to M. Antonius, Consul.

Were we not convinced of your good faith and friendly intentions towards us, we should not write you this letter, which, since you are in fact thus disposed, you will doubtless take in the best of part.

We are informed by letters that a large number of veterans has already gathered in Rome, and that a much larger number is expected before the Kalends of June.[1] It

maiorem. de te si dubitemus aut vereamur, simus nostri dissimiles. sed certe, cum ipsi in tua potestate fuerimus tuoque adducti consilio dimiserimus ex municipiis nostros necessarios, neque solum edicto sed etiam litteris id fecerimus, digni sumus quos habeas tui consili participes, in ea praesertim re quae ad nos pertinet. qua re petimus a te facias nos certiores tuae voluntatis in nos, putesne non tutos fore in tanta frequentia militum veteranorum, quos etiam de reponenda ara cogitare audimus; quod velle et probare vix quisquam posse videtur qui nos salvos et honestos velit.

2

Nos ab initio spectasse otium nec quicquam aliud libertate communi quaesisse exitus declarat. fallere nemo non potest nisi tu, quod certe abest ab tua virtute et fide; sed alius nemo facultatem habet decipiendi nos. tibi enim uni credidimus et credituri sumus. maximo timore de nobis adficiuntur amici nostri; quibus etsi tua fides explorata est, tamen illud in mentem venit, multitudinem veteranorum facilius impelli ab aliis quolibet quam a te retineri posse.

3

Rescribas nobis ad omnia rogamus. nam illud valde leve est ac nugatorium, ea re denuntiatum esse veteranis quod de commodis eorum mense Iunio laturus esses. quem enim impedimento futurum putas, cum de nobis certum sit nos quieturos? non debemus cuiquam videri nimium cupidi vitae cum accidere nobis nihil possit sine pernicie et confusione omnium rerum.

---

2 A funeral monument to Caesar in the Forum which became an object of popular cult until it was demolished by Dolabella.

would be out of character for us to entertain any doubt or apprehension concerning yourself. But having placed ourselves in your hands and dismissed our friends from the municipalities on your advice, having done that moreover not only by edict but in private letters, we surely deserve to share your confidence, particularly in a matter which concerns us. Therefore we request you to inform us of your disposition towards us, whether you think we shall be safe among such a multitude of veteran soldiers, who are actually thinking, so we hear, of replacing the altar.[2] It is not easy to believe that anyone who desires our security and dignity can desire and approve of that.

The event shows that peace has been our aim from the beginning, and that we have had no object in view but the freedom of the community. Nobody can deceive us except yourself, a thing surely abhorrent to your manly and honourable spirit. Still, no other man has the means to trick us, for we have trusted, and shall continue to trust, only you. Our friends are deeply anxious on our behalf. They have every confidence in your good faith, but it is in their minds that the crowd of veterans can more easily be impelled by others in any direction they please than held in check by you.

We request you to give us your reply on all points. As for the allegation that the veterans were summoned because you intended to bring matters to their advantage before the Senate in June, it is a quite frivolous and nugatory excuse. Who do you suppose is likely to be obstructive, since, as for ourselves, it is certain that we shall hold our peace? None should believe us overly anxious to preserve our lives, for nothing can happen to us without universal ruin and chaos.

330 (XVI.23)

Scr. in Tusculano ex. m. Mai., ut vid., an. 44

CICERO TIRONI S.

1   Tu vero confice professionem, si potes (etsi haec pecunia ex eo genere est ut professione non egeat, verum tamen). Balbus ad me scripsit tanta se ἐπιφορᾷ oppressum ut loqui non possit. Antonius de lege quod[1] egerit. liceat modo rusticari. ad Bithynicum scripsi.

2   De Servilio tu videris, qui senectutem non contemnis. etsi Atticus noster, quia quondam me commoveri πανικοῖς intellexit, idem semper putat nec videt quibus praesidiis philosophiae saeptus sim; et hercle, quod timidus ipse est, θορυβοποιεῖ. ego tamen Antoni inveteratam sine ulla offensione amicitiam retinere sane volo scribamque ad eum, sed non ante quam te videro. nec tamen te avoco a syngrapha; γόνυ κνήμης. cras exspecto Leptam et †n.†,[2] ad cuius rutam puleio mihi tui sermonis utendum est.

Vale.

---

[1] quid *(Lehmann)*   [2] nostrum *T.–P.*: eum *Wes.*

---

[1] Perhaps the public registration of a transfer of assets.

[2] Perhaps a bill for the distribution of all available public lands among veterans and the poor.   [3] Not necessarily Pompeius Bithynicus. The purpose of Cicero's letter is unknown.

[4] The elder Servilius Isauricus had recently died at a great age. Tiro seems to have relayed a talk with Atticus, who was afraid that Cicero might take fright at some current 'scare.' Tiro may have added that Cicero ought not to worry and that he would very likely live to a ripe old age, like Servilius.

330 (XVI.23)
CICERO TO TIRO

Tusculum, end of May (?) 44

From Cicero to Tiro greetings.

Yes, please get the declaration[1] done if you can, though with a sum of this sort no declaration is necessary—but do it all the same. Balbus writes to me that he has had an attack, so severe that he can't talk. Antony can do as he likes about the law,[2] so long as I am allowed to stay in the country. I have written to Bithynicus.[3]

Servilius I leave to you, since you think old age worth having.[4] To be sure our good Atticus, having found me susceptible to scares in the old days, still thinks it is so and doesn't see my proof armour of philosophy. And, truth to say, being a nervous fellow himself, he plays alarmist. However, I certainly want to keep my old-established friendship with Antony—we have never had a quarrel— and shall write to him, but not till I have seen you. Not that I am taking you away from your bond[5]— charity begins at home.[6] I expect Lepta tomorrow and *.[7] I shall need the sweet of your conversation to counteract the bitter[8] of his company.

Good-bye.

[5] Some private business of Tiro.

[6] Cicero quotes a Greek proverb meaning literally 'the knee is nearer than the shin.'

[7] The manuscripts are corrupt at this point, but the person concerned is probably either Q. Cicero senior or his son; cf. *Letters to Atticus* 404 (XV.26).1.

[8] Literally 'the penny royal . . . the rue.'

331 (VII.22)

Scr. Romae, fort. an. 46

CICERO TREBATIO S.

Illuseras heri inter scyphos, quod dixeram controversiam esse, possetne heres, quod furtum antea factum esset, furti recte agere. itaque, etsi domum bene potus seroque redieram, tamen id caput ubi haec controversia est notavi et descriptum tibi misi, ut scires id quod tu neminem sensisse dicebas Sex. Aelium, M'. Manilium, M. Brutum sensisse. ego tamen Scaevolae et Testae adsentior.

332 (VII.21)

Scr. in Tusculano parte post. m. Iun. an. 44

CICERO TREBATIO S.

Sili causam te docui. is postea fuit apud me. cum ei dicerem tibi videri sponsionem illam nos sine periculo facere posse, 'si bonorum Turpiliae possessionem Q. Caepio praetor ex edicto suo mihi dedit,' negare aiebat Servium tabulas testamenti esse eas quas instituisset is qui factionem testamenti non habuerit; hoc idem Offilium[1] dicere.

[1] officium

[1] I.e. in the interval between the testator's death and the heir's taking possession. A theft committed during the testator's lifetime was actionable.

[2] No doubt in Scaevola the Pontifex's great treatise on civil law.

331 (VII.22)
CICERO TO TREBATIUS

Rome, 46 (?)

From Cicero to Trebatius greetings.

You made game of me yesterday over our cups for saying that it was a moot point whether an heir can properly take action for theft in respect of a theft previously committed.[1] So when I got home, though late and well in tipple, I noted the relevant section[2] and send you a transcript. You will find that the view which, according to you, has never been held by anybody was in fact held by Sex. Aelius, Manius Manilius, and M. Brutus.[3] However, for my part I agree with Scaevola and Testa.

332 (VII.21)
CICERO TO TREBATIUS

Tusculum, June (latter half) 44

From Cicero to Trebatius greetings.

I have given you an account of Silius' case.[1] Since then he has been at my house. When I told him that in your opinion we could safely make the stipulation ('if Q. Caepio,[2] Praetor, under his edict has given me possession of the estate of Turpilia'), he said that Servius does not agree that the will of a person not possessing testamentary capacity has any existence in law, and that Offilius says the

[3] Three eminent second-century jurists.
[1] The legal details are too complicated to go into here.
[2] I.e. M. Brutus, the City Praetor.

tecum se locutum negabat meque rogavit ut se et causam suam tibi commendarem.

Nec vir melior, mi Testa, nec mihi amicior P. Silio quisquam est, te tamen excepto. gratissimum mihi igitur feceris si ad eum ultro veneris eique pollicitus eris; sed, si me amas, quam primum. hoc te vehementer etiam atque etiam rogo.

333 (VII.20)

Scr. Veliae XIII *Kal. Sext. an. 44*

CICERO TREBATIO S.

1   Amabilior mihi Velia fuit quod te ab ea sensi amari. sed quid ego dicam 'te,' quem quis non amat? Rufio me dius fidius tuus ita desiderabatur ut si esset unus e nobis. sed te ego non reprehendo qui illum ad aedificationem tuam traduxeris. quamquam enim Velia non est vilior quam Lupercal, tamen istuc malo quam haec omnia. tu,[1] si me audies quem soles, has paternas possessiones tenebis (nescio quid enim Velienses verebantur), neque Haletem, nobilem amnem, relinques nec Papirianam domum deseres. quamquam illa quidem habet lotum, a quo etiam advenae teneri

---

[1] tamen *C. Stephanus:* tu ⟨tamen⟩ *Lamb.:* ⟨at⟩ tu *coni. SB*

---

[1] Cicero was on his way to Athens, though he got no further than Syracuse; cf. *Letters to Atticus* 415 (XVI.7).1. It is not clear that he stayed in Trebatius' house.

[2] A slave or freedman of Trebatius.

[3] A grotto at the foot of the Palatine, where the she-wolf was

same. He told me that he has not spoken to you, and asked me to commend to you himself and his case.

My dear Testa, there is no better man alive than P. Silius and no better friend to me, yourself however excepted. I shall therefore be deeply obliged if you will go to see him and promise your services. But if you love me, no delay! I ask this as a most particular favour.

333 (VII.20)
CICERO TO TREBATIUS

Velia, 20 July 44

From Cicero to Trebatius greetings.

I have found Velia[1] all the more likeable a place because I saw how much Velia likes you. But I need not talk of you, who are liked by all the world—your man Rufio[2] is as much missed, my word upon it, as if he were one of ourselves. But I don't blame you for taking him along to your building operations. Velia is as respectable a place as the Lupercal,[3] but still I prefer Rome to everything down here. But if you will take my advice, as you generally do, you will hold on to your paternal property (the good folk of Velia are somewhat apprehensive), and not forsake the noble river Hales and the house of the Papirii.[4] To be sure it contains a lotus, a plant which captivates even strangers[5]—

---

supposed to have suckled Romulus and Remus. Presumably Trebatius was building in its vicinity. The jingle *velia . . . vilior* is hardly reproduceable.   [4] Presumably Trebatius' house, called after its previous owners.

[5] With allusion to the lotus eaters in the *Odyssey*.

2   solent; quem tamen si excideris, multum prospexeris. sed
in primis opportunum videtur, his praesertim temporibus,
habere perfugium, primum eorum urbem quibus carus
sis, deinde tuam domum tuosque agros, eaque remoto,
salubri, amoeno loco; idque etiam mea interesse, mi Trebati, arbitror. sed valebis meaque negotia videbis meque
dis iuvantibus ante brumam exspectabis.

3   Ego a Sex. Fadio, Niconis discipulo, librum abstuli
Νίκωνος περὶ Πολυφαγίας. o medicum suavem meque
docilem ad hanc disciplinam! sed Bassus noster me de hoc
libro celavit, te quidem non videtur.

     Ventus increbrescit. cura ut valeas.

     XIII Kal. Sext. Velia.

334 (VII.19)

Scr. Regii v Kal. Sext. an. 44

CICERO TREBATIO S.

     Vide quanti apud me sis (etsi iure id quidem, non enim
te amore vinco, verum tamen): quod praesenti tibi prope
subnegaram, non tribueram certe, id absenti debere non
potui. itaque ut primum Velia navigare coepi, institui Topi-
ca Aristotelea conscribere ab ipsa urbe commonitus aman-

---

6 Prescriptions by a physician so called are cited by Celsus.
Nothing else is known of Fadius or Bassus.

7 Perhaps with the implication that Trebatius knew all about
Heavy Eating.

1 In fact Cicero's *Topics* (on the sources of proof, *topoi*) is not
based on Aristotle's work of the same name, which he had perhaps

though if you cut it down, you will see a long way further
than your nose! But there is a great deal to be said, particularly in times like these, for having a refuge: a town full of
people who care for you and a house and land of your own,
that too in a retired, healthy, and pleasant locality. And I
feel that I myself have some stake in the matter, my dear
Trebatius. However, you must keep well and look after
my affairs and expect me back, Gods willing, before mid-
winter.

I have taken away a book, from Nico's[6] pupil Sex.
Fadius: 'Nico on Heavy Eating.' What a charming physician, and how docile a patient he would find me! But our
friend Bassus told me nothing about that book—though he
seems to have told you![7]

The wind is getting brisker. Take care of yourself.

20 July, Velia

334 (VII.19)
CICERO TO TREBATIUS

Regium, 28 July 44

From Cicero to Trebatius greetings.

This will show how highly I regard you—as indeed I
ought, for your affection is no less warm than my own; but
anyhow, that request of yours to which to your face I said
something a little like no, and at any rate did not say yes—
in your absence I could not let it go unanswered. As soon as
my boat left Velia, I set to work on writing up Aristotle's
Topics.[1] The town itself, in which you are so well-loved a

never seen. He seems to have used Antiochus of Ascalon, who
claimed to be following Aristotle.

tissima tui. eum librum tibi misi Regio, scriptum quam planissime res illa scribi potuit. sin tibi quaedam videbuntur obscuriora, cogitare debebis nullam artem litteris sine interprete et sine aliqua exercitatione percipi posse. non longe abieris: num ius civile vestrum ex libris cognosci potest? qui quamquam plurimi sunt, doctorem tamen usumque desiderant. quamquam tu, si attente leges, si saepius, per te omnia consequere ut recte[1] intellegas; ut vero etiam ipsi tibi loci proposita quaestione occurrant exercitatione consequere. in qua quidem nos te continebimus, si et salvi redierimus et salva ista offenderimus.

v Kal. Sext. Regio.

335 (XI.29)

Scr. fort. Anagniae in. m. Quint. an. 44

CICERO OPPIO S. D.

1   Dubitanti mihi, quod scit Atticus noster, de hoc toto consilio profectionis, quod in utramque partem in mentem multa veniebant, magnum pondus accessit ad tollendam dubitationem iudicium et consilium tuum. nam et scripsisti aperte quid tibi videretur et Atticus ad me sermonem tuum pertulit. semper iudicavi in te et in capiendo consilio prudentiam summam esse et in dando fidem, maximeque sum expertus cum initio civilis belli per litteras te consu-

---

[1] certe et *(K. Müller)*

[2] A somewhat defensive qualification. The *Topics* is the most difficult of Cicero's works, the examples being taken from Roman law in compliment to Trebatius.

figure, reminded me of you. I am sending the book to you from Regium, written in as clear a style as the material admits.[2] If you find it in places hard to follow, you must remember that no technical subject can be acquired by reading, without an interpreter and a certain amount of practice. You will not have far to go for an illustration: can your Civil Law be learned from books? There are any number of them, but they need a teacher and experience. However, if you read and reread carefully, you will understand everything correctly by your own efforts. But only practice will make the topics present themselves to your mind automatically when a question is proposed. I shall keep you hard at it, if I get back safely and find all safe in Rome.

28 July, Regium

335 (XI.29)
CICERO TO OPPIUS

Anagnia(?), July (beginning) 44

From Cicero to Oppius greetings.

As our friend Atticus knows, I have been hesitating about this whole project of going abroad, because many considerations occurred to me on either side. Your judgement and advice have now come massively into the scales to put an end to my indecision. You have written your opinion in plain terms and Atticus has reported to me what you said to him. I have always had the highest respect for your sagacity in framing advice and your honesty in giving it, which I experienced most notably when I wrote to you at

luissem quid mihi faciendum esse censeres, eundumne ad Pompeium an manendum in Italia. suasisti ut consulerem dignitati meae; ex quo quid sentires intellexi et sum admiratus fidem tuam et in consilio dando religionem, quod, cum aliud malle amicissimum tuum putares, antiquius tibi officium meum quam illius voluntas fuit.

2   Equidem et ante hoc tempus te dilexi et semper me a te diligi sensi; et cum abessem atque in magnis periculis essem, et me absentem et meos praesentis a te cultos et defensos esse memini, et post meum reditum quam familiariter mecum vixeris quaeque ego de te senserim et praedicarim omnis qui solent haec animadvertere testis habemus. gravissimum vero iudicium de mea fide et constantia fecisti cum post mortem Caesaris [et] totum te[1] ad amicitiam meam contulisti. quod tuum iudicium nisi mea summa benevolentia erga te omnibusque meritis comprobaro, ipse me hominem non putabo.

3   Tu, mi Oppi, conservabis amorem tuum (etsi more magis hoc quidem scribo quam quo te admonendum putem) meaque omnia tuebere; quae tibi ne ignota essent Attico mandavi. a me autem, cum paulum oti nacti erimus, uberiores litteras exspectato.

Da operam ut valeas. hoc mihi gratius facere nihil potes.

[1] te totum [te] *coni. SB*

the beginning of the Civil War to ask you what you thought I should do—join Pompey or stay in Italy. You recommended me to think of my reputation; from which I understood your opinion, and admired your scrupulous honesty as an adviser. For although you believed that your greatest friend[1] would have preferred it otherwise, you thought more of my duty than of his wishes.

For my part, I had a regard for you even before that time and have always felt that you had a regard for me. When I was away and in great danger, I remember how you cared for and protected my absent self and my family on the spot. To our familiar association since my return, and to my sentiments and public expressions about yourself, we can call everybody who notices such things to witness. But the weightiest tribute you paid to my good faith and consistency was after Caesar's death, when you gave me your friendship without reserve. If I do not justify your choice by the most hearty good will towards you and by all friendly offices in my power, I shall consider myself a poor creature indeed.

On your side, my dear Oppius, you will maintain your affection (I say this more as a conventional form than because I suppose you need any reminder), and give me your support in all my concerns. I have asked Atticus to make sure you don't lack information about them. Expect a more substantial letter from me as soon as I get a little time to spare.

Take care of your health—you can do me no greater favour.

[1] Caesar.

336 (XI.3)

Scr. Neapoli prid. Non. Sext. an. 44

BRUTUS ET CASSIUS PR. S. D. ANTONIO COS.

1 S. v. b.

Litteras tuas legimus simillimas edicti tui, contumeliosas, minacis, minime dignas quae a te nobis mitterentur. nos, Antoni, te nulla lacessi<i>mus[1] iniuria neque miraturum credidimus si praetores et ea dignitate homines aliquid edicto postulassemus a consule. quod si indignaris ausos esse id facere, concede nobis ut doleamus ne hoc quidem abs te Bruto et Cassio tribui.

2 Nam de dilectibus habitis et pecuniis imperatis, exercitibus sollicitatis et nuntiis trans mare missis quod te questum esse negas, nos quidem tibi credimus optimo animo te fecisse, sed tamen neque agnoscimus quicquam eorum et te miramur, cum haec reticueris, non potuisse continere iracundiam tuam quin nobis de morte Caesaris obiceres.

3 Illud vero quem ad modum ferendum sit tute cogita, non licere praetoribus concordiae ac libertatis causa per edictum de suo iure decedere quin consul arma minetur. quorum fiducia nihil est quod nos terreas. neque enim decet aut convenit nobis periculo ulli summittere animum nostrum neque est Antonio postulandum ut iis imperet

¹ *(Vict.)*

---

[1] Brutus and Cassius had put out an edict to the effect that they were inhibited from carrying out their duties as Praetors and were ready to retire into voluntary exile.

336 (XI.3)
M. BRUTUS AND CASSIUS TO ANTONY

Naples, 4 August 44

From Brutus and Cassius, Praetors, to Antonius, Consul, greetings.

We trust you are well.

We have read your letter. We find it very similar to your edict, offensive and menacing, a letter which ought never to have been sent by you to us. We, sir, have done nothing to provoke or annoy you, nor did we suppose that you would be surprised if, as Praetors and gentlemen of a certain station, we put forward in an edict a request to you as Consul. If you resent our venturing it, permit us to be sorry that you grudge even so small a licence to Brutus and Cassius.

You say that you have made no protest concerning our levies of troops and money, our tampering with the loyalty of the armed forces, and our dispatching of messengers overseas. We believe in the excellence of your motives, but at the same time we do not acknowledge any of these allegations; we also find it surprising that, having held your peace on these matters, you should not have been able to control your spleen so far as to refrain from throwing Caesar's death in our teeth.

One point we must ask you yourself to consider: is it tolerable that Praetors should not be permitted in the interests of concord and freedom to abate the rights of their office by edict[1] without a Consul threatening military violence? You must not count upon such a threat to intimidate us. It would be unworthy and unbecoming in us to be cowed by any personal danger; and you, sir, should not

quorum opera liber est. nos si alia hortarentur ut bellum
civile suscitare vellemus, litterae tuae nihil proficerent;
nulla enim minantis auctoritas apud liberos est. sed pulchre intellegis non posse nos quoquam impelli et fortassis
ea re minaciter agis ut iudicium nostrum metus videatur.

4   Nos in hac sententia sumus ut te cupiamus in libera re
publica magnum atque honestum esse, vocemus te ad nul-
las inimicitias, sed tamen pluris nostram libertatem quam
tuam amicitiam aestimemus. tu etiam atque etiam vide
quid suscipias, quid sustinere possis; neque quam diu vixe-
rit Caesar sed quam non diu regnarit fac cogites. deos
quaesumus consilia tua rei publicae salutaria sint ac tibi; si
minus, ut salva atque honesta re publica tibi quam minimum noceant optamus.

Prid. Non. Sext.

337 (XVI.21)

Scr. Athenis fort. m. Sext. an. 44

CICERO F. TIRONI SUO DULCISSIMO S.

1   Cum vehementer tabellarios exspectarem cottidie, aliquando venerunt post diem quadragesimum et sextum
quam a vobis discesserant. quorum mihi fuit adventus
exoptatissimus. nam cum maximam cepissem laetitiam ex
humanissimi et carissimi patris epistula, tum vero iucundissimae tuae litterae cumulum mihi gaudi attulerunt.
itaque me iam non paenitebat intercapedinem scribendi

claim authority over those to whom you owe your freedom. Suppose we desired on other grounds to stir up civil war, your letter would have no effect. Free men are not impressed by threats. But you are perfectly well aware that we cannot be driven into any course, and it may be that your present menacing behaviour is designed to make our deliberate choice look like fear.

To summarize our position, we are desirous to see you an important and respected member of a free commonwealth. We are not fastening any quarrel upon you, At the same time, our freedom means more to us than your friendship. On your part, consider well what you undertake and what you can sustain. Bear in mind, not only the length of Caesar's life, but the brevity of his reign. We pray heaven that your counsels may be salutary to the commonwealth and to you. If it should be otherwise, then we pray that they may bring you as little hurt as possible without detriment to the public safety and honour.

4 August.

337 (XVI.21)
M. CICERO JUNIOR TO TIRO

Athens, August (?) 44

From Cicero junior to his beloved Tiro greetings.

I was eagerly expecting couriers every day, and at last they have come, forty-five days after leaving home. I was delighted by their arrival. My kindest and dearest father's letter gave me great pleasure, and then your own most agreeable letter put the finishing touch to my happiness. I am no longer sorry to have made a break in our correspon-

fecisse, sed potius laetabar; fructum enim magnum humanitatis tuae capiebam ex silentio mearum litterarum. vehementer igitur gaudeo te meam sine dubitatione accepisse
excusationem.

2   Gratos tibi optatosque esse qui de me rumores ad-
feruntur non dubito, mi dulcissime Tiro, praestaboque et
enitar ut in dies magis magisque haec nascens de me duplicetur opinio. qua re quod polliceris te bucinatorem fore
existimationis meae, firmo id constantique animo facias
licet. tantum enim mihi dolorem cruciatumque attulerunt
errata aetatis meae ut non solum animus a factis sed aures
quoque a commemoratione abhorreant. cuius te sollicitudinis et doloris participem fuisse notum exploratumque
est mihi, nec id mirum; nam cum omnia mea causa velles
mihi successa, tum etiam tua. socium enim te meorum
3   commodorum semper esse volui. quoniam igitur tum ex
me doluisti, nunc ut duplicetur tuum ex me gaudium
praestabo.

Cratippo me scito non ut discipulum sed ut filium esse
coniunctissimum. nam cum [et]¹ audio illum libenter tum
etiam propriam eius suavitatem vehementer amplector.
sum totos dies cum eo noctisque saepe numero partem;
exoro enim ut mecum quam saepissime cenet. hac intro-
ducta consuetudine saepe inscientibus nobis et cenantibus
obrepit sublataque severitate philosophiae humanissime
nobiscum iocatur. qua re da operam ut hunc talem, tam
iucundum, tam excellentem virum videas quam primum.

¹ (Man.)

dence, rather the contrary, since as a result of my letters falling silent I am repaid by this example of your good nature. I am truly delighted that you have accepted my excuses without question.

I don't doubt that you are pleased with the reports you are hearing of me, dearest Tiro, and that they are such as you wished to hear. I shall make sure and work hard to see that this tiny new image of mine goes on getting bigger and bigger[1] as the days go by. So you can carry out your promise to be my publicity agent with every confidence. Young men make mistakes, and mine have brought me so much unhappiness and torment that I hate to think of what I did, or even hear it mentioned. Very well do I know that you shared my worry and unhappiness, as well you might, for you wanted all to go right for me not for my sake only but for your own too, because I have always wanted you to have a part in any good things that come my way. Well, since I gave you unhappiness then, I shall make sure to give you twice as much happiness now.

I can tell you that Cratippus and I are very close, more like father and son than teacher and pupil. I enjoy hearing him lecture, and quite delight in his own pleasant company. I spend all day with him and often part of the night, for I beg him into dining with me as frequently as possible. Now that he has got into the habit, he often drops in on us at dinner unawares, and then he puts off the grave philosopher and jokes with us in the most genial way. So you must try to meet him as soon as possible—he is such an agreeable, excellent man.

[1] Literally 'is doubled more and more,' a phrase of which Cicero senior would hardly have approved.

4   Nam quid ego de Bruttio dicam, quem nullo tempore a me patior discedere? cuius cum frugi severaque est vita tum etiam iucundissima convictio; non est enim seiunctus iocus a philologia et cottidiana συζητήσει. huic ego locum in proximo conduxi et, ut possum, ex meis angustiis illius

5   sustento tenuitatem. praeterea declamitare Graece apud Cassium institui, Latine autem apud Bruttium exerceri volo. utor familiaribus et cottidianis convictoribus quos secum Mytilenis Cratippus adduxit, hominibus et doctis et illi probatissimis. multum etiam mecum est Epicrates, princeps Atheniensium, et Leonides et horum ceteri similes. τὰ μὲν οὖν καθ᾽ ἡμᾶς τάδε.

6   De Gorgia autem quod mihi scribis, erat quidem ille in cottidiana declamatione utilis, sed omnia postposui dum modo praeceptis patris parerem; διαρρήδην enim scripserat ut eum dimitterem statim. tergiversari nolui, ne mea nimia σπουδὴ suspicionem ei aliquam importaret. deinde illud etiam mihi succurrebat, grave esse me de iudicio

7   patris iudicare. tuum tamen studium et consilium gratum acceptumque est mihi.

     Excusationem angustiarum tui temporis accipio; scio enim quam soleas esse occupatus. emisse te praedium vehementer gaudeo feliciterque tibi rem istam evenire cupio. hoc loco me tibi gratulari noli mirari; eodem enim fere loco tu quoque emisse te fecisti me certiorem. habes! deponendae tibi sunt urbanitates; rusticus Romanus factus es. quo modo ego mihi nunc ante oculos tuum iucun-

---

2 Nothing more known, but no doubt an Italian.
3 Another unknown professor of rhetoric.
4 Later a noted rhetorician in Rome, he is said in Plutarch's

As for Bruttius,[2] what can I say? I never let him out of my sight. He lives simply and strictly, and he is the best of company too. Fun goes hand in hand with literary study and daily disputation. I have rented a lodging for him near mine, and as he is a poor man, I help him as best I can out of my own meagre funds. Also I have started regular declamation in Greek with Cassius,[3] and I want to practise in Latin with Bruttius. Some people whom Cratippus brought over from Mytilene, scholars whom he entirely approves of, are my friends and daily associates. I see a lot of Epicrates too (a leading man in Athenian society), and Leonides, and people of that sort. So as to myself—*voilà!*

As for what you say about Gorgias,[4] he *was* useful to me in declamation practice, but I have put obedience to my father's directions above all other considerations. He had written telling me *sans phrase* to get rid of Gorgias at once. I thought I had better not boggle over it—if I made too much fuss, he might think it suspicious. Also it came to my mind that I should be taking a lot upon myself in judging my father's judgement. All the same, I am very grateful for your concern and advice.

I quite accept your excuse about shortage of time. I know how busy you generally are. I'm really delighted to hear that you have bought a property, and hope it turns out a successful investment. Don't be surprised at my congratulations coming at this stage in my letter—that was about the point where you put the news of your purchase. Well, you are a landed proprietor! You must shed your town-bred ways—you are now a Roman squire! How amusing to

Life of Cicero (24) to have led M. Cicero junior into bad ways and to have received an angry letter (in Greek) from his father.

dissimum conspectum propono! videor enim videre
ementem te rusticas res, cum vilico loquentem, in lacinia
servantem ex mensa secunda semina. sed, quod ad rem
pertinet, me tum tibi defuisse aeque ac tu doleo. sed noli
dubitare, mi Tiro, quin te sublevaturus sim, si modo Fortuna me, praesertim cum sciam communem nobis emptum
esse istum fundum.

8   De mandatis quod tibi curae fuit est mihi gratum. sed
peto a te ut quam celerrime mihi librarius mittatur,
maxime quidem Graecus. multum enim mihi eripitur
operae in exscribendis hypomnematis.

Tu velim in primis cures ut valeas, ut una συμφιλολο-
γεῖν possimus. Antherum[2] tibi commendo.

Vale.

338 (XVI.25)

Scr. Athenis fort. autumno an. 44

CICERO F. TIRONI SUO S.

Etsi iusta et idonea usus es excusatione intermissionis
litterarum tuarum, tamen id ne saepius facias rogo. nam
etsi de re publica rumoribus et nuntiis certior fio et de sua
in me voluntate semper ad me perscribit pater, tamen de
quavis minima re scripta a te ad me epistula semper fuit
gratissima. qua re, cum in primis tuas desiderem litteras,

---

[2] anterum H

---

[5] Presumably the slave who carried the letter. *Anterum,* usually read, would come from a hybrid form Anterus (instead of

picture the delightful sight of you now! I imagine you buying farm tackle, talking to the bailiff, hoarding pips at dessert in your pockets! But seriously, I am as sorry as you that I was not there to lend you a hand. However, dear Tiro, I *shall* help you, provided luck helps me, especially as I know you have bought the place to share with us.

Thank you for attending to my commissions. But do please get a clerk sent out to me, preferably a Greek. I waste a lot of time copying out my notes.

Take care of your health first and foremost, so that we can be students together. I commend Antherus[5] to you.

Good-bye.

338 (XVI.25)
M. CICERO JUNIOR TO TIRO

Athens, autumn (?) 44

From Cicero junior to his dear Tiro greetings.

Your excuse for letting your correspondence with me lapse is fair and sufficient, but I beg of you not to do this often. Even though I am kept informed of political rumours and reports and my father constantly writes to me about his kind feelings towards me,[1] a letter from you, no matter what or how trivial the topic, has always been most welcome to me. So since I miss your letters above all things,

Anterōs) also found in inscriptions; cf. *Letters to Atticus* 182 (IX.14).2, 211 (XI.1).1.

[1] Translating "ce qu'il me veut," Beaujeu infers that young Cicero continued to receive imperious and captious letters from his father (Vol. IX, p. 153). But *voluntas in (erga) aliquem* is standard for "attitude" (especially friendly) towards a person.

noli committere ut excusatione potius expleas officium
scribendi quam adsiduitate epistularum.

Vale.

339 (XII.20)

Scr. Romae fort. IV Non. Sept. an. 44

CICERO CORNIFICIO

Gratae mihi tuae litterae, nisi quod Sinuessanum de-
vers‹or›iolum[1] contempsisti. quam quidem contumeliam
villa pusilla iniquo animo feret, nisi in Cumano et Pompeiano reddideris πάντα περὶ πάντων. sic igitur facies,
meque amabis et scripto aliquo lacesses. ego enim respondere facilius possum quam provocare. quod si, ut es, ces-
sabis, lacessam, nec tua ignavia etiam ‹mihi›[2] inertiam
adferet. plura otiosus; haec cum essem in senatu exaravi.

340 (X.1)

Scr. Romae m. Sept. an. 44

CICERO PLANCO

1   Et afui proficiscens in Graeciam et, postea quam de

1 *(Lamb.)*
2 *(Lamb.)*

---

[1] Perhaps written at the sitting of the Senate on that day, after
Cornificius had set out for his province of Africa.

don't let your obligation to write be fulfilled in the making of excuses, but by a steady stream of letters.

Good-bye.

339 (XII.20)
CICERO TO CORNIFICIUS

Rome, 2 September 44 (?)[1]

From Cicero to Cornificius.

Thank you for your letter—but you should not have been so rude to my little lodge at Sinuessa.[2] The insult will rankle with my poor little house, unless you make an *amende honorable* at Cumae or Pompeii. So that is what you must do; also you must remember me kindly, and prod me with a literary effort. I find it easier to answer a challenge than to issue one. However, if you drag your feet (a tendency of yours), I shall be the one to prod. Your laziness will not make an idler of *me*. More when I have time to spare—I scribbled this in the Senate.

340 (X.1)
CICERO TO PLANCUS

Rome, September 44

From Cicero to Plancus.

I have been away, en route for Greece; and ever since

[2] Perhaps acquired from Lepta; cf. Letter 262. Evidently Cornificius had declined an invitation to use it on his way south.

me‹di›o[1] cursu rei publicae sum voce revocatus, numquam per M. Antonium quietus fui; cuius tanta est non insolentia (nam id quidem vulgare vitium est) sed immanitas non modo ut vocem sed ne vultum quidem liberum possit ferre cuiusquam. itaque mihi maximae curae est non de mea quidem vita, cui satis feci vel aetate vel factis vel, si quid etiam hoc ad rem pertinet, gloria, sed me patria sollicitat in primisque, mi Plance, exspectatio consulatus tui, quae ita longa est ut optandum ‹magis quam sperandum›[2] sit ut possimus ad id tempus rei publicae spiritum ducere. quae potest enim spes esse in ea re publica in qua hominis impotentissimi atque intemperantissimi armis oppressa sunt omnia et in qua nec senatus nec populus vim habet ullam nec leges ullae sunt nec iudicia nec omnino simulacrum aliquod ac vestigium civitatis?

2   Sed quoniam acta omnia mitti ad te arbitrabar, nihil erat quod singulis de rebus scriberem. illud autem erat amoris mei, quem a tua pueritia susceptum non servavi solum sed etiam auxi, monere te atque hortari ut in rem publicam omni cogitatione curaque incumberes. quae si ad tuum tempus perducitur, facilis gubernatio est; ut perducatur autem magnae cum diligentiae est tum etiam fortunae.

3   Sed et te aliquanto ante, ut spero, habebimus et, praeterquam quod rei publicae consulere debemus, tamen[3] tuae dignitati ita favemus ut omne nostrum consilium,

---

[1] (*Man.*)

[2] (*SB*: vix *Watt*)

[3] etiam *Wes*.

the voice of the commonwealth called me home half way through my journey, Mark Antony has not left me a quiet moment. His insolence—but that is a common fault, say rather his atrocity—has reached such proportions that he cannot bear anybody to look like a free man, let alone speak like one. My greatest concern is not for my own life. As for that, I have run my race, whether in respect of years or achievements or (if that too be relevant) glory. But the thought of my country, and above all the prospect of your Consulship,[1] my dear Plancus, makes me anxious—it is so far away that I must pray rather than hope to be granted breath until that time comes for the commonwealth. For what hope can there be in a commonwealth where all lies crushed by the armed force of a violent, licentious individual, where neither Senate nor People has any power, where neither laws nor law courts exist, nor any semblance or trace whatsoever of a free community?

Well, I imagine you are sent all the news of the day, so there is no point in my going into details. But the steadfast and indeed increasing affection I have entertained for you ever since you were a boy prompts me to urge and admonish you to consecrate all your thoughts and care to the commonwealth. If it lasts until your time comes, its guidance will be easy; but to make it last great fortune as well as great pains is required.

However, I hope we shall see you back some considerable time before then. Apart from my obligation to think of the commonwealth I also take a strong and sympathetic interest in your future dignity. My advice and zeal, my time

[1] By Caesar's appointment Plancus and D. Brutus were to hold the Consulship in 42.

studium, officium, operam, laborem, diligentiam ad am-
plitudinem tuam conferamus. ita facillime et rei publicae,
quae mihi carissima est, et amicitiae nostrae, quam sanc-
tissime nobis colendam puto, me intellego satis facturum.

4 Furnium nostrum tanti a te fieri quantum ipsius humanitas et dignitas postulat nec miror et gaudeo, teque hoc
existimare volo, quicquid in eum iudici officique contule-
ris, id ita me accipere ut in me ipsum te putem contulisse.

341 (X.2)

Scr. Romae c. XIII Kal. Oct. an. 44

CICERO PLANCO S.

1 Meum studium honori tuo pro necessitudine nostra
non defuisset si aut tuto in senatum aut honeste venire
potuissem; sed nec sine periculo quisquam libere de re
publica sentiens versari potest in summa impunitate gla-
diorum nec nostrae dignitatis videtur esse ibi sententiam
de re publica dicere ubi me et melius et propius audiant
armati quam senatores.

2 Quapropter in privatis rebus nullum neque officium
neque studium meum desiderabis; ne in publicis quidem,
si quid erit in quo me interesse necesse sit, umquam deero
ne cum periculo quidem meo dignitati tuae. in iis autem
rebus quae nihilo minus ut ego absim confici poterunt peto
a te ut me rationem habere velis et salutis et dignitatis
meae.

---

[1] Probably for a Supplication in honour of Plancus' military
successes in Rhaetia.

and service, my effort and industry, are entirely devoted to your advancement. Thus I conceive I shall most easily render what is due both to the commonwealth, which is most dear to me, and to our friendship, which I hold us bound religiously to maintain.

I am not surprised, but I am happy, that you value our friend Furnius as highly as his own goodness and high standing deserve. Please believe that any good opinion or good office you bestow upon him is in my estimation bestowed upon myself.

341 (X.2)
CICERO TO PLANCUS

Rome, ca. 19 September 44

From Cicero to Plancus greetings.

As a friend I should not have failed to support the decree in your honour,[1] had I been able to enter the Senate in security and dignity. But it is dangerous for any man of independent political views to move about in public when swords are drawn with complete impunity; and it does not seem to comport with my dignity to make a speech in a House where men-at-arms would hear me better and at shorter distance than members.

In private matters you shall find me always zealous to serve you; and even in matters public, if there be some compelling occasion for me to take part, I shall never fail you in your career, even at risk to myself. But in matters which can just as well be settled in my absence I would ask you to wish me to consider my own safety and dignity.

342 (XI.4)

Scr. in Gallia Cisalpina m. Sept. an. 44

D. BRUTUS IMP. COS. DESIG. S. D. CICERONI

1   Si de tua in me voluntate dubitarem, multis a te verbis peterem ut dignitatem meam tuerere. sed profecto est ita ut mihi persuasi, me tibi esse curae.

Progressus sum ad Inalpinos cum exercitu, non tam nomen imperatorium captans quam cupiens militibus satis
2   facere firmosque eos ad tuendas nostras res efficere; quod mihi videor consecutus; nam et liberalitatem nostram et animum sunt experti. cum omnium bellicosissimis bellum gessi. multa castella cepi, multa vastavi. non sine causa ad senatum litteras misi. adiuva nos tua sententia; quod cum facies, ex magna parte communi commodo inservieris.

343 (XI.6)

Scr. Romae c. ex. m. Sept. an. 44

M. CICERO S. D. D. BRUTO IMP. COS. DESIG.

Lupus noster cum Romam sexto die Mutina venisset, postridie me mane convenit; tua mihi mandata diligentissime exposuit et litteras reddidit. quod mihi tuam dignita-

342 (XI.4)

D. BRUTUS TO CICERO

Cisalpine Gaul, September 44

From D. Brutus, Imperator, Consul-Elect, to Cicero greetings.

If I had any doubt of your sentiments towards me, I should use many words in requesting you to defend my public standing; but the fact surely is as I am convinced, that you have my interests at heart.

I marched against the Alpine tribes, not so much in quest of the title Imperator, as desiring to satisfy my men and make them firm for the defence of our concerns. I think I have succeeded; for they have had practical experience of my liberality and spirit. I have made war on the bravest warriors in the world, taken many strong places, laid many areas waste. My dispatch to the Senate is not unwarranted. Support me with your voice in the House. In so doing you will be serving the common cause in no small measure.

343 (XI.6)

CICERO TO D. BRUTUS

Rome, ca. end of September

From M. Cicero to D. Brutus, Imperator, Consul-Elect, greetings.

Arriving in Rome five days after leaving Mutina, our friend Lupus had an interview with me the following morning, at which he set forth your message very carefully and delivered your letter. When you commend your public

139

tem commendas, eodem tempore existimo te mihi meam dignitatem commendare, quam mehercule non habeo tua cariorem. qua re mihi gratissimum facies si exploratum habebis tuis laudibus nullo loco nec consilium nec studium meum defuturum.

344 (XII.2)

Scr. Romae inter XIII Kal. Oct. et VI Non. Oct. an. 44

CICERO CASSIO S.

1   Vehementer laetor tibi probari sententiam et orationem meam. qua si saepius uti liceret, nihil esset negoti libertatem et rem publicam reciperare. sed homo amens et perditus multoque nequior quam ille ipse quem tu nequissimum occisum esse dixisti caedis initium quaerit nullamque aliam ob causam me auctorem fuisse Caesaris interficiendi criminatur nisi ut in me veterani incitentur; quod ego periculum non extimesco, modo vestri facti gloriam cum mea laude communicet. ita nec Pisoni, qui in eum primus invectus est nullo adsentiente, nec mihi, qui idem tricesimo post die feci, nec P. Servilio, qui me est consecutus, tuto in senatum venire licet. caedem enim gladiator quaerit eiusque initium a. d. XIII Kal. Oct. a me se facturum putavit; ad quem paratus venerat, cum in villa Metelli compluris dies commentatus esset. quae autem in lustris et in vino commentatio potuit esse? itaque omnibus

---

1 The First Philippic, Cicero's first public challenge to Antony, delivered on 2 September.   2 Metellus Scipio's villa at Tibur, bought by Antony after its confiscation.

ʃtanding to my care, I feel that you are also commending my own, which is truly no more precious to me than yours. Therefore you will gratify me highly if you will rest assured that my counsel and support shall at no point be lacking to promote your credit.

344 (XII.2)
CICERO TO CASSIUS

Rome, between 19 September and 2 October 44

From Cicero to Cassius greetings.

I am very glad to find that my vote and speech[1] meet with your approval. If I had been able to make such speeches often, the recovery of liberty and constitution would have been no problem. But a crazy desperado, far more wicked even than he whom you called the wickedest man ever killed, is looking for a starting point for a massacre. In charging me with having instigated Caesar's slaying he has no other object than to incite the veterans against me (a risk which I am not afraid to take so long as he honours me with a share in the glory of your exploit). Accordingly, neither Piso, who was the first to make an (unsupported) attack on him, nor I, who followed Piso's example a month later, nor P. Servilius, who came after me, can enter the Senate in safety. The gladiator is looking for a massacre, and thought to make a start with me on 19 September. He came prepared for the occasion, having spent several days in Metellus' villa[2] getting up a speech. How could that be done in an orgy of drink and debauchery? So,

est visus, ut ad te antea scripsi, vomere suo more, non dicere.

2 Qua re, quod scribis te confidere auctoritate et eloquentia nostra aliquid profici posse, non nihil ut in tantis malis est profectum. intellegit enim populus Romanus tris esse consularis qui, quia de re publica bene senserint, libere locuti sint, tuto in senatum venire non possint. nec est praeterea quod quicquam exspectes. tuus enim necessarius adfinitate nova delectatur, itaque iam non est studiosus ludorum infinitoque fratris tui plausu dirumpitur. alter item adfinis novis commentariis Caesaris delenitus est. sed haec tolerabilia, illud non ferendum, quod est qui vestro anno filium suum consulem futurum putet ob eamque

3 causam se huic latroni deservire prae se ferat. nam L. Cotta, familiaris meus, fatali quadam desperatione, ut ait, minus in senatum venit; L. Caesar, optimus et fortissimus civis, valetudine impeditur; Ser. Sulpicius, et summa auctoritate et optime sentiens, non adest. reliquos exceptis designatis—ignosce mihi, sed non numero consularis.

---

3 Antony's tendency to vomit in public is featured in the Second Philippic and attested in Plutarch's life of him.

4 L. Aemilius Paullus, whose brother Lepidus was married to a sister of Cassius' wife Junia Tertia. Lepidus' son had recently been betrothed to a daughter of Antony. Presumably Paullus was generally fond of shows, but now avoided them for fear of popular demonstrations.

5 C. Marcellus, Consul in 50, whose mother was a Junia, perhaps Junia Tertia's aunt.

6 L. Marcius Philippus, Consul in 56. His son of the same name was Praetor in 44 and so would be eligible for the Consulate in 41, which would be the earliest possible year for M. Brutus and Cassius.

as I wrote to you earlier, everyone thought he was not speaking but vomiting—according to habit![3]

You say you are confident that with my prestige and eloquence something can be achieved. Well, something *has* been achieved, if we allow for the deplorable state of affairs. The People of Rome realizes that there are three Consulars who cannot come to the Senate in safety because they felt as loyal citizens and spoke their minds. Beyond that you must expect nothing. Your relative[4] is delighted with his new connection, and so he is no longer interested in the Games, and is ready to burst at the endless applause they give your brother. Your other connection[5] likewise has been cajoled by new memoranda of Caesar's. Such things are tolerable, but it is surely not to be borne that a certain person[6] should expect the Consulship for his son in your and Brutus' year, and give out that he is this brigand's humble servant on that account. As for my good friend L. Cotta, to use his own phrase, he is in a state of fatalistic despair, and rarely comes to the Senate any more. L. Caesar, an excellent citizen and a brave man, is tied by ill health. Ser. Sulpicius has great prestige and loyal sentiments, but he is away. As for the rest,[7] the Designates[8] excepted, you'll forgive me[9] but I don't reckon them as

[7] Men appointed under Caesar's regime or recalled by him from exile.

[8] A. Hirtius and C. Vibius Pansa (for 43); also, but absent from Rome, D. Brutus and Plancus (for 42).

[9] The judgement logically applied to Cassius' connection by marriage, Lepidus, though he was absent from Rome; as also to P. Servilius, married to another sister of Junia Tertia, though Cicero includes him as a Consular above.

habes auctores consili publici. qui numerus etiam bonis rebus exiguus esset, quid censes perditis?

Qua re spes est omnis in vobis. qui si idcirco abestis ut sitis in tuto, ne in vobis quidem; sin aliquid dignum vestra gloria cogitatis, velim salvis nobis, sin id minus, res tamen publica per vos brevi tempore ius suum reciperabit.

Ego tuis neque desum neque deero. qui sive ad me referent <sive non[1] referent[2]>, mea tamen tibi benevolentia fidesque praestabitur.

Vale.

345 (XII.3)

Scr. Romae paulo post VI Non. Oct. an. 44

CICERO CASSIO S.

1   Auget tuus amicus furorem in dies. primum in statua quam posuit in rostris inscripsit 'parenti optime merito,' ut non modo sicarii sed iam etiam parricidae iudicemini. quid dico 'iudicemini'? iudicemur potius. vestri enim pulcherrimi facti ille furiosus me principem dicit fuisse. utinam quidem fuissem! molestus nobis non esset. sed hoc vestrum est; quod quoniam praeteriit, utinam haberem quid vobis darem consili! sed ne mihi quidem ipsi reperio quid faciendum sit. quid enim est quod contra vim sine vi fieri possit?

[1] (ς)   [2] (Or.)

---

[10] M. Brutus and Cassius. Both were leaving, or had already left, Italy for the East.   [1] Antony.   [2] Of Caesar.

Consulars. Such are the men to whom the country looks for guidance; even for good times an all too meagre number, but for desperate times—I say no more.

So all our hope lies in yourselves.[10] If you are keeping away for your safety's sake, even that hope fails. On the other hand, should you be planning something worthy of your glory, I hope I may be alive to see it; but if I am not, at any rate the commonwealth will soon regain its rights through you.

Your family can count on me now and in the future. Whether they consult me or not, my loyalty and good will to you shall not be wanting.

Good-bye.

345 (XII.3)
CICERO TO CASSIUS

Rome, soon after 2 October 44

From Cicero to Cassius greetings.

Your friend[1] gets crazier every day. To begin with he has inscribed the statue[2] which he set up on the Rostra 'To Father and Benefactor'—so that you are now set down, not only as assassins, but as parricides to boot! I say 'you,' but ought rather to say 'we,' for the madman declares that I was a leader in your noble enterprise. If only I had been! He would not be giving us any trouble. But all that is your responsibility, and now that it is past and gone, I only wish I had some advice to offer you. But I cannot even think what to do myself. What can be done against violence except by violence?

2   Consilium omne autem hoc est illorum ut mortem Caesaris persequantur. itaque a. d. VI Non. Oct. productus in
contionem a Cannutio turpissime ille quidem discessit,
sed tamen ea dixit de conservatoribus patriae quae dici
deberent de proditoribus; de me quidem non dubitanter
quin omnia de meo consilio et vos fecissetis et Cannutius
faceret. cetera cuius modi sint ex hoc iudica quod legato
tuo viaticum eripuerunt. quid eos interpretari putas cum
hoc faciunt? ad hostem scilicet portari.

O rem miseram! dominum ferre non potuimus, conser-
vo servimus. et tamen me quidem favente magis quam
sperante etiam nunc residet spes in virtute tua. sed ubi
sunt copiae? de reliquo malo te ipsum tecum loqui quam
nostra dicta cognoscere.

Vale.

346 (XII.22)

Scr. Romae post XIII *Kal. Oct. et fort. post* VI *Non. Oct.
an. 44*

CICERO CORNIFICIO S.

1   Nos hic cum homine gladiatore omnium nequissimo,
collega nostro, Antonio, bellum gerimus, sed non pari condicione, contra arma verbis. at etiam de te contionatur, nec
impune; nam sentiet quos lacessierit. ego autem acta ad te
omnia arbitror perscribi ab aliis; a me futura debes cognos-

---

3 Cassius had been appointed governor of Cyrene. The names
of his Legates are unknown.

1 As Augur.

Their whole plan is to avenge Caesar's death. On 2 October Antony was brought before a public meeting by Cannutius. He came off ignominiously indeed, but still he spoke of the country's saviours in terms appropriate to her betrayers. Of myself he declared unequivocally that everything you and your friends did and Cannutius is doing was on my advice. As a specimen of their behaviour in general, take the fact that they have deprived your Legate[3] of his travelling allowance. What do you suppose they imply by that? Presumably that the money was being conveyed to a public enemy.

It is a lamentable picture. We could not tolerate a master, so we are in bondage to our fellow slave. However, hope still remains in your valour (though for me it is a case of wishing rather than of hoping). But where are your forces? For the rest I prefer you to talk to yourself rather than listen to words of mine.

Good-bye.

346 (XII.22)
CICERO TO CORNIFICIUS

Rome, after 19 September or 2 October 44

From Cicero to Cornificius greetings.

Here I have a fight on my hands with a most rascally gladiator fellow, our colleague[1] Antony. But it is no fair match: words against weapons. However, he also makes speeches to public meetings, about you! Not with impunity: he shall find to his cost what sort of people he has provoked! However, I suppose you get details of all that *has* happened from other correspondents; it is my business to

cere, quorum quidem nunc[1] est difficilis coniectura.

2   Oppressa omnia sunt, nec habent ducem boni nostrique tyrannoctoni longe gentium absunt. Pansa et sentit bene et loquitur fortiter; Hirtius noster tardius convalescit. quid futurum sit plane nescio; spes tamen una est aliquando populum Romanum maiorum similem fore. ego certe rei publicae non deero et quicquid acciderit a quo mea culpa absit animo forti feram. illud profecto quoad potero: tuam famam et dignitatem tuebor.

347 (XII.23)

Scr. Romae c. VI *Id. Oct. an. 44*

<CICERO CORNIFICIO S.>

1   Omnem condicionem imperi tui statumque provinciae mihi demonstravit Tratorius. o multa intolerabilia locis omnibus! sed quo tua maior dignitas eo quae tibi acciderunt minus ferenda. neque enim quae tu propter magnitudinem et animi <et> ingeni moderate fers tibi ea non[1] ulciscenda sunt, etiam si non sunt dolenda. sed haec posterius.

2   Rerum urbanarum acta tibi mitti certo scio. quod ni ita putarem, ipse perscriberem, in primisque Caesaris Octaviani conatum. de quo multitudini fictum ab Antonio crimen videtur, ut in pecuniam adulescentis impetum faceret; prudentes autem et boni viri et credunt factum et

[1] non *(SB*)*
[1] teanon M: te ante *et* ate non χ *(SB, i.e.* ferstᵢeañ)

---

[1] To have Antony assassinated.

inform you of what is going to happen, and that is hard to guess at present.

The whole country is under heel. The honest men have no leader, our tyrannicides are at the other end of the earth. Pansa's sentiments are sound, and he talks boldly. Our friend Hirtius is making a slow recovery. What will come of it I simply don't know, but the only hope is that the People of Rome will at last show themselves like their ancestors. I at any rate shall not fail the commonwealth, and shall bear with courage whatever may befall, provided that I am not to blame for it. Of one thing you may be sure—I shall protect your reputation and prestige to the best of my ability.

347 (XII.23)
CICERO TO CORNIFICIUS

Rome, ca. 10 October 44

From Cicero to Cornificius greetings.

Tratorius has given me a comprehensive picture of your situation as governor and the state of your province. Outrages everywhere! But the higher your standing, the less you should acquiesce in what has happened to you. What your lofty spirit and intellect bear equably you should not on that account let go unpunished, even though it need not cause you pain. But of this later.

I feel sure that the city news is sent to you. If I thought otherwise, I should give you the particulars myself, especially about Caesar Octavian's attempt.[1] The general public thinks Antony has trumped up the charge because he wants to lay hands on the young man's money; but intelligent and honest men both believe in the fact and approve.

149

probant. quid quaeris? magna spes est in eo; nihil est quod
non existimetur laudis et gloriae causa facturus. Antonius
autem, noster familiaris, tanto se odio esse intellegit ut
cum interfectores suos domi comprenderit rem proferre
non audeat. itaque a. d. VII Id. Oct. Brundisium erat profectus obviam legionibus Macedonicis quattuor, quas sibi
conciliare pecunia cogitabat easque ad urbem adducere et
in cervicibus nostris collocare.

3   Habes formam rei publicae, si in castris potest esse res
publica. in quo[2] tuam vicem saepe doleo, quod nullam
partem per aetatem sanae et salvae rei publicae gustare
potuisti. atque antehac quidem sperare saltem licebat;
nunc etiam id ereptum est. quae enim est spes, cum in
contione dicere ausus sit Antonius Cannutium apud eos
locum sibi quaerere quibus se salvo locus in civitate esse
non posset?

4   Equidem et haec et omnia quae homini accidere possunt sic fero ut philosophiae magnam habeam gratiam,
quae me non modo ab sollicitudine abducit sed etiam contra omnis Fortunae impetus armat, tibique idem censeo
faciendum nec a quo culpa absit quicquam in malis nume-
randum. sed haec tu melius.

Tratorium nostrum cum semper probassem, tum
maxime in tuis rebus summam eius fidem, diligentiam
prudentiamque cognovi.

Da operam ut valeas. hoc mihi gratius facere nihil
potes.

[2] qua *(Ern.)*

In a word, high hopes are set on him. He will do anything, it is thought, for honour and glory. As for our friend Antony, he is so conscious of his unpopularity that after catching his would-be murderers in his house he does not dare to make the matter public. So on 9 October he set off for Brundisium to meet the four Macedonian legions.[2] He intends to buy their good will, and then to march them to Rome and set them on our necks.

Such is the political situation in outline, if a political situation can exist in an armed camp. I often feel sorry for you, because you are too young to have sampled any part of a free commonwealth in sound working order. Formerly it was at least possible to hope, but now even that has been torn from us. What hope is left, when Antony dares to say in a public meeting that Cannutius is trying to make a place for himself with people[3] who can have no place in the community so long as he, Antony, remains a member of it?

For my part, I take all this and whatever else can happen to mortal man with profound thankfulness to philosophy, which not only diverts me from anxiety but arms me against all assaults of fortune. I recommend you to do the same, and not to reckon as an evil anything devoid of culpability. But you know all this better than I.

I always thought well of our friend Tratorius, and I have been particularly impressed by his thorough loyalty, conscientiousness, and good sense in your affairs.

Take good care of your health. You can do nothing to please me more.

[2] Legions sent to Macedonia to take part in Caesar's projected war against Parthia and recently brought to Italy by Antony.

[3] Caesar's assassins.

348 (XI.27)

Scr. in Tusculano med. m. Oct., ut vid., an. 44

M. CICERO MATIO S.

1   Nondum satis constitui molestiaene plus an voluptatis attulerit mihi Trebatius noster, homo cum plenus offici tum utriusque nostrum amantissimus. nam cum in Tusculanum vesperi venissem, postridie ille ad me, nondum satis firmo corpore cum esset, mane venit. quem cum obiurgarem quod parum valetudini parceret, tum ille nihil sibi longius fuisse quam ut me videret. 'numquidnam' inquam 'novi?' detulit ad me querelam tuam.

2   De qua prius quam respondeo, pauca proponam. quantum memoria repetere praeterita possum, nemo est mihi te amicus antiquior. sed vetustas habet aliquid commune cum multis, amor non habet. dilexi te quo die cognovi, meque a te diligi iudicavi. tuus deinde discessus isque diuturnus, ambitio nostra et vitae dissimilitudo non est passa voluntates nostras consuetudine conglutinari. tuum tamen erga me animum agnovi multis annis ante bellum civile, cum Caesar esset in Gallia. quod enim vehementer mihi utile esse putabas nec inutile ipsi Caesari perfecisti, ut ille me diligeret, coleret, haberet in suis. multa praetereo quae temporibus illis inter nos familiarissime dicta, scripta,

348 (XI.27)
CICERO TO MATIUS

Tusculum, mid October (?) 44

From M. Cicero to Matius greetings.

I have not yet quite made up my mind whether our good Trebatius, a zealous and affectionate friend to both of us, has brought me more vexation or pleasure. He paid me an early morning visit at my house at Tusculum, where I had arrived the previous evening, although his health was still not fully restored. On my scolding him for not taking proper care of himself, he answered that he had never felt more impatience for anything than for an interview with me. 'Why, has something happened?' I asked. And he laid before me your grievance.

Before replying to that, I will make a few observations. As far back into the past as my memory extends, no friend of mine is older than yourself. But length of acquaintance is something which many share in some degree, affection is not. I cared for you from the first day we met and believed that you cared for me. Your subsequent departure for a long period, together with my pursuit of a political career and the difference between our modes of life, debarred us from cementing our friendly feelings by constant intercourse. But I had fresh evidence of your disposition towards me many years before the Civil War, when Caesar was in Gaul. Through your efforts Caesar came to look upon me as one of his circle, the object of his regard and friendly attentions; a result which you considered highly advantageous to me and not disadvantageous to Caesar himself. I pass over our many familiar interchanges in those days by word of mouth and correspondence, for

153

communicata sunt; graviora enim consecuta sunt.

3   [et]¹ Initio belli civilis cum Brundisium versus ires ad Caesarem, venisti ad me in Formianum. primum hoc ipsum quanti, praesertim temporibus illis! deinde oblitum me putas consili, sermonis, humanitatis tuae? quibus rebus interesse memini Trebatium. nec vero sum oblitus litterarum tuarum quas ad me misisti cum Caesari obviam venisses in agro, ut arbitror, Trebulano.

4   Secutum illud tempus est cum me ad Pompeium proficisci sive pudor meus coegit sive officium sive Fortuna. quod officium tuum, quod studium vel in absentem me vel in praesentis meos defuit? quem porro omnes mei et mihi et sibi te amiciorem iudicaverunt?

Veni Brundisium. oblitumne me putas qua celeritate, ut primum audieris, ad me Tarento advolaris, quae tua fuerit adsessio, oratio, confirmatio animi mei fracti communium miseriarum metu?

5   Tandem aliquando Romae esse coepimus. quid defuit nostrae familiaritati? in maximis rebus, quonam modo gererem me adversus Caesarem, usus tuo consilio sum, in reliquis officio.² cui tu tribuisti excepto Caesare praeter me ut domum ventitares horasque multas saepe suavissimo sermone consumeres, tum cum etiam, si meministi, ut haec φιλοσοφούμενα scriberem tu me impulisti? post Caesaris reditum quid tibi maiori curae fuit quam ut essem ego illi quam familiarissimus? quod effeceras.

¹ *delere noluit Wes.*: et ‹enim› *Or.*
² officiis *(Madvig)*

---

¹ Cf. *Letters to Atticus* 178 (IX.11).2.
² Presumably *Letters to Atticus* 184 (IX.15 a).

graver matters supervened.

At the outset of the Civil War, when you were on your way to join Caesar at Brundisium, you paid me a visit in my house at Formiae.[1] That to begin with meant a good deal, especially at such a time. And then, do you suppose I have forgotten your kindly advice and talk? I remember that Trebatius was present during all this. Nor have I forgotten the letter[2] you sent me after you had met Caesar in the Trebula district, I think it was.

Then followed the time when, whether impelled by my sensitivity to criticism or by obligation or by Fortune, I went to join Pompey. Your devoted service was never wanting either to me in my absence or to my family on the spot. In the judgement of them all, neither they nor I had a better friend.

I arrived in Brundisium. Do you think I have forgotten how swiftly, the moment you heard the news, you rushed over to me from Tarentum, how you sat beside me, talking and encouraging me in the dejection to which fear of the common calamities had reduced me?

At long last we took up residence in Rome. Our familiar friendship was now complete. In the most important matters, in determining how to conduct myself towards Caesar, I availed myself of your advice; in others, of your good offices. Was there any man but me, Caesar excepted, whose house you chose to frequent, and often spend many hours in the most delightful conversation? It was at that time, if you recall, that you prompted me to compose these philosophical works of mine. After Caesar's return I doubt if you had any object so much at heart as that I should be on the best possible footing with him. In that you had succeeded.

6   Quorsum igitur haec oratio longior quam putaram? quia sum admiratus te, qui haec nosse deberes, quicquam a me commissum quod esset alienum nostra amicitia credidisse. nam praeter haec quae commemoravi, quae testata sunt et illustria, habeo multa occultiora, quae vix verbis exsequi possum. omnia me tua delectant, sed maxime maxima,[3] cum fides in amicitia, consilium, gravitas, constantia tum lepos, humanitas, litterae.

7   Quapropter (redeo nunc ad querelam) ego te suffragium tulisse in illa lege primum non credidi; deinde, si credidissem, numquam id sine aliqua iusta causa existimarem te fecisse. dignitas tua facit ut animadvertatur quicquid facias, malevolentia autem hominum ut non nulla durius quam a te facta sunt proferantur. ea tu si non audis, quid dicam nescio. equidem si quando audio, tam defendo quam me scio a te contra iniquos meos solere defendi. defensio autem est duplex: alia sunt quae liquido negare soleam, ut de isto ipso suffragio, alia quae defendam a te pie fieri et humane, ut de curatione ludorum.

8   Sed te, hominem doctissimum, non fugit, si Caesar rex fuerit, quod mihi quidem videtur, in utramque partem de tuo officio disputari posse, vel in eam qua ego soleo uti, laudandam esse fidem et humanitatem tuam qui amicum etiam mortuum diligas, vel in eam qua non nulli utuntur,

---

[3] *dist. SB*

---

[3] A recent law, possibly one of Antony's redistributing provincial commands (certainly not Caesar's law on debt, as sometimes supposed).

[4] Celebrated by Octavian in memory of Caesar and in honour of his victory from 20 to 30 July; cf. *Letters to Atticus* 379 (XV.2).3.

You may wonder where all this discourse (longer than I had envisaged) is tending. The truth is, I am astonished that you, who ought to know all this, should have believed me guilty of any action against the spirit of our friendship. For besides the well attested and manifest facts which I have mentioned above, I have many others of a less conspicuous nature in mind, such as I cannot easily express in words. All about you delights me, but your most notable characteristics attract me most: loyalty in friendship, judgement, responsibility, steadfastness on the one hand, charm, humanity, literary culture on the other.

And so, to revert to your grievance, in the first place I did not believe you cast a vote on that law;[3] and in the second, if I had believed it, I should never have supposed you to have acted without some legitimate reason. Your standing brings all you do into notice, and the malice of the world sometimes presents your actions as more uncompromising than they really were. If such things don't come to your hearing, I don't know what to say. For my own part, if ever I hear anything, I defend you as I know you are in the habit of defending me against *my* ill-wishers. This I do in two ways: there are some things I deny outright, as this very matter of the vote, others in which I claim you are acting out of loyalty and good nature, for example your superintendence of the Games.[4]

But a scholar like yourself will not be unaware that if Caesar was a despot, which seems to me to be the case, your ethical position can be argued in two ways. On the one side it can be maintained (and this is the line I take) that in caring for your friend even after he is dead you show commendable loyalty and good feeling. According to the other view, which is adopted in some quarters, the free-

libertatem patriae vitae amici anteponendam. ex his sermonibus utinam essent delatae ad te disputationes meae! illa vero duo quae maxima sunt laudum tuarum quis aut libentius quam ego commemorat aut saepius, te et non suscipiendi belli civilis gravissimum auctorem fuisse et moderandae victoriae? in quo qui mihi non adsentiretur inveni neminem.

Qua re habeo gratiam Trebatio, familiari nostro, qui mihi dedit causam harum litterarum. quibus nisi credideris, me omnis offici et humanitatis exper⟨tem⟩ iudicaris, quo nec mihi gravius quicquam potest esse nec te alienius.

349 (XI.28)

Scr. Romae accepta ep. superiore

MATIUS CICERONI S.

1   Magnam voluptatem ex tuis litteris cepi, quod quam[1] speraram atque optaram habere te de me opinionem cognovi. de qua etsi non dubitabam, tamen, quia maximi aestimabam ut incorrupta maneret, laborabam. conscius autem mihi eram nihil a me commissum esse quod boni cuiusquam offenderet animum. eo minus credebam plurimis atque optimis artibus ornato tibi temere quicquam persuaderi potuisse, praesertim in quem mea propensa et perpetua fuisset atque esset benevolentia. quod quoniam

---

[1] cum

dom of one's country should come before a friend's life. I only wish that my argumentations arising from such talk had been conveyed to you. At any rate no one recalls more readily and more often than I the two facts which above all others redound to your honour, namely, that yours was the weightiest influence both against embarking on a civil war and in favour of a moderate use of victory. In this I have found nobody who did not agree with me.

So I am grateful to our good friend Trebatius for giving me occasion to write this letter. If you do not believe in its sincerity, you will be setting me down as a stranger to all sense of obligation and good feeling. Nothing can be more grievous to me than such a verdict, or more uncharacteristic of yourself.

349 (XI.28)
MATIUS TO CICERO

Rome, in reply to the foregoing

Matius to Cicero greetings.

Your letter gave me great pleasure, because it told me that you think of me as I had expected and desired. Although I was not in any doubt on this score, the high importance I attach to your good opinion made me anxious that it should remain unimpaired. My conscience assured me that I had not been guilty of any act which could give offence to any honest man. I was therefore all the less disposed to believe that a man of your great and many-sided attainments would let himself be persuaded of anything hastily, especially in view of my ready and never-failing good will towards yourself. Now that I know this is as I

159

ut volui scio esse, respondebo criminibus quibus tu pro
me, ut par erat pro tua singulari bonitate et amicitia nostra,
saepe restitisti.

2   Nota enim mihi sunt quae in me post Caesaris mortem
contulerint. vitio mihi dant quod mortem hominis necessari graviter fero atque eum quem dilexi perisse indignor;
aiunt enim patriam amicitiae praeponendam esse, proinde
ac si iam vicerint obitum eius rei publicae fuisse utilem.
sed non agam astute: fateor me ad istum gradum sapien-
tiae non pervenisse. neque enim Caesarem in dissensione
civili sum secutus, sed amicum, quamquam re offendebar,
tamen non deserui, neque bellum umquam civile aut
etiam causam dissensionis probavi, quam etiam nascen-
tem exstingui summe studui. itaque in victoria hominis
necessari neque honoris neque pecuniae dulcedine sum
captus, quibus praemiis reliqui, minus apud eum quam
ego cum possent, immoderate sunt abusi. atque etiam res
familiaris mea lege Caesaris deminuta est, cuius beneficio
plerique qui Caesaris morte laetantur remanserunt in civitate. civibus victis ut parceretur aeque ac pro mea salute
laboravi.

3   Possum igitur, qui omnis voluerim incolumis, eum a
quo id impetratum est perisse non indignari, cum praesertim idem homines illi et invidiae et exitio fuerint? 'plecte-
ris ergo' inquiunt, 'quoniam factum nostrum improbare
audes.' o superbiam inauditam! alios in facinore gloriari,
aliis ne dolere quidem impunite licere! at haec etiam servis

---

[1] On debt.
[2] Such as D. Brutus, who had 'taken immoderate advantage' of
their position as leading Caesarians.

hoped, I will make some reply to the charges which you, as befitted the singular kindness of your heart and the friendly relations between us, have often rebutted on my behalf.

I am well aware of the criticisms which people have levelled at me since Caesar's death. They make it a point against me that I bear the death of a friend hard and am indignant that the man I loved has been destroyed. They say that country should come before friendship—as though they have already proved that his death was to the public advantage. But I shall not make debating points. I acknowledge that I have not yet arrived at that philosophical level. It was not Caesar I followed in the civil conflict, but a friend whom I did not desert, even though I did not like what he was doing. I never approved of civil war or indeed of the origin of the conflict, which I did my very utmost to get nipped in the bud. And so, when my friend emerged triumphant, I was not caught by the lure of office or money, prizes of which others, whose influence with Caesar was less than my own, took immoderate advantage. My estate was actually reduced by a law of Caesar's,[1] thanks to which many who rejoice at his death are still inside the community. For mercy to our defeated fellow countrymen I struggled as for my own life.

Well then, can I, who desired every man's preservation, help feeling indignant at the slaughter of the man who granted it—all the more when the very persons[2] who brought him unpopularity were responsible for his destruction? 'Very well,' say they, 'you shall be punished for daring to disapprove of our action.' What unheard-of arrogance! Some may glory in the deed, while others may not even grieve with impunity! Even slaves have always had

161

semper libera fuerunt, ⟨ut sperarent⟩[2] timerent, gaude-
rent dolerent suo potius quam alterius arbitrio; quae nunc,
ut quidem isti dictitant, 'libertatis auctores' metu nobis ex-
4 torquere conantur. sed nihil agunt. nullis umquam periculi
terroribus ab officio aut ab humanitate desciscam. numquam enim honestam mortem fugiendam, saepe etiam
appetendam putavi.

Sed quid mihi suscensent si id opto ut paeniteat eos sui
facti? cupio enim Caesaris mortem omnibus esse acerbam.
at debeo pro civili parte rem publicam velle salvam. id quidem me cupere, nisi et ante acta vita et reliqua mea spes
5 tacente me probat, dicendo vincere non postulo. qua re
maiorem in modum te rogo ut rem potiorem oratione du-
cas mihique, si sentis expedire recte fieri, credas nullam
communionem cum improbis esse posse. an quod adulescens praestiti, cum etiam errare cum excusatione possem,
id nunc aetate praecipitata commutem ac me ipse re-
texam? non faciam, neque quod displiceat committam,
praeterquam quod hominis mihi coniunctissimi ac viri am-
plissimi doleo gravem casum. quod si aliter essem animatus, numquam quod facerem negarem, ne et in peccando
improbus et in dissimulando timidus ac vanus existimarer.
6 At ludos quos Caesaris victoriae Caesar adulescens
fecit curavi. at id ad privatum officium, non ad statum rei
publicae, pertinet. quod tamen munus et hominis amicissi-
mi memoriae atque honoribus praestare etiam mortui

[2] *(Lehmann)*

---

[3] I.e. subversive elements. Matius is here asserting his loyalty
to established order.

liberty to feel hope or fear or joy or sorrow of their own impulse, not someone else's. That freedom the 'authors of our liberty,' as these persons like to describe themselves, are trying to snatch from us by intimidation. But they are wasting their breath. No threats of danger shall ever make me false to obligation and good feeling. I never thought an honourable death a thing to shun, indeed I should often have welcomed it.

Why are they angry with me for praying that they may be sorry for what they have done? I want every man's heart to be sore for Caesar's death. But I shall be told that as a citizen I ought to wish the good of the commonwealth. Unless my past life and hopes for the future prove that I so desire without words of mine, then I do not ask anyone to accept it because I say so. Therefore I earnestly request you to consider facts rather than words, and, if you perceive that it is to my advantage that things go as they should, to believe that I cannot have any part or lot with rascals.[3] Is it likely that in my declining years I should reverse the record of my youth (*then* I might have been pardoned for going astray) and undo the fabric of my life? I shall not do that, nor shall I give any offence, except that I grieve for the tragic fate of a great man to whom I was intimately bound. But if I were differently disposed, I should never deny what I was doing, and risk being thought a rascal for my misconduct and a cowardly hypocrite for trying to conceal it.

Well, but I superintended the Games for Caesar's Victory given by his young heir. That was a matter of private service, which has nothing to do with the state of the commonwealth. It was, however, an office which I owed to the memory and distinction of a dear friend even after his

163

debui et optimae spei adulescenti ac dignissimo Caesare
7 petenti negare non potui. veni etiam consulis Antoni domum saepe salutandi causa; ad quem qui me parum patriae amantem esse existimant rogandi quidem aliquid aut
auferendi causa frequentis ventitare reperies. sed quae
haec est adrogantia, quod Caesar numquam interpellavit
quin quibus vellem atque etiam quos ipse non diligebat
tamen iis uterer, eos qui mihi amicum eripuerunt carpen-
do me efficere conari ne quos velim diligam!
8 Sed non vereor ne aut meae vitae modestia parum vali-
tura sit in posterum contra falsos rumores aut ne etiam ii
qui me non amant propter meam in Caesarem constantiam
non malint mei quam sui similis amicos habere. mihi quidem si optata contingent, quod reliquum est vitae in otio
Rhodi degam. sin casus aliquis interpellarit, ita ero Romae
ut recte fieri semper cupiam.

Trebatio nostro magnas ago gratias quod tuum erga me
animum simplicem atque amicum aperuit et quod eum
quem semper libenter dilexi quo magis iure colere atque
observare deberem fecit.

Bene vale et me dilige.

death, and one which I could not deny to the request of a most promising young man, thoroughly worthy of the name he bears. Also I have often called on Consul Antony to pay my respects; and you will find that those who think *me* a poor patriot are continually flocking to his house to make their petitions or carry off his favours. The presumption of it! Caesar never put any obstacle in the way of my associating with whom I pleased, even persons whom he himself did not like. And shall the people who have robbed me of my friend try to stop me with their carping tongues from liking whom I choose?

However, I don't doubt that the moderation of my career will be a strong enough defence against false reports in time to come; and I am equally confident that even those who do not love me because of my loyalty to Caesar would rather have friends like me than like themselves. If my prayers are granted, I shall spend the remainder of my days quietly in Rhodes; but if some chance interferes with my plan, I shall live in Rome as one whose desire will ever be that things go as they should.

I am most grateful to our friend Trebatius for revealing the straightforward and amicable nature of your sentiments towards me, thus adding to the reasons why I ought to pay respect and attention to one whom I have always been glad to regard as a friend.

I bid you good-bye and hope to have your affection.

350 (XVI.24)

Scr. in Arpinati med. m. Nov. an. 44

TULLIUS TIRONI S.

1   Etsi mane Harpalum miseram, tamen, cum haberem
cui recte darem litteras, etsi novi nihil erat, isdem de rebus
volui ad te saepius scribere, non quin confiderem diligentiae tuae, sed rei me magnitudo movebat. mihi prora
et puppis, ut Graecorum proverbium est, fuit a me tui
dimittendi ut rationes nostras explicares. Offilio et Aurelio
utique satis fiat. a Flamma, si non potes omne, partem aliquam velim extorqueas, in primisque ut expedita sit pensio
Kal. Ian. de attributione conficies, de repraesentatione
videbis.

2   De domesticis rebus hactenus. de publicis omnia mihi
certa, quid Octavius,[1] quid Antonius, quae hominum opinio, quid futurum putes. ego vix teneor quin accurram, sed
litteras tuas exspecto. et scito Balbum tum fuisse Aquini
cum tibi est dictum et postridie Hirtium; puto utrumque
ad aquas. sed quod egerint. Dolabellae procuratores fac ut
admoneantur. appellabis etiam Papiam.

Vale.

[1] octavianus H

350 (XVI.24)
CICERO TO TIRO

Arpinum, November (middle) 44

From Tullius to Tiro greetings.

I sent Harpalus to you this morning, but having a suitable bearer, though nothing new to say, I thought I would write to you again on the same subjects—not that I doubt your conscientiousness, but the thing is so important. The fore and aft (as the Greek saying has it) of my letting you go away was that you should put my affairs straight. Offilius and Aurelius must be satisfied at all costs. If you cannot extract the full amount from Flamma,[1] I hope you will get some part of it. Above all the payment on the Kalends of January must be cleared. Settle the assignment and use your judgement about the cash payment. So much for domesticities.

As for public affairs send me full, reliable reports—on Octavian, on Antony, on the state of public opinion, on what you think will happen. I can hardly stop myself hurrying up to town, but I am waiting to hear from you. You may be interested to know that Balbus *was* at Aquinum when you were told so, and Hirtius the next day; both on their way to the waters, I suppose—but let them do what they like. See that Dolabella's agents get a reminder. You will also ask Papia[2] for payment.

Good-bye.

---

[1] On these transactions see *Letters to Atticus* 294 (XII.52).1.

[2] Probably Latinized from Papias, a slave or freedman of Dolabella's.

351 (XVI.26)

Scr. loco et an. incerto

Q. CICERO[1] TIRONI SUO P. S. D.

1   Verberavi te cogitationis tacito dumtaxat convicio quod fasciculus alter ad me iam sine tuis litteris perlatus est. non potes effugere huius culpae poenam te patrono; Marcus est adhibendus, isque diu et multis lucubrationibus commentata oratione vide ut probare possit te non peccasse.

2   plane te rogo, sic ut olim matrem nostram facere memini, quae lagonas etiam inanis obsignabat ne dicerentur inanes aliquae fuisse quae furtim essent exsiccatae, sic tu, etiam si quod scribas non habebis, scribito tamen, ne furtum cessationis quaesivisse videaris. valde enim mi semper et vera et dulcia tuis epistulis nuntiantur.

     Ama nos et vale.

352 (XVI.27)

Scr. fort. in Gallia Cisalpina ex. m. Dec. an. 44

Q. CICERO TIRONI SUO S. P. D.

1   Mirificam mi verberationem cessationis epistula dedisti. nam quae parcius frater perscripserat, verecundia videlicet et properatione, ea tu sine adsentatione ut erant ad

---

[1] Q. MDH: Cicero V (ς)*

---

[1] The letter usually has been assigned to 44, but may be much earlier, perhaps written during Quintus' service in Gaul.

351 (XVI.26)
Q. CICERO TO TIRO

Place and date unknown[1]

From Quintus to his dear Tiro best greetings.

A second packet has reached me with no letter from you, and my thoughts have drubbed you with reproaches, though I say nothing. You cannot hope to escape punishment for this offence if you conduct your own case. You must call Marcus in and see whether he can prove you innocent with a speech long pondered in the watches of many a night. I really do beg of you—I remember how our mother in the old days used to seal up the empty bottles, so that bottles drained on the sly could not be included with the empties—so you likewise write, even though you have nothing to write about, so that you are not suspected of having scraped an excuse to cover your idleness. Your letters always tell me things most true and agreeable.

Love us and good-bye.

352 (XVI.27)
Q. CICERO TO TIRO

Cisalpine Gaul (?), end of December 44

From Q. Cicero to his dear Tiro best greetings.

By your letter you have given me a fine drubbing for my idleness. My brother wrote more charily, no doubt because he did not like to say too much and was pressed for time. You handle the same material, but give the naked truth

me scripsisti, et maxime de cos. designatis; quos ego penitus novi, libidinum et languoris plenos, effeminatissimi
animi.[1] qui nisi a gubernaculis recesserint, maximum ab
2   universo naufragio periculum est. incredibile est quae ego
illos scio oppositis Gallorum castris in aestivis fecisse; quos
ille latro, nisi aliquid firmius fuerit, societate vitiorum
deleniet. res est aut tribuniciis aut privatis consiliis mu-
nienda; nam isti duo vix sunt digni quibus alteri Caesenam,
alteri Cossutianarum tabernarum fundamenta credas.

Te, ut dixi, fero ⟨in⟩[2] oculis. ego vos a. d. III Kal. video
tuosque oculos, etiam si te veniens in medio foro videro,
dissaviabor.

Me ama. vale.

353 (XI.5)

Scr. Romae v Id. Dec. vel paulo post, an. 44

M. CICERO S. D. D. BRUTO IMP. COS. DESIG.

1   Lupus, familiaris noster, cum a te venisset cumque
Romae quosdam dies commoraretur, ego eram in iis locis
in quibus maxime tuto me esse arbitrabar. eo factum est ut
ad te Lupus sine meis litteris rediret, cum tamen curasset

---

[1] ⟨et⟩ eff- *Cortius*
[2] *(Ern.)*

---

[1] Antony.
[2] Caesena was a small town in Cisalpine Gaul south of Ravenna. Cossutius' taverns were probably in the same area, which
produced a noted wine. Possibly Quintus was staying there. He

without varnish, especially about the Consuls-Elect. I
know them through and through. They are riddled with
lusts and languor, utter effeminates at heart. Unless they
retire from the helm, there is every risk of universal ship-
wreck. It is incredible the things they did to my knowledge
on active service, with the Gauls encamped right opposite.
Unless a firm line is taken, that bandit[1] will woo them over
by comradeship in vice. The position must be fortified by
the Tribunes or by private initiative. As for that precious
pair, you would hardly trust one with Caesena or the other
with the cellars of Cossutius' taverns.[2]

As I have said, you are the apple of my eye. I shall see
you all on the 30th and smother *your* eyes in kisses, even
though I first sight you in the middle of the Forum.

Love me. Good-bye.

353 (XI.5)
CICERO TO D. BRUTUS

Rome, 9 December (or shortly after) 44

From M. Cicero to D. Brutus, Imperator, Consul-Elect,
greetings.

When our friend Lupus arrived from you and spent
some days in Rome, I was where I thought I should be
safest.[1] That is how it came about that Lupus went back
without a letter from me, although he had seen to it that I

seems to mean that Hirtius was feeble and incompetent, Pansa a
drunkard; cf. *Letters to Atticus* 409 (XVI.1).4.

[1] In Arpinum.

tuas ad me perferendas. Romam autem veni a.d. v Id.[1]
Dec., nec habui quicquam antiquius quam ut Pansam statim convenirem; ex quo ea de te cognovi quae maxime
optabam.

Qua re hortatione tu quidem non eges, si ne in illa
quidem re quae a te gesta est post hominum memoriam
2 maxima hortatorem desiderasti. illud tamen breviter significandum videtur, populum Romanum omnia a te exspectare atque in te aliquando reciperandae libertatis
omnem spem ponere. tu si dies noctesque memineris,
quod te facere certo scio, quantam rem gesseris, non obli-
viscere profecto quantae tibi etiam nunc gerendae sint. si
enim iste provinciam nactus erit, cui quidem ego semper
amicus fui ante quam illum intellexi non modo aperte sed
etiam libenter cum re publica bellum gerere, spem reli-
quam nullam video salutis.

3 Quam ob rem te obsecro, iisdem precibus quibus senatus populusque Romanus, ut in perpetuum rem publicam
dominatu regio liberes, ut principiis consentiant exitus.
tuum est hoc munus, tuae partes; a te hoc civitas, vel omnes potius gentes, non exspectant solum sed etiam postulant. quamquam, cum hortatione non egeas, ut supra
scripsi, non utar ea pluribus verbis; faciam illud quod
meum est, ut tibi omnia mea officia, studia, curas, cogita-
tiones ⟨in res omnis⟩[2] pollicear quae ad tuam laudem et
gloriam pertinebunt. quam ob rem velim tibi ita persuadeas, me cum rei publicae causa, quae mihi vita mea est
carior, tum quod tibi ipsi faveam tuamque dignitatem

---

[1] v (*melius* xv) Kal. *Ruete*
[2] (*Andresen*)

received yours. I returned to Rome on 9 December and made it my first business to meet Pansa without delay. From him I received news of you such as I was most desirous to hear.

You stand in no need of encouragement, any more than you wanted it in your late exploit, the greatest in history. Yet I think I should briefly intimate that the People of Rome look to you to fulfil all their aspirations, and pin upon you all their hope of eventually recovering their freedom. If you bear in mind day and night, as I am sure you do, how great a thing you have accomplished, you will not be likely to forget how much remains for you still to do. If the personage[2] with whom you have to deal obtains a province (I was always his friend until I saw him waging war upon the commonwealth not only without concealment but with relish), I see no further hope of survival.

Therefore I implore you (and I am echoing the entreaty of the Senate and People of Rome) to liberate the commonwealth forever from despotic rule. Let the end chime with the beginning. Yours is this task, yours the role. Our community, or rather all nations of the earth, expect this of you, indeed they demand it. But as I have already said, you need no encouragement, so I shall not spend many words in offering it. That which properly concerns me I will do, namely, promise you all my devoted service, all my care and consideration, in all that shall tend to your credit and glory. Therefore I hope you will believe that both for the sake of the commonwealth, which is dearer to me than my life, and also because I wish you well personally and desire

---

[2] Antony, who had marched north in order to dispossess D. Brutus of Cisalpine Gaul.

amplificari velim, me tuis optimis consiliis, amplitudini, gloriae nullo loco defuturum.

354 (XI.7)

Scr. Romae med. m. Dec. an. 44

M. CICERO S. D. D. BRUTO IMP. COS. DESIG.

1   Cum adhibuisset domi meae Lupus me et Libonem et Servium, consobrinum tuum, quae mea fuerit sententia cognosse te ex M. Seio arbitror, qui nostro sermoni interfuit; reliqua, quamquam statim Seium Graeceius est subsecutus, tamen ex Graeceio poteris cognoscere.

2   Caput autem est hoc, quod te diligentissime percipere et meminisse volam, ut ne in libertate et salute populi Romani conservanda auctoritatem senatus exspectes nondum liberi, ne et tuum factum condemnes (nullo enim publico consilio rem publicam liberavisti, quo etiam est res illa maior et clarior) et adulescentem, vel puerum potius, Caesarem iudices temere fecisse qui tantam causam publicam privato consilio susceperit, denique homines rusticos sed fortissimos viros civisque optimos dementis fuisse iudices, primum milites veteranos, commilitones tuos, deinde legionem Martiam, legionem quartam, quae suum consulem hostem iudicaverunt seque ad salutem rei

---

[1] Settled in Caesar's Campanian colonies. They had rallied to Octavian early in November and were later joined by two of the four legions that came from Macedonia, the Martian and Fourth.

your further advancement, I shall not fail at any point to support your patriotic designs, your greatness, and your glory.

354 (XI.7)
CICERO TO D. BRUTUS

Rome, mid December 44

From M. Cicero to D. Brutus, Imperator, Consul-Elect, greetings.

Lupus asked myself, Libo, and your cousin Servius to meet him at my house. I think you will have heard the view I expressed from M. Seius, who was present at our colloquy. Other matters you will be able to learn from Graeceius, although he left just after Seius.

The main point, which I want you thoroughly to grasp and remember in the future, is that in safeguarding the liberty and welfare of the Roman People you must not wait to be authorized by a Senate which is not yet free. If you did, you would be condemning your own act, for you did not liberate the commonwealth by any public authority—a fact which makes the exploit all the greater and more glorious. You would also be implying that the young man, or rather boy, Caesar had acted inconsiderately in taking upon himself so weighty a public cause on his private initiative. Further, you would be implying that the soldiers, country folk but brave men and loyal citizens, had taken leave of their senses—that is to say firstly, the veterans,[1] your own comrades in arms, and secondly the Martian and Fourth Legions, which branded their Consul as a public enemy and rallied to the defence of the commonwealth.

publicae defendendam contulerunt. voluntas senatus pro auctoritate haberi debet cum auctoritas impeditur metu.

3 postremo suscepta tibi causa iam bis est ut non sit integrum, primum Idibus Martiis, deinde proxime exercitu novo et copiis comparatis. quam ob rem ad omnia ita paratus, ita[1] animatus debes esse, non ut nihil facias nisi iussus sed ut ea geras quae ab omnibus summa cum admiratione laudentur.

355 (X.3)

Scr. Romae paulo post v Id. Dec. an. 44

CICERO PLANCO S.

1 Cum ipsum Furnium per se vidi libentissime tum hoc libentius quod illum audiens te videbar videre.[1] nam et in re militari virtutem et in administranda provincia iustitiam et in omni genere prudentiam mihi tuam exposuit et praeterea mihi non ignotam in consuetudine et familiaritate suavitatem tuam; adiunxit praeterea summam erga se liberalitatem. quae omnia mihi iucunda, hoc extremum etiam gratum fuit.

2 Ego, Plance, necessitudinem constitutam habui cum domo vestra ante aliquanto quam tu natus es, amorem autem erga te ab ineunte pueritia tua, confirmata iam aetate familiaritatem cum studio meo tum iudicio tuo constitutam. his de causis mirabiliter faveo dignitati tuae, quam

[1] sit *(Man.)*
[1] audire *(SB)*

The will of the Senate should be accepted in lieu of authority when its authority is trammelled by fear. Lastly, you are already committed, for you have twice taken the cause upon yourself—first on the Ides of March, and again recently when you raised a new army and forces. Therefore you should be ready for every contingency. Your attitude must be, not that you will do nothing except on orders, but that you will take such action as will earn the highest praise and admiration from us all.

355 (X.3)
CICERO TO PLANCUS

Rome, shortly after 9 December 44

From Cicero to Plancus greetings.

I was delighted to see Furnius for his own sake, and all the more so because as I listened to him I felt I was seeing you. He gave me an account of your military prowess, your rectitude in the administration of your province, and your good sense in all spheres. He spoke further of your agreeable personality in familiar intercourse, which was no news to me, and added that you had treated him most handsomely. All this I heard with pleasure, the last item with gratitude as well.

My friendly connection with your family, my dear Plancus, came into being some time before you were born. My affection towards yourself dates from your early childhood. When you became a grown man, my desire and your choice established a familiar friendship. For these reasons I take the most lively interest in your standing in the world, which I hold to be mine also. Guided by ability and accom-

me[2] tecum statuo habere[3] communem. omnia summa consecutus es virtute duce, comite Fortuna, eaque es adeptus adulescens multis invidentibus, quos ingenio industriaque fregisti. nunc, me amantissimum tui, nemini concedentem qui tibi vetustate necessitudinis potior possit esse, si audies, omnem tibi reliquae vitae dignitatem ex optimo rei publicae statu acquires.

3   Scis profecto (nihil enim te fugere potuit) fuisse quoddam tempus cum homines existimarent te nimis servire temporibus; quod ego quoque existimarem, te si ea quae patiebare probare etiam arbitrarer. sed cum intellegerem quid sentires, prudenter te arbitrabar videre quid posses. nunc alia ratio est. omnium rerum tuum iudicium est idque liberum. consul es designatus, optima aetate, summa eloquentia, ⟨in⟩[4] maxima orbitate rei publicae virorum talium. incumbe, per deos immortalis, in eam curam et cogitationem quae tibi summam dignitatem et gloriam adferat; unus autem est, hoc praesertim tempore, per tot annos re publica divexata, rei publicae bene gerendae cursus ad gloriam.

4   Haec amore magis impulsus scribenda ad te putavi quam quo te arbitrarer monitis et praeceptis egere. sciebam enim ex iisdem te haec haurire fontibus ex quibus ipse hauseram. qua re modum faciam. nunc tantum significandum putavi, ut potius amorem tibi ostenderem meum quam ostentarem prudentiam. interea quae ad dignitatem

[2] mihi *(SB)*
[3] habere V: -re esse M: -re et esse DH
[4] *(Ern.)**

panied by good fortune you have achieved the highest success in everything you attempted, and you have gained these triumphs as a young man in the face of much jealousy, which you have overcome by capacity and energy. Now, if you will listen to me, your truly affectionate friend, who could allow no man pride of place with you in virtue of old association, you will derive all further advancement to the end of your days from the establishment of the best form of constitution.

You are of course aware, for nothing could escape you, that there was a period when the world thought you too much at the service of the times. I should have held that opinion myself, if I had taken acquiescence on your part for approval. But, perceiving your sentiments as I did, I considered that you took a realistic view of your power to influence events. Now the case is altered. You will form your own judgement on all questions, and it will be unconstrained. You are Consul-Elect, in the prime of life and the flower of oratorical talent, at a time when the commonwealth is so sorely bereft of men of such calibre. In heaven's name, throw your thoughts and solicitude into the channel which will bring you to the highest honour and glory. To glory there is only one path, especially now, when the body politic has so many years been torn asunder: good statesmanship.

Affection, rather than any notion that you were in need of admonition and advice, made me think fit to write to you in this strain. I know you drink in such ideas from the fountains at which I myself imbibed them. Therefore I will go no further. At this time I thought I ought to intimate that much, to advise you of my affection rather than to advertise my wisdom. Meanwhile I shall most zealously and

tuam pertinere arbitrabor studiose diligenterque curabo.

356 (XI.6a)

Scr. Romae XIII *Kal. Ian. an.* 44

⟨M. CICERO S. D. D. BRUTO IMP. COS. DESIG.⟩

1   Cum tribuni pl. edixissent senatus adesset a.d. XIII Kal. Ian. haberentque in animo de praesidio consulum designatorum referre, quamquam statueram in senatum ante Kal. Ian. non venire, tamen, cum eo die ipso edictum tuum propositum esset, nefas esse duxi aut ita haberi senatum ut de tuis divinis in rem publicam meritis sileretur, quod factum esset nisi ego venissem, aut etiam, si quid de te honorifice diceretur, me non adesse.

2   Itaque in senatum veni mane. quod cum esset animadversum, frequentissimi senatores convenerunt. quae de te in senatu egerim, quae in contione maxima dixerim, aliorum te litteris malo cognoscere; illud tibi persuadeas velim, me omnia quae ad tuam dignitatem augendam pertinebunt, quae est per se amplissima, summo semper studio suscepturum et defensurum. quod quamquam intellego me cum multis esse facturum, tamen appetam huius rei principatum.

---

[1] In which D. Brutus declared that he would hold Cisalpine Gaul for the Senate and People (cf. *Philippics* 3.8).

[2] The Third Philippic was delivered at this meeting.

[3] The Fourth Philippic.

faithfully attend to any matters which I judge to bear upon your personal standing.

356 (XI.6a)
CICERO TO D. BRUTUS

Rome, 20 December 44

From M. Cicero to D. Brutus, Imperator, Consul-Elect, greetings.

The Tribunes summoned a meeting of the Senate by proclamation for 20 December with the intention of bringing the question of a bodyguard for the Consuls-Elect before the House. I had determined not to come to the Senate before the Kalends of January, but seeing that your proclamation[1] was published on that very day, I felt I should never forgive myself if the meeting passed without any reference to your immortal services to the commonwealth (which would have happened if I had not attended), or even if you did come in for honorific mention and I were not there.

Accordingly, I arrived at the House early. When my presence was noticed, members gathered in large numbers. Of my part in the Senate's proceedings concerning you[2] and my subsequent speech[3] before a large public meeting I prefer you to learn from other correspondents. But I hope you will believe that I shall always take up and maintain with the utmost enthusiasm whatever may tend to the advancement of your public standing, which is already of the highest. I know that I shall have many fellow labourers in this field, but I shall strive for the foremost place among them.

181

357 (XII.22a) ˙

Scr. Romae c. xii *Kal. Ian. an. 44*

<CICERO CORNIFICIO S.>

1   A. d. xiii Kal. Ian. senatus [aut] frequens mihi est adsensus cum de ceteris rebus magnis et necessariis tum de provinciis ab iis qui obtinerent retinendis neque cuiquam tradendis nisi qui ex senatus consulto successisset. hoc ego cum rei publicae causa censui tum mehercule in primis retinendae dignitatis tuae. quam ob rem te amoris nostri causa rogo, rei publicae causa hortor ut ne cui quicquam iuris in tua provincia esse patiare atque ut omnia referas ad

2   dignitatem, qua nihil esse potest praestantius. vere tecum agam, ut necessitudo nostra postulat: in Sempronio, si meis litteris obtemperasses, maximam ab omnibus laudem adeptus esses. sed illud et praeteriit et levius est, haec magna res est. fac ut provinciam retineas in potestate rei publicae.

    Plura scripsissem nisi tui festinarent. itaque Chaerippo nostro me velim excuses.

357 (XII.22a)
CICERO TO CORNIFICIUS

Rome, ca. 21 December 44

From Cicero to Cornificius greetings.

On 20 December a well attended meeting of the Senate accepted my proposals on certain urgent and important matters, including one to the effect that provincial governors should remain at their posts and hand over authority only to successors appointed by senatorial decree. I made this motion in the public interest, but I assure you that I was also actuated in no small measure by concern for the preservation of your personal consequence. Accordingly, I would ask you for the sake of our affection and exhort you for the sake of the commonwealth to allow no person any jurisdiction in your province and always to make your own public standing your primary consideration—and no man could stand higher. I will be candid, as our friendship requires. In the matter of Sempronius[1] you would have gained a great deal of credit in all quarters if you had paid heed to my letter. But that is a thing of the past and of no great moment: this is really important: be sure to keep your province in the control of the commonwealth.

I should have written more if your people had not been in a hurry. So please make my excuses to our friend Chaerippus.

[1] Perhaps C. Sempronius Rufus. His matter is obscure (cf. Letters 373.3, 433.2).

358 (X.4)

Scr. in Gallia Transalpina ex. m. Dec. an. 44

PLANCUS CICERONI

1   Gratissimae mihi tuae litterae fuerunt, quas ex Furni sermone te scripsisse animadverti. ego autem praeteriti temporis excusationem adfero quod te profectum audieram nec multo ante redisse scivi quam ex epistula tua cognovi. nullum enim in te officium ne minimum quidem sine maxima culpa videor posse praeterire, in quo tuendo habeo causas plurimas vel paternae necessitudinis vel meae a pueritia observantiae vel tui erga me mutui amoris.

2   Qua re, mi Cicero, quod mea tuaque patitur aetas, persuade tibi te unum esse in quo ego colendo patriam mihi constituerim sanctitatem. omnia igitur tua consilia mihi non magis prudentiae plena, quae summa est, videntur quam fidelitatis, quam ego ex mea conscientia metior. qua re, si aut aliter sentirem, certe admonitio tua me reprimere aut, si dubitarem, hortatio impellere posset ut id sequerer quod tu optimum putares. nunc vero quid est quod me in aliam partem trahere possit? quaecumque in me bona sunt aut Fortunae beneficio tributa aut meo labore parta, etsi a te propter amorem carius sunt aestimata, tamen vel inimicissimi iudicio tanta sunt ut praeter bonam famam nihil desiderare videantur.

3   Qua re hoc unum tibi persuade, quantum viribus eniti, consilio providere, auctoritate monere potuero, hoc omne

358 (X.4)
PLANCUS TO CICERO

Transalpine Gaul, December (end) 44

From Plancus to Cicero.

Very many thanks for your letter, which I notice you wrote as a result of your talk with Furnius. As for myself, I have an excuse to plead for the time I have allowed to go by—I heard you had set out, but did not know of your return much before I was apprised of it in your letter. I mention this because even the slightest failure in due attention to you could not but make me feel most deeply to blame. I have many reasons to be punctilious—your relations with my father, the respect I have paid you since childhood, your reciprocal affection for me.

Therefore, my dear Cicero, be assured that (as our respective ages allow) in cultivating your friendship I have invested you, and only you, with the sacred character of a father. Your counsels all appear to me full no less of sincerity, which I measure by my own conscience, than of the wisdom for which you are distinguished. If my disposition were otherwise, your admonition would assuredly suffice to check it; and if I were hesitating, your exhortation would be enough to urge me forward in pursuit of what *you* hold to be best. But as it is, what is there to draw me in a different direction? Your affection leads you to estimate such advantages as I possess (whether the gift of kindly Fortune or the product of my own effort) beyond their worth; but even my worst enemy would admit that only the world's good opinion seems wanting.

Therefore rest assured of one thing: all that my strength can compass, my prudence foresee, and my counsel sug-

rei publicae semper futurum. non est ignotus mihi sensus tuus; neque, si facultas optabilis mihi quidem tui praesentis esset, umquam a tuis consiliis discreparem nec nunc ‹c›om‹m›ittam ut ullum meum factum reprehendere iure possis.

4   Sum in exspectatione omnium rerum, quid in Gallia citeriore, quid in urbe mense Ianuario geratur; ‹fac igitur›[1] ut sciam. interim maximam hic sollicitudinem curamque sustineo, ne inter aliena vitia hae gentes nostra mala suam putent occasionem. quod si proinde ut ipse mereor mihi successerit, certe et tibi, cui maxime cupio, et omnibus viris bonis satis faciam.

Fac valeas meque mutuo diligas.

359 (X.5)

Scr. Romae med. m. Ian. an. 43

CICERO PLANCO S.

1   Binas a te accepi litteras eodem exemplo, quod ipsum argumento mihi fuit diligentiae tuae. intellexi enim te laborare ut ad me mihi exspectatissimae litterae perferrentur. ex quibus cepi fructum duplicem mihique in comparatione difficilem ad iudicandum, amoremne erga me tuum an animum in re‹m› publicam pluris aestimandum putarem. est omnino patriae caritas meo quidem iudicio maxima, sed amor voluntatisque coniunctio plus certe ha-

[1] *(Lehmann)*

gest, shall ever be at the service of the commonwealth. I am not unaware of your sentiments. If I could have you with me in person, as I should so much wish, I should never dissent from your policies; and as it is, I shall take good care not to let any of my actions give you fair ground for censure.

I am waiting for news of all manner of things—what is toward in Cisalpine Gaul, and what in Rome this January. Please inform me. Meanwhile I have a heavy and anxious task on my hands here, to guard (while others misbehave themselves) against the danger that the peoples of this country may see their opportunity in our calamities. If I am as successful in this as I deserve, I shall assuredly not disappoint you, whom I am most especially anxious to content, or the whole body of honest men.

Keep well and remember me kindly, as I do you.

359 (X.5)
CICERO TO PLANCUS

Rome, January (middle) 43

From Cicero to Plancus greetings.

I have received two letters from you, duplicates. That in itself showed me how punctilious you are. I appreciated your anxiety that the letter I so eagerly awaited should duly reach me. The letter itself gave me a twofold satisfaction; and when I try to make a comparison, I find it hard to decide which I should esteem the more precious, your affection for me or your spirit of patriotism. To be sure (in my judgement at all events) love of country transcends all other sentiments; but affection and friendly attachment

bet suavitatis. itaque commemoratio tua paternae necessitudinis benevolentiaeque eius quam erga me a pueritia
contulisses ceterarumque rerum quae ad eam sententiam
2 pertinebant incredibilem mihi laetitiam attulerunt.[1] rursus declaratio animi tui quem haberes de re publica
quemque habiturus esses mihi erat iucundissima, eoque
maior erat haec laetitia quod ad illa superiora accedebat.

Itaque te non hortor solum, mi Plance, sed plane etiam
oro, quod feci iis litteris quibus tu humanissime respondis-
ti, ut tota mente omnique animi impetu in rem publicam
incumbas. nihil est quod tibi maiori fructui gloriaeque esse
possit, nec quicquam ex omnibus rebus humanis est praeclarius aut praestantius quam de re publica bene mereri.
3 adhuc enim (patitur tua summa humanitas et sapientia me
quid[2] sentiam libere dicere) Fortuna suffragante videris
res maximas consecutus; quod quamquam sine virtute fieri
non potuisset, tamen ex maxima parte ea quae es adeptus Fortunae temporibusque tribuuntur. his temporibus
difficillimis rei publicae quicquid subveneris, id erit totum
et proprium tuum. incredibile est omnium civium latronibus exceptis odium in Antonium, magna spes in te et in tuo
exercitu, magna exspectatio; cuius, per deos, gratiae gloriaeque cave tempus amittas. sic moneo ut filium, sic faveo
ut mihi, sic hortor ut et pro patria et amicissimum.

[1] attulit, *deinde* attulerat *Man.*
[2] quod *(Wes.)*

[1] Antony and his followers are often referred to as *latrones*
(brigands), as being in arms against the public peace.

undeniably exercise a greater charm. And so your reminder of my relations with your father, of the good will you have bestowed upon me since your childhood, and of other points relevant to the theme, made me a happier man than you can well believe. But, again, the declaration of your political attitude, now and in time to come, pleased me exceedingly. My happiness was all the greater because this came as an addition to what had gone before.

So I urge you, my dear Plancus, nay more, I beg you, as I did in the letter to which you have replied so kindly, to bend all your thoughts and mental energy upon public affairs. There is nothing that can so richly reward you or so redound to your glory; nor in the whole range of human activities is there one more splendid and excellent than service to the commonwealth. Hitherto (your admirable good nature and good sense allow me to put my thoughts freely into words) you appear to have won brilliant success with luck on your side. That would not, it is true, have been possible without merit. None the less, the greater part of your achievements is credited to Fortune and circumstances. But if you come to the aid of the commonwealth in the very difficult circumstances of today, all you do will be properly your own. The universal hatred of Antony (bandits[1] excepted) is extraordinary. Great is the hope pinned upon you and the army under your command, great the expectancy. Do not, in the name of heaven, lose the opportunity to render yourself popular and renowned. I admonish you as a son, I hope for you as for myself, I urge you as one addressing a very dear friend in his country's cause.

360 (XI.8)

Scr. Romae ex. m. Ian. an. 43

M. CICERO S. D. D. BRUTO IMP. COS. DESIG.

1   Eo tempore Polla tua misit ut ad te si quid vellem darem litterarum cum quid scriberem non habebam; omnia enim erant suspensa propter exspectationem legatorum, qui quid egissent nihildum nuntiabatur. haec tamen scribenda existimavi: primum senatum populumque Romanum de te laborare non solum salutis suae causa sed etiam dignitatis tuae; admirabilis enim est quaedam tui nominis caritas amorque in te singularis omnium civium. ita enim sperant atque confidunt, ut antea rege, sic hoc tempore
2 regno te rem publicam liberaturum. Romae dilectus habetur totaque Italia, si hic dilectus appellandus est cum ultro se offerunt omnes; tantus ardor animos hominum occupavit desiderio libertatis odioque diuturnae[1] servitutis. de reliquis rebus a te iam exspectare litteras debemus, quid ipse agas, quid noster Hirtius, quid Caesar meus; quos spero brevi tempore societate victoriae tecum copulatos fore.

    Reliquum est ut de me id scribam quod te ex tuorum litteris et spero et malo cognoscere, me neque deesse ulla in re neque umquam defuturum dignitati tuae.

---

[1] diutinae*

---

[1] Three senior Consulars, Ser. Sulpicius Rufus, L. Calpurnius Piso, and L. Marcius Philippus, had been sent by the Senate to convey its behests to Antony, now besieging D. Brutus in Mutina (Modena). They returned about 1 February, Sulpicius having died on the mission.

360 (XI.8)
CICERO TO D. BRUTUS

Rome, late January 43

From M. Cicero to D. Brutus, Imperator, Consul-Elect, greetings.

I have had word from your lady Polla to give the bearer a letter for you if I wished to send something, but at this particular time I have nothing to write. Everything is in suspense while we wait to hear the result of the embassy,[1] of which nothing is reported as yet. However, I think I should tell you to begin with that the Senate and People of Rome are much concerned about you, not only for their own safety's sake but for that of your prestige. The emotion your name inspires is extraordinary. The whole citizen community feels a peculiar affection towards you, hoping and believing that you will now free our country from tyranny as you have already freed her from a tyrant. The levy is proceeding in Rome and all over Italy, if 'levy' is the right word to use when the whole population is freely volunteering in a flush of enthusiasm inspired by craving for liberty and disgust of their long servitude. On other matters it is time for us to be expecting a letter from you with news of yourself and our friend Hirtius and my young friend Caesar. I trust it will not be long before they are joined with you in the bond of a common victory.

I have only to add concerning myself something which I hope and prefer you learn from the letters of those near to you, that my support for your public standing is not and never shall be wanting on any occasion.

Scr. Romae ex. m. Ian. an. 43

‹CICERO CORNIFICIO S.›

1   Ego nullum locum praetermitto (nec enim debeo) non modo laudandi tui sed ne ornandi quidem; sed mea studia erga te et officia malo tibi ex tuorum litteris quam ex meis esse nota. te tamen hortor ut omni cura in rem publicam incumbas. hoc est animi, hoc est ingeni tui, hoc eius spei quam habere debes amplificandae dignitatis tuae.

2   Sed hac de re alias ad te pluribus. cum enim haec scribebam in exspectatione erant omnia. nondum legati redierant quos senatus non ad pacem deprecandam sed ad denuntiandum bellum miserat nisi legatorum nuntio paruisset. ego tamen, ut primum occasio data est meo pristino more rem publicam defen‹den›di,[1] me principem senatui populoque Romano professus sum, nec, postea quam suscepi causam libertatis, minimum tempus amisi tuendae salutis libertatisque communis. sed haec quoque te ex aliis malo.

[1] *(Ern.)*

361 (XII.24)
CICERO TO CORNIFICIUS

Rome, late January 43

From Cicero to Cornificius greetings.

I do not (and in duty I should not) lose any opportunity of singing your praises and, what is more, of securing practical recognition for you. But I prefer you to learn of my efforts and good offices from the letters of your domestic correspondents rather than from mine. I would, however, urge you to throw your whole mind into the public service. That is worthy of your spirit and intellect, and of the hope of increased prestige which you ought to entertain.

But of this more at some other time. As I write, everything hangs in suspense. The envoys sent by the Senate (not to beg for peace but to give notice of war if he did not comply with their message) have not yet returned. However, on the first occasion that presented itself to defend the commonwealth in my old style I offered myself to the Senate and People of Rome as their leader,[1] and, since I first took up the cause of freedom, I have not let slip the smallest opportunity to champion our corporate existence and liberties. But of this too I would rather you learned from others.

[1] In the Third Philippic, delivered on 20 December 44.

362 (IX.24)

Scr. Romae m. Ian., ut vid., an. 43

CICERO PAETO S. D.

1   Rufum istum, amicum tuum, de quo iterum iam ad me
scribis, adiuvarem quantum possem etiam si ab eo laesus
essem cum te tanto opere viderem eius causa laborare;
cum vero et ex tuis litteris et ex illius ad me missis intelle-
gam et iudicem magnae curae ei salutem meam fuisse, non
possum ei non amicus esse, neque solum tua commendatione, quae apud me, ut debet, valet plurimum, sed etiam
voluntate ac iudicio meo. volo enim te scire, mi Paete,
initium mihi suspicionis et cautionis et diligentiae fuisse
litteras tuas, quibus litteris congruentes fuerunt aliae postea multorum. nam et Aquini et Fabrateriae consilia sunt
inita de me, quae te video inaudisse, et quasi divinarent
quam iis molestus essem futurus, nihil aliud egerunt nisi
me ut opprimerent. quod ego non suspicans incautior fuissem nisi a te admonitus essem. quam ob rem iste tuus amicus apud me commendatione non eget. utinam ea Fortuna
rei publicae sit ut ille me[um]¹ gratissimum possit cognoscere! sed haec hactenus.

2   Te ad cenas itare desisse moleste fero; magna enim te
delectatione et voluptate privasti. deinde etiam vereor

¹ *(Wes.)*

---

[1] Otherwise unknown. Rufus is probably the commonest *cog-nomen*.

[2] Partisans of Mark Antony. We hear something of plots

362 (IX.24)
CICERO TO PAPIRIUS PAETUS

Rome, January (?) 43

Cicero to Paetus greetings.

I should assist your friend Rufus,[1] about whom you now write to me for the second time, to the best of my ability, even if he had done me an injury, seeing how concerned you are on his behalf. But understanding and concluding as I do both from your letters and from one he has sent me himself that he has been greatly exercised about my safety, I cannot but be his friend, not only because of your recommendation (which carries the greatest weight with me, as is right and proper) but from my personal inclination and judgement. For I want you to know, my dear Paetus, that my suspicions and diligent precautions all started with your letter, which was followed by letters to like effect from many other correspondents. Plots were laid against me both at Aquinum and at Fabrateria of which something evidently came to your ears. They[2] put all their energies into catching me unawares, as though they had a presentiment of what a thorn in their flesh I was to become. Unsuspecting as I was, I might have laid myself open but for your admonition. Therefore this friend of yours needs no recommendation to me. I only hope the Fortune of the commonwealth may be such as to enable him to discover that gratitude is a strong point with me. So much for that.

I am sorry to hear that you have given up dining out. You have deprived yourself of a great deal of amusement

against Cicero's person by L. Antonius in the summer of 44; cf. *Letters to Atticus* 385 (XV.8).2, 390 (XV.12).2, *Philippics* 12.20.

(licet enim verum dicere) ne nescio quid illud quod scie-
bas[2] dediscas et obliviscare cenulas facere. nam si tum cum
habebas quos imitarere non multum proficiebas, quid
nunc te facturum putem? Spurinna quidem, cum ei rem
demonstrassem et vitam tuam superiorem exposuissem,
magnum periculum summae rei publicae demonstrabat
nisi ad superiorem consuetudinem tum cum Favonius
flaret revertisses; hoc tempore ferri posse, si forte tu frigus
ferre non posses.

3   Et mehercule, mi Paete, extra iocum moneo te, quod
pertinere ad beate vivendum arbitror, ut cum viris bonis,
iucundis, amantibus tui vivas. nihil est aptius vitae, nihil ad
beate vivendum accommodatius. nec id ad voluptatem
refero sed ad communitatem vitae atque victus remissio-
nemque animorum, quae maxime sermone efficitur familiari, qui est in conviviis dulcissimus, ut sapientius nostri
quam Graeci; illi 'συμπόσια' aut 'σύνδειπνα,' id est com-
potationes aut concenationes,[3] nos 'convivia,' quod tum
maxime simul vivitur. vides ut te philosophando revocare
coner ad cenas.

       Cura ut valeas; id foris cenitando facillime consequere.
4   Sed cave, si me amas, existimes me quod iocosius scribam abiecisse curam rei publicae. sic tibi, mi Paete, persuade, me dies et noctes nihil aliud agere, nihil curare, nisi
ut mei cives salvi liberique sint. nullum locum praetermit-

[2] solebas *(SB)*
[3] id est . . . concen- *del. Lamb.*

---

[3] The west wind, harbinger of spring.
[4] 'Symposia,' 'syndeipna.'
[5] *Convivia.*

and pleasure. Furthermore (you will not mind my being candid), I am afraid you will unlearn what little you used to know, and forget how to give little dinner parties. For if you made such small progress in the art when you had models to imitate, what am I to expect of you now? When I laid the facts before Spurinna and explained to him your former mode of life, he pronounced a grave danger to the supreme interests of the commonwealth unless you resume your old habits when Favonius[3] starts to blow; at the present time of year he said he thought it might be borne, if you could not bear the cold.

And really, my dear Paetus, all joking apart I advise you, as something which I regard as relevant to happiness, to spend time in honest, pleasant, and friendly company. Nothing becomes life better, or is more in harmony with its happy living. I am not thinking of physical pleasure, but of community of life and habit and of mental recreation, of which familiar conversation is the most effective agent; and conversation is at its most agreeable at dinner parties. In this respect our countrymen are wiser than the Greeks. They use words meaning literally 'co-drinkings' or 'co-dinings,'[4] but we say 'co-livings,'[5] because at dinner parties more than anywhere else life is lived in company. You see how I try to bring you back to dinners by philosophizing!

Take care of your health—which you will most easily compass by constantly dining abroad.

But do not suppose, if you love me, that because I write rather flippantly I have put aside my concern for the commonwealth. You may be sure, my dear Paetus, that my days and nights are passed in one sole care and occupation—the safety and freedom of my countrymen. I lose no opportunity of admonition or action or precaution. Finally it is my

to monendi, agendi, providendi. hoc denique animo sum,
ut, si in hac cura atque administratione vita mihi ponenda
sit, praeclare actum mecum putem.

Etiam atque etiam vale.

363 (XII.4)

Scr. Romae IV vel III Non. Febr., ut vid., an. 43

CICERO CASSIO S.

1   Vellem Idibus Martiis me ad cenam invitasses; profecto
reliquiarum nihil fuisset. nunc me reliquiae vestrae exer-
cent, et quidem praeter ceteros me. quamquam egregios
consules habemus, sed turpissimos consularis; senatum
fortem, sed infimo quemque honore fortissimum. populo
vero nihil fortius, nihil melius, Italiaque universa, nihil autem foedius Philippo et Pisone legatis, nihil flagitiosius.
qui cum essent missi ut Antonio ex senatus sententia certas
res nuntiarent,[1] cum ille earum rerum nulli paruisset, ultro
ab illo ad nos intolerabilia postulata rettulerunt. itaque
ad nos concurritur, factique iam in re salutari populares
sumus.

2   Sed tu quid ageres, quid acturus, ubi denique esses
nesciebam. fama nuntiabat te esse in Syria, auctor erat
nemo. de Bruto quo propius est eo firmiora videntur esse
quae nuntiantur. Dolabella valde vituperabatur ab hominibus non insulsis quod tibi tam cito succederet, cum tu vix-

---

[1] denunt- *Gron.*

---

[1] M. Brutus was now in Macedonia.

feeling that, if I must lay down my life in my present care
and direction of public affairs, I shall consider myself very
fortunate in my destiny.

Once again, good-bye.

363 (XII.4)
CICERO TO CASSIUS

Rome, 2 or 3 February (?) 43

From Cicero to Cassius greetings.

A pity you did not invite me to dinner on the Ides of
March! Assuredly there would have been no leavings! As it
is, *your* leavings are giving me plenty of trouble—yes, me
in particular. True, we have an excellent pair of Consuls,
but the Consulars are a shocking collection. The Senate is
firm, but firmest in the lowest rank. As for the people, they
are magnificently firm and loyal, so is the whole of Italy.
The envoys Philippus and Piso have played a disgusting,
scandalous role. They were sent to announce certain spe-
cific items to Antony according to the will of the Senate.
After he had refused to obey any of these, they took it upon
themselves to bring back a set of intolerable demands from
him to us. Accordingly there is a rally to me, and I have
now become a popular favourite in a good cause.

But what you are doing or going to do, or even where
you are, I don't know. Rumour reports you in Syria, but nobody vouches for it. Reports of Brutus[1] appear more trustworthy in so far as he is nearer Italy. Dolabella is severely
censured by persons with some claim to wit for relieving
you in such a hurry, when you had been barely thirty days

dum xxx dies in Syria fuisses. itaque constabat eum recipi
in Syriam non oportere. summa laus et tua et Bruti est
quod exercitum praeter spem existimamini comparasse.
scriberem plura si rem causamque nossem. nunc quae
scribo scribo ex opinione hominum atque fama. tuas litteras avide exspecto.

Vale.

364 (X.28)

Scr. Romae iv *Non. Febr. vel paulo post, an. 43*

CICERO TREBONIO S.

1   Quam vellem ad illas pulcherrimas epulas me Idibus
Martiis invitasses! reliquiarum nihil haberemus. at nunc
cum iis tantum negoti est ut vestrum illud divinum ⟨in⟩
rem publicam beneficium non nullam habeat querelam.
quod vero a te, viro optimo, seductus est tuoque beneficio
adhuc vivit haec pestis, interdum, quod mihi vix fas est, tibi
subirascor; mihi enim negoti plus reliquisti uni quam praeter me omnibus.

Ut enim primum post Antoni foedissimum discessum
senatus haberi libere potuit, ad illum animum meum reverti pristinum quem tu cum civi acerrimo, patre tuo, in

---

² Under the lex Cornelia a governor must leave his province
within thirty days of the arrival of his successor. Cassius, as it
seemed, was not to be allowed thirty days from the *start* of his tenure. The joke seems to lie in the fact that Cassius had no legal
claim to Syria, which had been assigned to Dolabella.

in Syria![2] It is accordingly agreed that he ought not to be let into the province. You and Brutus are highly commended because you are supposed to have raised an army, which nobody expected. I should write more if I knew the facts of the case. As it is, what I write is based on public opinion and rumour. I am eagerly waiting to hear from you.

Good-bye.

364 (X.28)
CICERO TO TREBONIUS

Rome, 2 February or shortly after, 43

From Cicero to Trebonius greetings.

How I wish you had invited me to that splendid feast on the Ides of March! We should then have had no leftovers! As it is, we are having so much trouble with these that the immortal service which you and your friends rendered the commonwealth leaves room for some criticism. And when I think that it was your excellent self who drew that noxious creature[1] aside and that he has you to thank that he is still alive, I sometimes grow half angry with you, which for me is almost sinful.[2] For you have left *me* with more trouble on my hands than everybody else put together.

As soon as the Senate was able to meet in freedom after Antony's ignominious departure,[3] my old spirit returned to me, the spirit which you and that ardent loyalist, your

---

[1] Antony, who had been kept in conversation by Trebonius while the other plotters were disposing of Caesar.

[2] Because of the obligations rehearsed in Letter 207 (XV.21).

[3] For Cisalpine Gaul on 28 November.

2   ore et amore semper habuisti. nam cum senatum a. d. XIII
Kal. Ian. tribuni pl. vocavissent deque alia re referrent,
totam rem publicam sum complexus egique acerrime
senatumque iam languentem et defessum ad pristinam
virtutem consuetudinemque revocavi magis animi quam
ingeni viribus. hic dies meaque contentio atque actio spem
primum populo Romano attulit libertatis reciperandae.
nec vero ipse postea tempus ullum intermisi de re publica
non cogitandi solum sed etiam agendi.

3   Quod nisi res urbanas actaque omnia ad te perferri
arbitrarer, ipse perscriberem, quamquam eram maximis
occupationibus impeditus. sed illa cognosces ex aliis, a me
pauca et ea summatim. habemus fortem senatum, consularis partim timidos, partim male sentientis. magnum dam-
num factum est in Servio. L. Caesar optime sentit, sed,
quod avunculus est, non acerrimas dicit sententias. consules egregii, praeclarus D. Brutus, egregius puer Caesar, de
quo spero equidem reliqua; hoc vero certum habeto, nisi
ille veteranos celeriter conscripsisset legionesque duae de
exercitu Antoni ad eius se auctoritatem contulissent atque
is oppositus esset terror Antonio, nihil Antonium sceleris,
nihil crudelitatis praeteriturum fuisse.

    Haec tibi, etsi audita esse arbitrabar, volui tamen notio-
ra esse. plura scribam si plus oti habuero.

father, always praised and admired. The Tribunes had summoned a meeting on 20 December and put another matter to the House. I then entered upon a comprehensive survey of the whole political situation. I did not mince my words, and, more by will power than by oratorical skill, I recalled the weak and weary Senate to its old, traditional vigour. That day, and my energy, and the course I took, brought to the Roman People the first hope of recovering their freedom. And from that time forward I have used every possible moment, not only in thought but in action, on behalf of the commonwealth.

If I did not suppose you to be receiving all the city affairs and official proceedings, I should recount them myself, although I am immersed in pressing business. But you will learn all that from others—from me, only a few items, and those in brief. We have a courageous Senate, but of the Consulars some are timid and others disloyal. Servius was a great loss. L. Caesar is thoroughly sound, but as Antony's uncle he does not speak very forcibly in the House. The Consuls are admirable, D Brutus is splendid, young Caesar admirable—I for one have good hopes of him in the future. This much at any rate you may take as certain; if he had not rapidly enrolled veterans, if two of Antony's legions had not put themselves under his orders,[4] and if Antony had not been confronted with this menace, he would have stopped at no crime or cruelty.

Although I suppose you have heard all this, I wished you to know it better. I shall write further as soon as I have more leisure.

[4] Cf. Letter 354, n.

365 (XII.5)

Scr. Romae c. Id. Febr. an. 43

CICERO CASSIO S.

1   Hiemem credo adhuc prohibuisse quo minus de te certum haberemus quid ageres maximeque ubi esses. loque-
bantur omnes tamen (credo, quod volebant) in Syria te
esse, habere copias. id autem eo facilius credebatur quia
simile veri videbatur. Brutus quidem noster egregiam laudem est consecutus. res enim tantas gessit tamque inopi-
natas ut eae cum per se gratae essent tum ornatiores propter celeritatem. quod si tu ea tenes quae putamus, magnis
subsidiis fulta res publica est. a prima enim ora Graeciae
usque ad Aegyptum optimorum civium imperiis muniti
erimus et copiis.

2   Quamquam, nisi me fallebat, res se sic habebat ut totius
belli omne discrimen in D. Bruto positum videretur. qui
si, ut sperabamus, erupisset Mutina, nihil belli reliqui fore
videbatur. parvis omnino iam copiis obsidebatur, quod
magno praesidio Bononiam tenebat Antonius. erat autem
Claternae noster Hirtius, ad Forum Cornelium Caesar,
uterque cum firmo exercitu, magnasque Romae Pansa
copias ex dilectu Italiae compararat. hiems adhuc rem geri
prohibuerat. Hirtius nihil nisi considerate, ut mihi crebris
litteris significat, acturus videbatur. praeter Bononiam,
Regium Lepidi, Parmam totam Galliam tenebamus stu-
diosissimam rei publicae. tuos etiam clientis Transpadanos

---

[1] Why the Transpadanes are called clients of Cassius is unknown. They were indebted to Caesar the Dictator for Roman
citizenship.

365 (XII.5)
CICERO TO CASSIUS

Rome, ca. 13 February 43

From Cicero to Cassius greetings.

I dare say it is the winter weather that has so far prevented us getting any certain news of you—your doings and, above all, your whereabouts. But everybody is saying (I imagine because they would like it to be so) that you are in Syria at the head of a force. This report gains the readier credence because it has a ring of probability. Our friend Brutus has won golden opinions. His achievements have been no less important than unexpected, so that, welcome as they are intrinsically, they are enhanced by their rapidity. If you hold the areas we think you do, the national cause has massive forces at its back. From the shores of Greece down to Egypt we shall have a rampart of commands and armies in thoroughly patriotic hands.

And yet, if I am not in error, the position is that the decision of the whole war depends entirely on D. Brutus. If, as we hope, he breaks out of Mutina, it seems unlikely that there will be any further fighting. In fact the forces besieging him are now small, because Antony is holding Bononia with a large garrison. Our friend Hirtius is at Claterna, Caesar at Forum Cornelium, both with a strong army; and Pansa has got together a large force in Rome, raised by levy throughout Italy. The winter has so far prevented action. Hirtius seems determined to leave nothing to chance, as he intimates in frequent letters to me. Except for Bononia, Regium Lepidi, and Parma, all Gaul is in our hands, enthusiastically loyal to the commonwealth. Even your clients[1]

mirifice coniunctos cum causa habebamus. erat firmis-
simus senatus exceptis consularibus, ex quibus unus L.
3 Caesar firmus est et rectus. Ser. Sulpici morte magnum
praesidium amisimus. reliqui partim inertes, partim improbi. non nulli invident eorum laudi quos in re publica
probari vident. populi vero Romani totiusque Italiae mira
consensio est.

Haec erant fere quae tibi nota esse vellem. nunc autem
opto ut ab istis Orientis partibus virtutis tuae lumen elu-
ceat.

Vale.

366 (XII.11)

Scr. in castris Taricheis Non. Mart. an. 43

C. CASSIUS PRO COS. S. D. M. CICERONI
1 S. v. b.; e. e. q. v.

In Syriam me profectum esse scito ad L. Murcum et Q.
Crispum imp. viri fortes optimique cives, postea quam au-
dierunt quae Romae gererentur, exercitus mihi tradide-
runt ipsique mecum una fortissimo animo rem publicam
administrant. item legionem quam Q. Caecilius Bassus habuit ad me venisse scito, quattuorque legiones quas A.
Allienus ex Aegypto eduxit traditas ab eo mihi esse scito.

---

[1] L. Staius Marcus had been sent to Syria by Caesar with an
army to suppress Caecilius Bassus. Q. Marcius Crispus, governor
of Bithynia, had come with another army to his assistance.

beyond the Po are marvellously attached to the cause. The Senate is thoroughly resolute, except for the Consulars, of whom only L. Caesar is staunch and straight. With Servius Sulpicius' death we have lost a tower of strength. The rest are without energy or without principle. Some are jealous of the credit of those whose statesmanship they see gaining approval. But the unanimity of the People of Rome and of all Italy is quite remarkable.

That is about all I wanted you to know. I pray now that from those lands of the sunrise the light of your valour may shine.

Good-bye.

366 (XII.11)
CASSIUS TO CICERO

Camp at Tarichea, 7 March 43

From C. Cassius, Proconsul, to M. Cicero greetings.

I trust you are well, as I am and my army.

Let me inform you that I am leaving for Syria to join Generals L. Murcus and Q. Crispus.[1] These gallant and loyal gentlemen, having heard of events in Rome, have handed their armies over to me, and are themselves discharging their public duties jointly with me in the most resolute spirit. I beg further to inform you that the legion commanded by Q. Caecilius Bassus has joined me, and likewise that the four legions which A. Allienus[2] led from Egypt have been handed over to me by him.

[2] As Dolabella's Legate he was sent to Egypt to bring four legions stationed there to Syria.

Nunc te cohortatione non puto indigere ut nos absentis remque publicam, quantum est in te, defendas. scire te volo firma praesidia vobis senatuique non deesse ut optima spe et maximo animo rem publicam defendas. reliqua tecum aget L. Carteius, familiaris meus.

Vale.

D. Non. Mart. ex castris Taricheis.

367 (XII.7)

Scr. Romae ex. m. Febr. an. 43

CICERO CASSIO S.

1   Quanto studio dignitatem tuam et in senatu et ad populum defenderim ex tuis te malo quam ex me cognoscere. quae mea sententia in senatu facile valuisset, nisi Pansa vehementer obstitisset. ea sententia dicta productus sum in contionem a tribuno pl. M. Servilio. dixi de te quae potui, tanta contentione quanta meorum ⟨laterum⟩[1] est, tanto clamore consensuque populi ut nihil umquam simile viderim. id velim mihi ignoscas quod invita socru tua fecerim. mulier timida verebatur ne Pansae animus offenderetur. in contione quidem Pansa dixit matrem quoque tuam et fratrem illam a me sententiam noluisse dici. sed me haec non

[1] *(Watt)*

---

[1] That Cassius should be put in charge of operations against Dolabella. For the wording see *Philippics* 11.29 f. Pansa put through a decree assigning the war to himself and Hirtius after D. Brutus had been relieved.   [2] This speech has not survived.

Affairs thus standing, I do not suppose you need any encouragement to defend us in our absence and the commonwealth also, so far as in you lies. I want you to know that you and your friends and the Senate are not without powerful supports, so you can defend the state in the best of hope and courage. On other matters my friend L. Carteius will speak to you.

Good-bye.

Dispatched Nones of March from camp at Tarichea.

367 (XII.7)
CICERO TO CASSIUS

Rome, end of February 43

From Cicero to Cassius greetings.

How zealously I have defended your position both in the Senate and before the People I prefer you to learn from your domestic correspondents than from myself. My motion[1] in the Senate would have gone through with ease but for Pansa's strong opposition. After delivering my speech, I was presented to a public meeting by Tribune M. Servilius. I said what I could about you to the full power of my lungs, amid unanimous shouts of approval from the crowd.[2] I have never seen anything like it. I hope you will forgive me for doing this against your mother-in-law's[3] wishes. She is a nervous lady, and was afraid that Pansa might take umbrage. In fact Pansa told a public meeting that your mother[4] and brother too had been against my

---

[3] M. Brutus' mother and Cato's sister, Servilia.

[4] Name unknown.

movebant, alia malebam; favebam et rei publicae, cui semper favi, et dignitati ac gloriae tuae.

2   Quod autem et in senatu pluribus verbis disserui ‹et›
dixi in contione, in eo velim fidem meam liberes. promisi
enim et prope confirmavi te non exspectasse nec exspecta-
turum decreta nostra, sed te ipsum tuo more rem publicam defensurum. et quamquam nihildum audieramus nec
ubi esses nec quas copias haberes, tamen sic statuebam,
omnis quae in istis partibus essent opes copiaeque tuas
esse, per teque Asiam provinciam confidebam iam rei
publicae reciperatam. tu fac in augenda gloria te ipsum
vincas.
    Vale.

368 (X.31)

Scr. Cordubae XVII *Kal. Apr. an. 43*

C. ASINIUS POLLIO CICERONI S. D.

1   Minime mirum tibi debet videri nihil me scripsisse
de re publica postea quam itum est ad arma. nam saltus
Castulonensis, qui semper tenuit nostros tabellarios, etsi
nunc frequentioribus latrociniis infestior factus est, tamen
nequaquam tanta in mora est quanta qui locis omnibus dis-
positi ab utraque parte scrutantur tabellarios et retinent.
itaque, nisi nave perlatae litterae essent, omnino nescirem
quid istic fieret. nunc vero nactus occasionem, postea
quam navigari coeptum est, cupidissime et quam creber-
rime potero scribam ad te.

making my motion. But all this did not affect me; I had other considerations more at heart. I was for the commonwealth, as always, and for your dignity and glory.

I hope you will redeem the pledge I gave in the Senate, at some length of discourse, and at the public meeting. I promised, indeed almost guaranteed, that you had not waited and would not wait for our decrees, but would defend the commonwealth on your own initiative in your wonted fashion. Although no news has yet reached us of your whereabouts and the forces at your disposal, I am resolved that all resources and troops in that part of the world are yours, and am confident that you have already recovered the province of Asia for the commonwealth. You must now surpass yourself in adding to your glory.

Good-bye.

368 (X.31)
POLLIO TO CICERO

Corduba, 16 March 43

C. Asinius Pollio to Cicero greetings.

You must not think it at all strange that I have written nothing on public affairs since war broke out. The pass of Castulo, which has always held up my couriers, has become more dangerous than ever with increasing banditry. Even so, that does not cause nearly so much delay as the pickets posted everywhere by both sides, which examine couriers and stop them proceeding. Had not letters got through by sea, I should be totally ignorant of affairs in Rome. But now that the opening of navigation gives me the chance, I shall write to you most eagerly and as often as I can.

2   Ne movear[1] eius sermonibus quem, tametsi nemo est
qui videre velit, tamen nequaquam proinde ac dignus est
oderunt homines, periculum non est. adeo est enim invi-
sus mihi ut nihil non acerbum putem quod commune cum
illo sit. natura autem mea et studia trahunt me ad pacis
et libertatis cupiditatem. itaque illud initium civilis belli
saepe deflevi. cum vero non liceret mihi nullius partis esse
quia utrubique magnos inimicos habebam, ea castra fugi in
quibus plane tutum me ab insidiis inimici sciebam non futurum. compulsus eo quo minime volebam, ne in extremis
3   essem, plane pericula non dubitanter adii. Caesarem vero,
quod me in tanta fortuna modo cognitum vetustissimorum
familiarium loco habuit, dilexi summa cum pietate et fide.
quae mea sententia gerere mihi licuit ita feci ut optimus
quisque maxime probarit;[2] quod iussus sum eo tempore
atque ita feci ut appareret invito imperatum esse. cuius
facti iniustissima invidia erudire me potuit quam iucunda
libertas et quam misera sub dominatione vita esset.

Ita, si id agitur ut rursus in potestate omnia unius sint,
quicumque is est, ei me profiteor inimicum; nec periculum
est ullum quod pro libertate aut refugiam aut deprecer.
4   sed consules neque senatus consulto neque litteris suis
praeceperant mihi quid facerem; unas enim [post][3] Id.
Mart. demum a Pansa litteras accepi, in quibus hortatur

[1] moveare *(Man.)*
[2] probaret *Stroth*
[3] *(SB: lac. ante* Id. *ind. Watt)*

---

[1] Almost certainly the Quaestor (strictly Proquaestor) L. Cornelius Balbus the younger; cf. Letter 415.
[2] He cannot be identified.

There is no danger of my being influenced by the talk of an individual[1] whom nobody wants in his sight, but who even so is by no means as unpopular as he deserves to be. My own dislike of him is such that anything in common with him would be disagreeable to me. Furthermore, my nature and pursuits lead me to crave for peace and freedom. The outbreak of the former civil war cost me many a tear. But since I could not remain neutral because I had powerful enemies on both sides, I avoided the camp where I well knew I should not be safe from my enemy's[2] plots. Finding myself forced whither I would not, and having no wish to trail in the rear, I certainly did not hang back from dangerous work. As for Caesar, I loved him in all duty and loyalty, because in his greatness he treated me, a recent acquaintance, as though I had been one of his oldest intimates. Where I was allowed to manage as I thought best, my actions were calculated to win cordial approval in the most respectable quarters. Where I obeyed orders, it was at a time and in a manner which made it clear that I had received them with reluctance. The ill will thereby incurred, highly unjust as it was, was enough to teach me how pleasant a thing is freedom and how miserable life under despotic rule.

If, therefore, we have an attempt to place supreme power once again in the hands of one man, I profess myself his enemy, whoever he is. There is no danger on behalf of freedom from which I shrink or seek to be excused. But the Consuls had not instructed me how to act, either by senatorial decree or by letter. I have finally received one letter, from Pansa, on the Ides of March, in which he urges me to write to the Senate that I and the army under my command

213

me ut senatu scribam me et exercitum in potestate eius futurum. * * *[4] quod, cum Lepidus contionaretur atque omnibus scriberet se consentire cum Antonio, maxime contrarium fuit. nam quibus commeatibus invito illo per illius provinciam legiones ducerem? aut si cetera transissem, num etiam Alpis poteram transvolare, quae praesidio illius tenentur? adde huc quod perferri litterae nulla condicione potuerunt; sescentis enim locis excutiuntur, 5 deinde etiam retinentur ab Lepido tabellarii. illud me Cordubae pro contione dixisse ne‹mo› vocabit in dubium, provinciam me nulli nisi qui ab senatu missus venisset traditurum. nam de legione tricesima tradenda quantas con‹ten›tiones[5] habuerim quid ego scribam? qua tradita quanto pro re publica infirmior fuerim futurus quis ignorat? hac enim legione noli acrius aut pugnacius quicquam putare esse. qua re eum me existima esse qui primum pacis cupidissimus sim (omnis enim civis plane studeo esse salvos), deinde qui et me et rem publicam vindicare in libertatem paratus sim.

6   Quod familiarem meum tuorum numero habes, opinione tua mihi gratius est. invideo illi tamen quod ambulat et iocatur tecum. quaeres quanti[6] aestimem; si umquam licuerit vivere in otio, experieris. nullum enim vestigium abs te discessurus sum.

    Illud vehementer admiror, non scripsisse te mihi manendo in provincia an ducendo exercitum in Italiam rei

---

[4] *lac. ind. SB ita fere supplendam*: quod me iam pridem facere oportuisse significat   [5] *(Man.)*   [6] quanti ‹id› *Or.*

---

[3] Something like 'which he intimates I should have done at an earlier stage' seems to have dropped out of the text.

will be at their disposal * * *.[3] That would have been very
unhelpful, since Lepidus was declaring in public speeches
and in letters to all and sundry that he saw eye to eye with
Antony. Where would I get provisions if I led my legions
through his province against his will? Or even if I had
passed the earlier stages, could I fly across the Alps, which
are held by his troops? Add the fact that it was quite impossible for a letter to get through. Couriers are searched
at any number of points, and then are actually detained by
Lepidus. One thing nobody will question, that before a
public meeting in Corduba I declared that I would hand
over my province to none but an emissary of the Senate.
There is no need for me to describe the struggle I have had
about handing over the Thirtieth Legion.[4] Had I done so,
nobody can be unaware how greatly my power to aid the
national cause would have been enfeebled. For I assure
you that the keenness and fighting spirit of that legion is
quite outstanding. So you must think of me as one who is,
first, most eager for peace (I am unashamedly anxious that
none of our fellow countrymen should perish) and, second, ready to defend my country's freedom and my own.

I am more gratified than you imagine by your taking my
friend[5] into your circle. But I envy him his walks and jests
with you. You will ask how highly I value that privilege: if
we are ever allowed to live in peace, you will find out by
experience. I shall not stir a yard from your side.

What does very much surprise me is that you have not
written to me whether I shall help the commonwealth
more by staying in my province or by leading my own army

[4] To Lepidus.
[5] Probably the poet C. Cornelius Gallus; cf. Letter 415.5.

publicae magis satis facere possim. ego quidem, etsi mihi
tutius ac minus laboriosum est manere, tamen, quia video
tali tempore multo magis legionibus opus esse quam provinciis, quae praesertim reciperari nullo negotio possunt,
constitui, ut nunc est, cum exercitu proficisci. deinde ex
litteris quas Pansae misi cognosces omnia; nam tibi earum
exemplar misi.

XVII Kal. Apr. Corduba.

369 (X.27)

Scr. Romae XIII Kal. Apr. an. 43

CICERO LEPIDO S.

1   Quod mihi pro summa erga te benevolentia magnae
curae est ut quam amplissima dignitate sis, moleste tuli te
senatui gratias non egisse cum esses ab eo ordine ornatus
summis honoribus. pacis inter civis conciliandae te cupi-
dum esse laetor. eam si a servitute seiungis, consules et rei
publicae et dignitati tuae; sin ista pax perditum hominem
in possessionem impotentissimi dominatus restitutura est,
hoc animo scito omnis sanos ut mortem servituti antepo-
2 nant. itaque sapientius meo quidem iudicio facies si te in

---

6 Yet earlier in his letter Pollio represented that it was quite
impossible for him to get to Italy through Lepidus' province without Lepidus' consent; and there is nothing to suggest that this
would now be forthcoming. Perhaps he was thinking of a sea
route. The letter to Pansa may have made matters clear.

1 On Cicero's motion at the beginning of the year the Senate
had passed a vote of thanks to Lepidus for his successful conclu-

to Italy. As for myself, although it is safer and easier for me to stay here, I perceive that at a time like this legions are needed much more than provinces, especially as the latter can be recovered without trouble. So I have decided, as matters stand, to march.[6] Further, you will learn everything from the letter I have sent to Pansa—I am sending you a copy.

16 March, from Corduba.

369 (X.27)
CICERO TO LEPIDUS

Rome, 20 March 43

From Cicero to Lepidus greetings.

The great good will I bear you makes me very anxious for you to enjoy the highest measure of public esteem. For that reason I was pained by your omission to thank the Senate after having been signally honoured by that body.[1] I am glad that you are desirous of restoring peace between your fellow countrymen. If you draw a line between peace and slavery, you will do a service to the state and your own reputation. But if the peace you have in view is one which is going to put unbridled autocratic power back into the hands of a desperado, then you should understand that all sane men are of a mind to prefer death to slavery. You will

sion of negotiations with Sex. Pompeius and decreed the erection of a gilded equestrian statue on the Rostra, an extraordinary distinction. On 20 March the Senate considered letters from Lepidus and Plancus (see next letter) advocating peace. Cicero dealt with the former in his Thirteenth Philippic (the speech as we have it makes no mention of Plancus).

istam pacificationem non interpones, quae neque senatui neque populo nec cuiquam bono probatur.

Sed haec audies ex aliis aut certior fies litteris. tu pro tua prudentia quid optimum factu sit videbis.

370 (X.6)

Scr. Romae XIII *Kal. Apr. an. 43*

CICERO PLANCO

1   Quae locutus est Furnius noster de animo tuo in rem publicam ea gratissima fuerunt senatui, populo Romano probatissima. quae autem tuae recitatae litterae sunt in senatu nequaquam consentire cum Furni oratione visae sunt. pacis enim auctor eras, cum collega tuus, vir clarissimus, a foedissimis latronibus obsideretur; qui aut positis armis pacem petere debent aut, si pugnantes eam postulant, victoria pax, non pactione, parienda est. sed de pace litterae vel Lepidi vel tuae quam in partem acceptae sint ex viro optimo, fratre tuo, et ex C. Furnio poteris cognoscere.

2   me autem impulit tui caritas ut, quamquam nec tibi ipsi consilium deesset et fratris Furnique benevolentia fidelisque prudentia tibi praesto esset futura, vellem tamen meae quoque auctoritatis pro plurimis nostris necessitudinibus praeceptum ad te aliquod pervenire.

Crede igitur mihi, Plance, omnis quos adhuc gradus

---

1 See Letter 369, n.

2 D. Brutus.

3 L. Plotius Plancus.

therefore, in my opinion at least, be wiser not to involve yourself in a kind of peacemaking which is unacceptable to the Senate, the People, and every honest man.

However, you will be hearing all this from others, or will be informed by your correspondents. Your own good sense will tell you what is best to do.

370 (X.6)
CICERO TO PLANCUS

Rome, 20 March 43

From Cicero to Plancus.

Our friend Furnius' account of your political disposition was most agreeable to the Senate and warmly approved by the Roman People. But your letter,[1] which was read out in the Senate, appeared by no means in accordance with Furnius' statement. You wrote as an advocate of peace, at a time when your distinguished colleague[2] is under siege by a band of the foulest brigands. Either they ought to lay down their arms and sue for peace, or, if they demand it fighting, then peace must be had by victory, not by negotiation. However, you will be able to learn from your excellent brother[3] and from C. Furnius how letters about peace have been received, whether yours or Lepidus'. You are well able to think for yourself; and the good will and loyal good sense of your brother and Furnius will be at your call. None the less, my affection for you prompts me to wish that a word of advice, to which the many ties between us ought to lend some weight, should also reach you from myself.

So, believe me, Plancus, when I say that all the stages of

dignitatis consecutus sis (es autem adeptus amplissimos)
eos honorum vocabula habituros, non dignitatis insignia,
nisi te cum libertate populi Romani et cum senatus auctoritate coniunxeris. seiunge te, quaeso, aliquando ab iis cum
quibus te non tuum iudicium sed temporum vincla con-
3 iunxerunt. complures in perturbatione rei publicae consules dicti, quorum nemo consularis habitus nisi qui animo
exstitit in rem publicam consulari. talem igitur te esse
oportet qui primum te ab impiorum civium tui dissimilli-
morum societate seiungas, deinde te[1] senatui bonisque
omnibus auctorem, principem, ducem praebeas, postremo ut[2] pacem esse iudices non in armis positis sed in
abiecto armorum et servitutis metu. haec si et ages et sen-
ties, tum eris non modo consul et consularis sed magnus
etiam consul et consularis; sin aliter, tum in istis amplissimis nominibus honorum non modo dignitas nulla erit sed
erit summa deformitas.

Haec impulsus benevolentia scripsi paulo severius;
quae tu [in] experiendo in ea ratione quae te digna est vera
esse cognosces.

D. XIII Kal. Apr.

[1] et *(Man.)*
[2] *num delendum?*

advancement which you have hitherto attained—and most splendid they are—will count but as so many official titles, not as symbols of public esteem, unless you ally yourself with the freedom of the Roman People and the authority of the Senate. At long last pray dissociate yourself from those to whom no choice of yours but bonds forged by circumstances have attached you. In this period of political turmoil a number of persons have been called Consuls, none of whom has been considered a Consular unless he displayed a patriotism worthy of the office. Such a patriot you should show yourself: firstly, in dissociating yourself from all connection with disloyal citizens, persons utterly unlike you; secondly, in offering yourself to the Senate and all honest men as adviser, principal, leader; lastly, in judging peace to consist, not in the mere laying down of weapons, but in the banishment of the fear of weapons and servitude. If such are your acts and sentiments, you will be not only a Consul and a Consular, but a great Consul and Consular. If otherwise, there will be no honour in these splendid official designations; rather they will carry the direst disgrace.

Prompted by good will, I have written rather gravely. You will prove the truth of my words by experience, in that path of conduct which is worthy of you.

Dispatched 20 March.

371 (X.8)

Scr. in Gallia Transalpina c. XIII Kal. Apr. an. 43

PLANCUS IMP. COS. DESIG. S. D. COS. PR. TR. PL. SENA-
TUI POPULO PLEBIQUE ROMANAE

1   Si cui forte videor diutius et hominum exspectationem
et spem rei publicae de mea voluntate tenuisse suspensam,
huic prius excusandum me esse arbitror quam de inse-
quenti officio quicquam ulli pollicendum. non enim prae-
teritam culpam videri volo redemisse sed optimae mentis
cogitata iam pridem maturo tempore enuntiare.

2   Non me praeteribat in tanta sollicitudine hominum et
tam perturbato statu civitatis fructuosissimam esse professionem bonae voluntatis magnosque honores ex ea re compluris consecutos videbam. sed cum in eum casum me
Fortuna demisisset ut aut celeriter pollicendo magna mihi
ipse[1] ad proficiendum impedimenta opponerem aut, si in
eo mihi temperavissem, maiores occasiones ad opitulan-
dum haberem, expeditius iter communis salutis quam
meae laudis esse volui. nam quis in ea fortuna quae mea
est et ab ea vita quam in me cognitam hominibus arbitror
et cum ea spe quam in manibus habeo aut sordidum
3   quicquam pati aut perniciosum concupiscere potest? sed
aliquantum nobis temporis et magni labores et multae
impensae opus fuerunt ut quae rei publicae bonisque

---

[1] -na in spe *(Rut.)*

371 (X.8)

PLANCUS TO THE MAGISTRATES, SENATE, AND PEOPLE

Transalpine Gaul, ca. 20 March 43

From Plancus, Imperator, Consul-Elect, to the Consuls, Praetors, Tribunes of the Plebs, Senate, and People and Plebs of Rome.

Before I make any promise to any man as to my duty in time to come, it will, I think, be proper to offer my excuses to those, if any there be, who feel that I have kept public expectancy and the hopes of the commonwealth concerning my political sentiments too long in suspense. For I do not wish to appear to have made amends for past shortcomings, but rather to be enunciating in the fulness of time thoughts long pondered in a loyal heart.

I was not unconscious that at such a time of grave public anxiety and national upheaval the profession of loyal sentiments is highly rewarding, and I saw that a number of persons had gained signal honours by this means. Fortune, however, had placed me in a dilemma. I had to choose whether to make promises without delay and thereby create obstacles to my own possibilities of usefulness, or, if I restrained myself in that particular, to gain larger opportunities for service. I preferred to smooth the path of national deliverance rather than that of my personal glory. A man enjoying a position such as mine, after a life such as I think I am generally known to have led, and with such a prospect as I now see before me, is not likely to submit to anything degrading or entertain a mischievous ambition. But a certain amount of time, a great deal of effort, and substantial expenditure of money were requisite if I was in

223

omnibus polliceremur exitu praestaremus neque ad auxilium patriae nudi cum bona voluntate sed cum facultatibus
accederemus. confirmandus erat exercitus nobis magnis
saepe praemiis sollicitatus, ut ab re publica potius modera-
ta quam ab uno infinita speraret; confirmandae complures
civitates, quae superiore anno largitionibus concessioni-
busque praemiorum erant obligatae, ut et illa vana putarent et eadem a melioribus auctoribus petenda existimarent; eliciendae etiam voluntates reliquorum, qui finitimis
provinciis exercitibusque praefuerunt, ut potius cum pluribus societatem defendendae libertatis iniremus quam
cum paucioribus funestam orbi terrarum victoriam parti-
4 remur. muniendi vero nosmet ipsi fuimus aucto exercitu
auxiliisque multiplicatis, ut, cum praeferremus sensus
aperte, tum etiam invitis quibusdam sciri quid defensuri
essemus non esset periculosum.

Ita numquam diffitebor multa me, ut ad effectum
horum consiliorum pervenirem, et simulasse invitum et
dissimulasse cum dolore, quod praematura denuntiatio
boni civis imparati quam periculosa esset ex casu collegae
5 videbam. quo nomine etiam C. Furnio legato, viro forti
atque strenuo, plura etiam verbo quam scriptura mandata
dedimus, ut et tectius ad vos perferrentur et nos essemus

---

[1] Not the Antonians. Plancus assumes that the Republic will
triumph anyhow, but the more of his fellow commanders who join
its cause the less costly the victory. He is thinking of Lepidus and
Pollio.

[2] D. Brutus, under siege in Mutina.

the end to make good my promises to the state and to all honest men, and to bring to the national cause, not empty hands and loyal sentiments, but the means to aid. I had to confirm the loyalty of the men under my command, who had been repeatedly tempted by lavish offers, inducing them to look to the commonwealth for a moderate recompense rather than to an individual for unlimited bounty. I had to confirm the loyalty of a number of communities which during the previous year had been obligated by means of gifts and grants of privileges, inducing them to regard those concessions as void and to make up their minds to seek the same from those better qualified to bestow them. I had to elicit the sentiments of my fellow governors and commanders in adjoining provinces; for I wished to join with many partners in a league for the defence of freedom, not to share with a few[1] the fruits of a victory disastrous to the world. I had also to strengthen my own position by increasing the size of my army and the numbers of its auxiliary forces, so that, when I came to make open declaration of my views, there might be no danger in the cause I intended to support becoming common knowledge, even though the announcement might be unwelcome in certain quarters.

So I shall never deny that, in order to bring those plans into effect, I made many reluctant pretences and distressful concealments; for I saw from my colleague's[2] predicament how dangerous it was for a loyal citizen to proclaim himself without preparing the ground. That is why the greater part of the communication which I entrusted to my Legate C. Furnius, a gallant and energetic officer, was by word of mouth rather than in writing, in order that it might reach you with less publicity and that I might run less risk.

tutiores, quibusque rebus et communem salutem muniri
et nos armari conveniret praecepimus. ex quo intellegi potest curam rei publicae summae defendendae iam pridem
apud nos excubare.

6 Nunc, cum deum benignitate ab omni re sumus para-
tiores, non solum bene sperare de nobis homines sed ex-
plorate iudicare volumus. legiones habeo quinque sub signis et sua fide virtuteque rei publicae coniunctissimas et
nostra liberalitate nobis obsequentis, provinciam omnium
civitatum consensu paratissimam et summa contentione
ad officia certantem, equitatus auxiliorumque tantas copias quantas hae gentes ad defendendam suam salutem libertatemque conficere possunt. ipse ita sum animo paratus ut vel provinciam tueri vel ire quo res publica vocet vel
tradere exercitum, auxilia provinciamque vel omnem impetum belli in me convertere non recusem, si modo meo
casu aut confirmare patriae salutem aut periculum possim
morari.

7 Haec si iam expeditis omnibus rebus tranquilloque statu civitatis polliceor, in damno meae laudis rei publicae
commodo laetabor; sin ad societatem integerrimorum et
maximorum periculorum accedam, consilia mea aequis iu-
dicibus ab obtrectatione invidorum defendenda commendo. mihi quidem ipsi fructus meritorum meorum in rei publicae incolumitate satis magnus est paratus. eos vero qui
meam auctoritatem et multo magis vestram fidem secuti

---

[3] His soldiers.

Therein I gave advice as to the measures requisite for the
protection of the common safety and for my own equip-
ment, from which it can be seen that the defence of the
supreme interests of the commonwealth has for a long
time past been my vigilant concern.

Now, by the grace of heaven, I am in every way better
prepared; and I wish my countrymen not only to entertain
good hope of me, but to make up their minds in full assurance. I have five legions under the standards; their own
loyalty and valour closely attach them to the commonwealth, and my liberality has secured their obedience to
myself. My province is in full readiness; all its constituent
communities are of one mind, and there is the keenest
rivalry in rendering services. I have cavalry and auxiliary
forces in such strength as these peoples can muster for the
defence of their lives and liberties. As for my personal
resolution, I am prepared to defend my province, or to go
wherever the public interest may summon, or to hand over
my army, auxiliaries, and province, or to turn the whole
brunt of the conflict upon myself, if only by such personal
hazard I can assure my country's safety or hold back the
danger that threatens her.

It may be that I make these professions when the
clouds have already dispersed and national tranquillity has
been restored. In that case my credit will be the less, but I
shall rejoice in the public good. If, however, I come to take
my share in dire and quite undiminished dangers, I commend the defence of my conduct from the malice of jealous tongues to equitable judges. For myself, I can look
forward to the preservation of the commonwealth as an
ample enough return for my services. But I think I ought to
ask you to regard as recommended to your favour those[3]

nec ulla spe decipi nec ullo metu terreri potuerunt ut commendatos vobis habeatis petendum videtur.

372 (X.7)

Scr. in Gallia Transalpina c. XIII Kal. Apr. an. 43

PLANCUS CICERONI

1   Plura tibi de meis consiliis scriberem rationemque
omnium rerum redderem verbosius, quo magis iudicares
omnia me rei publicae praestitisse quae et tua exhorta-
tione excepi et mea adfirmatione tibi recepi (non minus
enim a te probari quam diligi semper volui, nec te magis in
culpa defensorem mihi paravi quam praedicatorem meritorum meorum esse volui); sed breviorem me duae res
faciunt, una, quod publicis litteris omnia sum persecutus,
altera, quod M. Varisidium, equitem Romanum, familiarem meum, ipsum ad te transire iussi, ex quo omnia
cognoscere posses.

2   Non me dius fidius mediocri dolore adficiebar cum alii
occupare possessionem laudis viderentur; sed usque mihi
temperavi dum perducerem eo rem ut dignum aliquid
et consulatu meo et vestra exspectatione efficerem. quod
spero, si me Fortuna non fefellerit, me consecuturum, ut
maximo praesidio rei publicae nos fuisse et nunc sentiant
homines et in posterum memoria teneant. a te peto ut

who, in deference to me and (what counts for much more) in reliance upon your good faith, have resisted all blandishments and defied all threats.

372 (X.7)
PLANCUS TO CICERO

Transalpine Gaul, ca. 20 March 43

From Plancus to Cicero.

I should be writing at greater length about my plans and rendering you a more extended account of all particulars, thus enabling you better to judge how faithfully I have discharged to the commonwealth all that I took upon myself at your instigation and to which I am pledged by my solemn word to you given—I have always wanted your approval no less than your affection, and if in you I have secured a defender when at fault, I have also wished you to be the herald of my good works—but two things make me comparatively brief: first, I have dealt with everything in an official dispatch; second, I have told M. Varisidius, a Roman Knight and my close friend, to come over to you in person, so that you can learn it all from him.

I have felt no small chagrin, I give you my word, when others appeared to be staking out claims to glory ahead of me. But I made myself wait until I should have brought the situation to the point when I could achieve something worthy of my Consulship and the expectations of my friends in Rome. That aim, if Fortune does not disappoint me, I hope to accomplish, so that contemporaries shall recognize and posterity remember me as one who has rendered signal service to the commonwealth at need. Let me ask of you to

dignitati meae suffrageris et quarum rerum spe ad laudem me vocasti harum fructu in reliquum facias alacriorem. non minus posse te quam velle exploratum mihi est.

Fac valeas meque mutuo diligas.

373 (XII.25)

Scr. Romae c. XIII Kal. Apr. an. 43

<CICERO CORNIFICIO S.>

1   Liberalibus litteras accepi tuas, quas mihi Cornificius altero vicesimo die, ut dicebat, reddidit. eo die non fuit senatus neque postero. Quinquatribus frequenti senatu causam tuam egi, non invita Minerva; etenim eo ipso die senatus decrevit ut Minerva nostra, custos urbis, quam turbo deiecerat, restitueretur. Pansa tuas litteras recitavit. magna senatus approbatio consecuta est cum summo <meo>[1] gaudio et offensione Minotauri, id est Calvisi et Tauri. factum de te senatus consultum honorificum. postulabatur ut etiam illi notarentur, sed Pansa clementior.

1 *(Baiter)*

---

[1] Perhaps son of Cicero's correspondent.
[2] *Non invita Minerva;* see Letter 64.1.
[3] Just before leaving Rome for exile in 58 Cicero dedicated a small statue of Minerva Guardian of the City (= Athene Polias) in the temple of Jupiter Capitolinus.   [4] On 28 November 44 Antony had put through a senatorial decree reassigning provincial commands, under which Africa was given to its former governor C. Calvisius Sabinus, a former officer of Caesar's with a distin-

support my public standing and to render me more ardent in the further pursuit of glory by the enjoyment of those rewards which you set before my eyes when you called me to that endeavour. That your power is no less than your will I am well assured.

Take care of your health and remember me as affectionately as I do you.

373 (XII.25)
CICERO TO CORNIFICIUS

Rome, ca. 20 March 43

From Cicero to Cornificius greetings.

I received your letter on Bacchus' Day. Cornificius[1] handed it to me three weeks after dispatch, so he told me. There was no meeting of the Senate that day or the next. On Minerva's Day I pleaded your cause at a well attended session, not without the Goddess' good will[2]—my statue of her as Guardian of Rome[3] had been blown down in a gale, and that very day the Senate passed a decree to set it up again. Pansa read your dispatch. The House highly approved of it, to my great delight and the discomfiture of the Minotaur (Calvisius and Taurus).[4] A decree in honorific terms was voted concerning you. There was a demand that *they* should be censured as well, but Pansa took a more lenient view.

guished career ahead of him as a partisan of Octavian. Taurus may be T. Statilius Taurus, later to command Octavian's land forces at Actium. The nature of his association with Calvisius is unknown, as is the relevance of the first half of the nickname.

2   Ego, mi Cornifici, quo die primum in spem libertatis
ingressus sum et cunctantibus ceteris a. d. XIII Kal. Ian.
fundamenta ieci rei publicae, eo ipso die providi multum
atque habui rationem dignitatis tuae; mihi enim est adsensus senatus de obtinendis provinciis. nec vero postea
destiti labefactare eum qui summa cum tua iniuria contu-
meliaque rei publicae provinciam absens obtinebat. itaque
crebras, vel potius cottidianas compellationes meas non
tulit seque in urbem recepit invitus, neque solum spe sed
certa re iam et possessione deturbatus est meo iustissimo
honestissimoque convicio.
        Te tuam dignitatem summa tua virtute tenuisse pro-
vinciaeque honoribus amplissimis adfectum vehementer
3   gaudeo. quod te mihi de Sempronio purgas, accipio excusationem; fuit enim illud quoddam caecum tempus
servitutis. ego tuorum consiliorum auctor dignitatisque
fautor iratus temporibus in Graeciam desperata libertate
rapiebar, cum me etesiae quasi boni cives relinquentem
rem publicam prosequi noluerunt austerque adversus
maximo flatu me ad tribulis tuos Regium rettulit, atque
inde ventis remis in patriam omni festinatione properavi
4   postridieque in summa reliquorum servitute liber unus
fui. sic sum in Antonium invectus ut ille non ferret
omnemque suum vinulentum furorem in me unum effun-
deret meque tum elicere vellet ad caedis causam, tum

---

[5] Calvisius.
[6] Cf. Letter 357, n.
[7] The First Philippic.

For my part, my dear Cornificius, the day I first embarked upon the hope of liberty, that 20th of December on which I laid the foundations of the commonwealth while all the rest hung back, that very day I looked carefully ahead and took account of your personal standing; for the Senate acceded to my proposal about the provincial governorships' remaining in their present hands. Ever since then I have delivered blow after blow at the position of the person[5] who was acting as governor in absentia—a gross insult to yourself and a defiance of the commonwealth. My frequent, I might say daily, denunciations were too much for him. Unwillingly he returned to Rome, and was evicted not merely from the prospect of the province but from the actuality, the possession, by my most just and proper invective.

I am indeed delighted that you have held your distinguished post so ably and have received the highest honours the province has to offer. As for your apologia about Sempronius,[6] I accept it. In those days of slavery we lived in a land of mist. I myself, the inspiration of your conduct and the well-wisher of your public career, was letting myself be carried off to Greece in a mood of anger against the times and despair of freedom, when the Etesian winds, like loyal citizens, refused to escort a deserter of the commonwealth and a contrary southerly gale brought me back to your fellow tribesmen of Regium. From there I hastened back to my country as fast as sail and oar could take me, and the day after my arrival I was the one free man in an assembly of abject slaves. I delivered an attack[7] upon Antony which was more than he could stand. So he poured out all his drunken fury on my single person, at one time trying to provoke me into giving him a pretext for blood-

temptaret insidiis. quem ego ructantem et nauseantem
conieci[2] in Caesaris Octaviani plagas. puer enim egregius
praesidium sibi primum et nobis, deinde summae rei
5 publicae comparavit. qui nisi fuisset, Antoni reditus a
Brundisio pestis patriae fuisset. quae deinceps acta sint
scire te arbitror. sed redeamus illuc unde devertimus: accipio excusationem tuam de Sempronio. neque enim statuti
quid in tanta perturbatione habere potuisti.

'Nunc hic dies aliam vitam adfert, alios mores postulat,'
ut ait Terentius. quam ob rem, mi Quinte, conscende nobiscum et quidem ad puppim. una navis est iam bonorum
omnium, quam quidem nos damus operam ut rectam
teneamus, utinam prospero cursu! sed quicumque venti
erunt, ars nostra certe non aberit. quid enim praestare
aliud virtus potest? tu fac ut magno animo sis et excelso
cogitesque omnem dignitatem tuam cum re publica
coniunctam esse debere.

374 (XII.28)

Scr. Romae c. VIII *Kal. Apr. an.* 43

<CICERO CORNIFICIO S.>

1 Adsentior tibi eos quos scribis Lilybaeo minari istic

---

[2] confeci (*Man.*)

---

[8] In *The Girl from Andros* (189).

[9] In such addresses Cicero occasionally uses a *cognomen*
which he normally avoids, as Testa instead of Trebati and Rufe in-

shed, at another laying traps to catch me. I flung the belching, vomiting brute into Caesar Octavian's toils. This extraordinary youngster has raised a force to defend himself and us in the first place and the supreme interests of the commonwealth in the second. But for him Antony's return from Brundisium would have been the downfall of Rome. The sequel I think you know. But to return: I accept your explanation about Sempronius. In such confusion you could not have any definite code.

'Now this day brings new life, demands new modes,' as Terence has it.[8] So, my dear Quintus,[9] come aboard with us and stand at the poop. All honest men are now in the same boat. I am trying to keep her on course, and I pray we have a fair voyage. But whatever winds may blow, my skill shall not be wanting. What more can virtue guarantee? Do you keep a brave spirit and a lofty one. Remember that all your personal consequence should be bound up with the common weal.

374 (XII.28)
CICERO TO CORNIFICIUS

Rome, ca. 25 March 43

From Cicero to Cornificius greetings.

I agree with you that the individuals who you say are threatening Lilybaeum[1] ought to have been brought to

stead of Caeli. The *praenomen* here seems analogous, Cornificius having no *cognomen*.

[1] Apparently certain Antonian partisans in Africa had been detected in a plot to descend on Sicily.

poenas dare debuisse. sed metuisti, ut ais, ne nimis liber in ulciscendo viderere. metuisti igitur ne ⟨nimis⟩[1] gravis civis, ne nimis fortis, ne nimis te dignus viderere.

2   Quod societatem rei publicae conservandae tibi mecum a patre acceptam renovas gratum est; quae societas inter nos semper, mi Cornifici, manebit. gratum etiam illud, quod mihi tuo nomine gratias agendas non putas; nec enim id inter nos facere debemus. senatus saepius pro dignitate tua appellaretur si absentibus consulibus umquam nisi ad rem novam cogeretur. itaque nec de HS ⌈XX⌉ nec de HS $\overline{\text{DCC}}$ quicquam agi nunc per senatum potest. tibi autem ex senatus consulto imperandum mutuumve[2] sumendum censeo.

3   In re publica quid agatur credo te ex eorum litteris cognoscere qui ad te acta debent perscribere. ego sum spe bona. consilio, cura, labore non desum, omnibus inimicis rei publicae esse me acerrimum hostem prae me fero. res neque nunc difficili loco mihi videtur esse et fuisset facillimo[3] si culpa a quibusdam afuisset.

[1] *(SB)*
[2] -umque *(Or.)*
[3] -ima *(Man.)*

book in Africa. But you were afraid, so you say, of seeming too little inhibited in punitive proceedings; which means that you were afraid of seeming too responsible a citizen, too brave, too worthy of yourself.

I am glad you are reviving for yourself that partnership with me in the preservation of the commonwealth which you have inherited from your father. That partnership will always remain in being between us, my dear Cornificius. I am also glad you feel that expressions of thanks to me on your account are out of place—you and I do not have to do that between ourselves. The Senate would have been reminded more often of what is due to your position but for the fact that in the absence of the Consuls it is only convoked in emergencies. So nothing can be done through the Senate at present either about the HS2,000,000 or the HS700,000. I advise you to levy a tax on the basis of the Senate's decree, or to raise a loan.

I expect you are kept informed of what is going on politically by your correspondents, who should be sending you details of public proceedings. I am hopeful. I am not behind with advice, solicitude, and hard work. I declare myself a deadly foe to all enemies of the commonwealth. In my view the situation is not a difficult one as it stands; it would have been a very easy one, if certain parties had not been to blame.[2]

[2] Probably a reflection on the Consuls; cf. *Letters to Marcus Brutus* 1 (2.1).1.

375 (X.10)

Scr. Romae III *Kal. Apr. an.* 43

CICERO PLANCO

1   Etsi satis ex Furnio nostro cognoram quae tua voluntas, quod consilium de re publica esset, tamen tuis litteris lectis liquidius de toto sensu tuo iudicavi. quam ob rem, quamquam in uno proelio omnia[1] Fortuna rei publicae disceptat (quod quidem cum haec legeres iam decretum arbitrabar fore), tamen ipsa fama quae de tua voluntate percrebruit magnam es laudem consecutus. itaque, si consulem Romae habuissemus, declaratum esset ab senatu cum tuis magnis honoribus quam gratus esset conatus et apparatus tuus. cuius rei non modo non praeteriit tempus sed ne maturum quidem etiam nunc meo quidem iudicio fuit. is enim denique honos mihi videri solet qui non propter spem futuri benefici sed propter magna merita claris viris defertur et datur.

2   Qua re, sit modo aliqua res publica in qua honos elucere possit, omnibus, mihi crede, amplissimis honoribus abundabis. is autem qui vere appellari potest honos non invitamentum ad tempus sed perpetuae virtutis est praemium. quam ob rem, mi Plance, incumbe toto pectore ad laudem, subveni patriae, opitulare collegae, omnium gentium consensum et incredibilem conspirationem adiuva. me tuorum consiliorum adiutorem, dignitatis fautorem, omnibus in rebus tibi amicissimum fidelissimumque cog-

---

[1] omnis *(SB)*

---

[1] Lost.

375 (X.10)
CICERO TO PLANCUS

Rome, 30 March 43

From Cicero to Plancus.

Although sufficiently apprised of your political sentiments and intentions by our friend Furnius, I have reached a clearer assessment of your whole attitude after reading your letter.[1] The Fortune of the commonwealth is deciding all points at issue in a single battle (when you read these lines I expect its outcome will have been determined). None the less the widespread report of your sentiments has in itself redounded greatly to your credit. Had we had a Consul in Rome, the Senate would have declared its appreciation of your efforts and preparations and conferred high honours upon yourself. But the time for that has not gone by; indeed, in my judgement it was not yet ripe. For I always consider an honour to be really and truly such when offered and given, not in the expectation of future benefit, but to persons whose great services have made them illustrious.

And so, provided always that some form of free society exists wherein honours can shine, all the highest, trust me, shall be yours in abundance. But an honour truly so called is not an allurement offered at a crisis, but the reward of constant merit. Therefore, my dear Plancus, strive heart and soul for glory, bring aid to your country, succour to your colleague, support to the marvellous union of all nations banded together in spirit. In me you will find one to help your counsels and further your advancement, an ever loyal and loving friend in all things. For to the bonds

nosces. ad eas enim causas quibus inter nos amore sumus, officiis, vetustate coniuncti patriae caritas accessit, eaque effecit ut tuam vitam anteferrem meae.

III Kal. Apr.

376 (XII.6)

Scr. Romae ex. m. Mart. vel in. m. Apr. an. 43

CICERO CASSIO S.

1   Qui status rerum fuerit tum cum has litteras dedi scire poteris ex C. Tidio Strabone, viro bono et optime de re publica sentiente; nam quid dicam 'cupidissimo tui,' qui domo et fortunis relictis ad te potissimum profectus sit? itaque eum tibi ne commendo quidem. adventus ipsius ad te satis eum commendabit.

2   Tu velim sic existimes tibique persuadeas, omne perfugium bonorum in te et Bruto esse positum si, quod nolim, adversi quid evenerit. res, cum haec scribebam, erat in extremum adducta discrimen. Brutus enim Mutinae vix iam sustinebat. qui si conservatus erit, vicimus; sin, quod di omen avertant, omnis omnium cursus est ad vos. proinde fac animum tantum habeas tantumque apparatum quanto opus est ad universam rem publicam reciperandam.

Vale.

of affection, good offices, and old acquaintance that link us
to one another the love of country has been added, to make
your life more precious to me than my own.

30 March.

376 (XII.6)
CICERO TO CASSIUS

Rome, March (end) or April (beginning) 43

From Cicero to Cassius greetings.

You will be able to find out the state of affairs at the time
this letter was dispatched from C. Tidius Strabo,[1] a good
man and an excellent patriot—that he is most anxious to
serve you I need hardly say, seeing that he has left home
and career expressly in order to join you. I do not even recommend him to you. His own arrival will be recommendation enough.

Of one thing I hope you are thoroughly convinced,
that honest men can look for refuge solely to yourself and
Brutus, should any reverse unfortunately take place. As I
write, the ultimate crisis is upon us. Brutus[2] is hard put to
it to hold out any longer at Mutina. If he is saved, we
have won. If not, which heaven forfend, there is only one
road for us all—to you. Your courage and preparations
must be on the scale needed for the recovery of the whole
commonwealth.

Good-bye.

[1] Cf. Letter 281, n.

[2] D. Brutus, distinguished from M. Brutus (above) by the con-
text.

Scr. Romae III Id. Apr. an. 43

CICERO PLANCO

1   Etsi rei publicae causa maxime gaudere debeo tantum ei te praesidi, tantum opis attulisse extremis paene temporibus, tamen ita te victorem complectar re publica reciperata ut magnam partem mihi laetitiae tua dignitas adfert, quam et esse iam et futuram amplissimam intellego. cave enim putes ullas umquam litteras gratiores[1] quam tuas in senatu esse recitatas; idque contigit cum meritorum tuorum in rem publicam eximia quadam magnitudine tum verborum sententiarumque gravitate. quod mihi quidem minime novum, qui et te nossem et tuarum litterarum ad me missarum promissa meminissem et haberem a Furnio nostro tua penitus consilia cognita; sed senatui maiora visa sunt quam erant <ex>spectata, non quo umquam de tua voluntate dubitasset, sed nec quantum facere posses nec quo progredi velles exploratum satis habebat.

2   Itaque, cum a. d. VII Id. Apr. mane mihi tuas litteras M. Varisidius reddidisset easque legissem, incredibili gaudio sum elatus; cumque magna multitudo optimorum virorum et civium me domo deduceret, feci continuo omnis participes meae voluptatis. interim ad me venit Munatius noster, ut consuerat. at ego ei litteras tuas, nihildum enim sciebat;

---

[1] gravi- *(Man.)*

---

[1] Letter 371.
[2] Or 'letter;' perhaps the lost letter referred to in Letter 375.1.

377 (X.12)
CICERO TO PLANCUS

Rome, 11 April 43

From Cicero to Plancus.

I must heartily rejoice for our country's sake that you have brought such large resources to her defence and aid at an almost desperate hour. And yet, as truly as I hope to embrace you victorious in a restored commonwealth, a great part of my happiness is in your prestige, which I know is already of the highest and will so remain. I assure you that no dispatch ever read in the Senate was more favourably received than yours,[1] an effect due not only to the peculiar importance of your public services but also to the impressiveness of the words and sentiments. It was all no novelty to me, who knew you and remembered the promises you made in your letters[2] to me and had been thoroughly apprised of your intentions by our friend Furnius; but the Senate felt that their expectations had been surpassed—not that they ever doubted your good will, but they were not altogether clear as to how much you could do or how far you wished to go.

Accordingly, when M. Varisidius gave me your letter on the morning of 7 April and I read it, I was transported with delight; and as I was escorted from my house by a large throng of loyal patriots, I lost no time in making all of them sharers in my pleasure. Meanwhile our friend Munatius[3] called on me as usual, so I showed him your letter—he knew nothing about it beforehand, because Varisidius had

---

[3] Who this T. Munatius (cf. end of letter) was and how related to Plancus is unknown.

nam ad me primum Varisidius, idque sibi a te mandatum esse dicebat. paulo post idem mihi Munatius eas litteras
3 legendas dedit quas ipsi miseras et eas quas publice. placuit nobis ut statim ad Cornutum, praetorem urbanum, litteras deferremus, qui, quod consules aberant, consulare munus sustinebat more maiorum. senatus est continuo convocatus frequensque convenit propter famam atque exspectationem tuarum litterarum. recitatis litteris oblata religio Cornuto est pullariorum admonitu non satis diligenter eum auspiciis operam dedisse; idque a nostro collegio comprobatum est. itaque res dilata est in posterum. eo autem die magna mihi pro tua dignitate contentio cum Servilio; qui cum gratia effecisset ut sua sententia prima pronuntiaretur, frequens eum senatus reliquit et in alia omnia discessit, meaeque sententiae, quae secunda pronuntiata erat, cum frequenter adsentiretur senatus, rogatu
4 Servili P. Titius intercessit. res in posterum dilata. venit paratus Servilius Iovi ipsi iniquus, cuius in templo res agebatur. hunc quem ad modum fregerim quantaque contentione Titium intercessorem abiecerim ex aliorum te litteris malo cognoscere, unum hoc ex meis: senatus gravior, constantior, amicior tuis laudibus esse non potuit quam tum fuit, nec vero tibi senatus amicior quam cuncta civitas. mirabiliter enim populus Romanus universus et omnium generum ordinumque consensus ad liberandam rem publicam conspiravit.
5   Perge igitur ut agis, nomenque tuum commenda im-

---

4 The Augurs.
5 Proverbial for violent anger or truculence; cf. *Letters to Atticus* 165 (VIII.15).2.

come to me first, on your instructions as he said. A little
later the same Munatius gave me the letter you had sent
him together with your official dispatch for me to read. We
decided to lay the dispatch immediately before Cornutus,
the City Praetor, who in the absence of the Consuls is discharging consular functions according to traditional practice. The Senate was convoked at once and met in large
numbers, attracted by the report of your dispatch and their
eagerness to hear it. After the dispatch had been read out,
a religious scruple arose: Cornutus was apprised by the
Keepers of the Chickens of an inadvertence in his taking of
the auspices, and their representations were confirmed by
our College.[4] Business was therefore deferred till the following day, on which I had a great struggle with Servilius
so that you should get your due. By personal influence he
managed to get his motion taken first, but a large majority
of the Senate left him and voted against it. My motion,
which was taken second, was gaining widespread assent,
when P. Titius at Servilius' request interposed his veto.
The matter was adjourned to the day following. Servilius
arrived ready for the fray, 'wrath with Jove himself,'[5] in
whose temple the meeting was taking place. How I tamed
him and how vigorously I put down Titius with his veto I
prefer you to learn from other correspondents. One thing,
though, you may learn from me: the Senate could not have
been more responsible, resolute, and disposed to hear
your praises than it was on that occasion; and the community at large is no less well disposed towards you than the
Senate. Marvellous indeed is the unanimity with which the
entire Roman People, and every type and order therein,
has rallied to the cause of freedom.

Continue then in your present course, and hand down

mortalitati atque haec omnia quae habent speciem gloriae
collectam inanissimis splendoris insignibus contemne;
brevia, fucata, caduca existima. verum decus in virtute positum est, quae maxime illustratur magnis in rem publicam
meritis. eam facultatem habes maximam; quam quoniam
complexus es, tene. perfice ut ne minus res publica tibi
quam tu rei publicae debeas. me tuae dignitatis non modo
fautorem sed etiam amplificatorem cognosces. id cum rei
publicae, quae mihi vita est mea carior, tum nostrae neces-
situdini debere me iudico. atque in his curis quas contuli
ad dignitatem tuam cepi magnam voluptatem quod bene
cognitam mihi T. Munati prudentiam et fidem magis etiam
perspexi in eius incredibili erga te benevolentia et diligentia.

III Id. Apr.

378 (X.30)

Scr. in castris ad Mutinam a. d. XVII Kal. Mai. an. 43

GALBA CICERONI S.

1   A. d. XVII(I)[1] Kal. Mai., quo die Pansa in castris Hirti
erat futurus, cum quo ego eram (nam ei obviam processe-
ram millia passus centum quo maturius veniret), Antonius
legiones eduxit duas, secundam et quintam tricesimam, et
cohortis praetorias duas, unam suam, alteram Silani, evo-

---

[1] *(Ruete)*

---

[1] An account of the battle of Forum Gallorum. On 27 April

your name to eternity. Despise all these prizes that have only the semblance of glory, deriving from meaningless badges of distinction; hold them for brief, unreal, perishable things. True dignity lies in virtue; and virtue is most conspicuously displayed in eminent services to the commonwealth. Such you have a splendid opportunity to render. You have grasped it; do not let it slip. Make your country's debt to you no less than yours to her. You shall find me prompt not only to support but to amplify your standing. That I consider I owe both to the commonwealth, which is dearer to me than my life, and to our friendship. Let me add that in my recent endeavours for your credit I have had great pleasure in perceiving more clearly what I already knew well—the sound sense and loyalty of T. Munatius, shown in his truly remarkable good will and devotion to yourself.

11 April.

378 (X.30)
GALBA TO CICERO[1]

Camp at Mutina, 15 April 43

Galba to Cicero greetings.

On 14 April, that being the day Pansa was to have joined Hirtius' camp (I was with him, having gone 100 miles to meet him and expedite his arrival), Antony led out two legions, the Second and Thirty-Fifth, and two praetorian cohorts, one his own and the other Silanus', together

---

Antony suffered a second defeat (in which, however, the Consul Hirtius was killed) and was forced to raise the siege of Mutina.

catorum partem. ita obviam venit nobis, quod nos quattuor legiones tironum habere solum arbitrabatur. sed noctu, quo tutius venire in castra potuissemus, legionem Martiam, cui ego praeesse solebam, et duas cohortis praetorias miserat Hirtius nobis.

2 Cum equites Antoni apparuissent, contineri neque legio Martia neque cohortes praetoriae potuerunt; quas sequi coepimus coacti, quoniam retinere eas non potueramus. Antonius ad Forum Gallorum suas copias continebat neque sciri volebat se legiones habere; tantum equitatum et levem armaturam ostendebat. postea quam vidit se invito legionem ire Pansa, sequi se duas legiones iussit tironum. postea quam angustias paludis et silvarum transiimus, acies est instructa a nobis XII cohortium. nondum
3 venerant legiones duae. repente Antonius in aciem suas copias de vico produxit et sine mora concurrit. primo ita pugnatum est ut acrius non posset ex utraque parte pugnari; etsi dexterius cornu, in quo ego eram cum Martiae legionis cohortibus octo, impetu primo fugaverat legionem XXXV Antoni, ut amplius passus D ultra aciem, quo loco steterat, processerit. itaque, cum equites nostrum cornu circumire vellent, recipere me coepi et levem armaturam opponere Maurorum equitibus, ne aversos nostros adgrederentur. interim video me esse inter Antonianos Antoniumque post me esse aliquanto. repente equum immisi ad eam legionem tironum quae veniebat ex castris, scuto reiecto. Antoniani me insequi; nostri pila coicere velle. ita

with part of his reservists. In this strength he advanced to meet us, thinking that we had only four legions of recruits. But the previous night Hirtius had sent us the Martian Legion, which used to be under my command, and the two praetorian cohorts for our better security on the march to his camp.

When Antony's cavalry came into sight, there was no holding the Martian Legion and the praetorian cohorts. We started to follow them willy-nilly, since we had not been able to hold them back. Antony kept his forces at Forum Gallorum, wanting to conceal the fact that he had the legions; he only showed his cavalry and light-armed. When Pansa saw the legion advancing contrary to his intention, he ordered two legions of recruits to follow him. Having traversed a narrow route through marsh and woodland, we drew up a battle line of twelve cohorts; the two legions had not yet come up. Suddenly Antony led his forces out of the village, drew them up and immediately engaged. Both sides at first fought as fiercely as men could fight. But the right wing, where I was placed with eight cohorts of the Martian Legion, threw back Antony's Thirty-Fifth at the first charge, and advanced more than half a mile from its original position in the line. The cavalry then tried to surround our wing, so I started to retire, setting our light-armed against the Moorish horse to stop them attacking our men in the rear. Meanwhile I found myself in the thick of the Antonians, with Antony some distance behind me. All at once I rode at a gallop towards a legion of recruits which was on its way up from our camp, throwing my shield over my shoulders. The Antonians chased me, while our men were about to hurl their javelins. In this predica-

nescio quo fato sum servatus, quod sum cito a nostris cognitus.

4   In ipsa Aemilia, ubi cohors Caesaris praetoria erat, diu pugnatum est. cornu sinisterius, quod erat infirmius, ubi Martiae legionis duae cohortes erant et cohors praetoria, pedem referre coeperunt quod ab equitatu circumibantur, quo vel plurimum valet Antonius. cum omnes se recepissent nostri ordines, recipere me novissimus coepi ad castra. Antonius tamquam victor castra putavit se posse capere. quo cum venit, compluris ibi amisit nec egit quicquam.

Audita re Hirtius cum cohortibus XX veteranis redeunti Antonio in sua castra occurrit copiasque eius omnis delevit fugavit, eodemque loco ubi erat pugnatum, ad Forum Gallorum. Antonius cum equitibus hora noctis quarta se in
5   castra sua ad Mutinam recepit. Hirtius in ea castra redi<i>t unde Pansa exierat, ubi duas legiones reliquerat quae ab Antonio erant oppugnatae. sic partem maiorem suarum copiarum Antonius amisit veteranarum; nec id tamen sine aliqua iactura cohortium praetoriarum nostrarum et legionis Martiae fieri potuit. aquilae duae, signa LX sunt relata Antoni. res bene gesta est.

A. d. X<V>II² Kal. Mai. ex castris.

² *(Ruete)*

ment some providence came to my rescue—I was quickly recognized by our men.

On the Aemilian Way itself, where Caesar's praetorian cohort was stationed, there was a long struggle. The left wing, which was weaker, consisting of two cohorts of the Martian Legion and one praetorian cohort, began to give ground, because they were being surrounded by cavalry, which is Antony's strongest arm. When all our ranks had withdrawn, I started to retreat to the camp, the last to do so. Having won the battle, as he considered, Antony thought he could take the camp, but when he arrived he lost a number of men there and achieved nothing.

Having heard what had happened, Hirtius with twenty veteran cohorts met Antony on his way back to his camp and completely destroyed or routed his forces, on the very ground of the previous engagement near Forum Gallorum. Antony withdrew with his horse to his camp at Mutina about 10 o'clock at night. Hirtius then returned to the camp from which Pansa[2] had marched out and where he had left two legions, which had been assaulted by Antony. So Antony has lost the greater part of his veteran troops; but this result could not be achieved without some losses in the praetorian cohorts and the Martian Legion. Two eagles and sixty standards of Antony's have been brought in. It is a victory.

15 April, from camp.

---

[2] Pansa had been taken to Bononia (Bologna), fatally wounded. Galba had evidently not heard of this.

379 (X.9)

Scr. in Gallia Narbonensi c. v Kal. Mai. an. 43

PLANCUS CICERONI S.

1   Nihil me tibi temere aut te ceteris de me frustra recepisse laetor. certe hoc maius habes testimonium amoris
mei quo[1] maturius tibi quam ceteris consilia mea volui esse
nota. in dies vero meritorum meorum fieri accessiones
pervidere te spero, cogniturum magis recipio.

2   Quod ad me attinet, mi Cicero (ita ab imminentibus
malis res publica me adiuvante liberetur!), sic honores
praemiaque vestra suspicio, conferenda certe cum immor-
talitate, ut sine iis nihil de meo studio perseverantiaque
sim remissurus. nisi in multitudine optimorum civium impetus animi mei fuerit singularis et opera praecipua, nihil
ad meam dignitatem accedere volo suffragatione vestra.
concupisco autem nihil mihi, contra quod ipse pugno; et
temporis et rei te moderatorem facile patior esse. nihil aut
sero aut exigue a patria civi tributum potest videri.

Exercitum a. d. vi Kal. Mai. Rhodanum traieci magnis
itineribus, Vienna⟨m⟩ equites mille[2] via breviore praemisi. ipse, si ab Lepido non impediar, celeritate satis faciam.
si autem is[3] itineri meo se opposuerit, ad tempus consilium
capiam. copias adduco et numero et genere et fidelitate

---

[1] quod *coni. SB*   [2] equitum III milia *Wes.*
[3] in *(R. Klotz)*

---

[1] Or (reading *quod* for *quo*) 'you have so much the greater evidence of my affection in that I wished . . .'

[2] I.e. personal ambition like Antony's.

379 (X.9)
PLANCUS TO CICERO

Gallia Narbonensis, ca. 27 April 43

From Plancus to Cicero greetings.

I am happy to feel that the pledges I made to you were not hasty, and that those you gave to others concerning me have not proved idle. At any rate, the earlier I wished you to know my plans before anyone else the greater evidence you have of my affection.[1] I hope you observe how the tale of my services lengthens every day; that you will learn of them in the future I do not hope so much as guarantee.

As for myself, my dear Cicero (so may the commonwealth be relieved with my assistance from impending evils), I prize the honours and rewards which you and those with you have to bestow as gifts surely no less precious than immortality itself; at the same time my zeal and perseverance will be no whit relaxed without them. Only if amid the throng of good patriots *my* enthusiasm and exertions shine conspicuous do I wish my standing to be enhanced by your collective support. For myself I covet nothing—that[2] is exactly what I am fighting against. When and what are questions which I am well content to leave to your discretion. No gift that a man receives from his country can appear tardy or trivial.

By dint of forced marches I have taken my army across the Rhone this 26th of April, and have sent a thousand horse ahead to Vienne by a shorter route. I myself shall not fail in the matter of speed, if I am not held up by Lepidus; but if he blocks my way, I shall act as circumstances suggest. The forces I am bringing are very strong in numbers, character, and loyalty. I ask you to remember me affection-

firmissimas. te ut diligas me, si mutuo te facturum scis,
rogo.

Vale.

380 (XI.9)

Scr. in castris Regii III Kal. Mai. an. 43

D. BRUTUS S. D. M. CICERONI

1 Pansa amisso quantum detrimenti res publica acceperit
non te praeterit. nunc auctoritate et prudentia tua prospi-
cias oportet ne inimici nostri consulibus sublatis sperent se
convalescere posse. ego ne consistere possit in Italia Antonius dabo operam. sequar eum confestim. utrumque me
praestaturum spero, ne aut Ventidius elabatur aut Antonius in Italia moretur. in primis rogo te ad hominem vento-
sissimum, Lepidum, mittas, ne bellum nobis redintegrare
possit Antonio sibi coniuncto. nam de Pollione Asinio puto
te perspicere quid facturus sit. multae et bonae et firmae
sunt legiones Lepidi et Asini.

2 Neque haec idcirco tibi scribo quod te non eadem
animadvertere sciam, sed quod mihi persuasissimum est
Lepidum recte facturum numquam, si forte vobis id de
hoc dubium est. Plancum quoque confirmetis oro; quem
spero pulso Antonio rei publicae non defuturum. si se
Alpis Antonius traiecerit, constitui praesidium in Alpibus
collocare et te de omni re facere certiorem.

---

[1] He was bringing up three legions from Picenum in support
of Antony whom he eventually joined at Vada Sabatia (cf. Letter
385.3). [2] I.e. join Antony if he got the chance.

ately, if you know that I shall do the like for you.
   Good-bye.

380 (XI.9)
D. BRUTUS TO CICERO

Camp at Regium Lepidum, 29 April 43

From D. Brutus to M. Cicero greetings.

   How serious a loss the state has sustained in Pansa you
doubtless appreciate. It now behoves you to apply your authority and foresight to ensuring that the removal of the
Consuls does not give rise to hopes of possible recovery
among our enemies. For my part, I shall try to see that Antony is unable to maintain himself in Italy. I shall be after
him immediately. I trust I can stop Ventidius[1] slipping
away on the one hand, and Antony remaining in Italy on
the other. Let me especially ask you to send word to that
arrant weathercock Lepidus, so that he does not let Antony
join him and perhaps make us fight the war all over again.
As for Pollio Asinius, I expect you see well enough what he
is likely to do.[2] The legions under Lepidus and Asinius are
good and strong, and there are many of them.

   I do not write to you thus because I am not sure that
these same points have occurred to yourself, but because I
am firmly convinced that Lepidus will never behave well,
in case you people in Rome feel any doubt about the matter. I also beg you to stiffen Plancus. After Antony's defeat I
trust he will not fail the public cause. If Antony gets over
the Alps, I have decided to station a force there and to
inform you on all points.

III Kal. Mai. ex castris Regio.[1]

381 (XI.13b)

Scr. in castris Parmae prid. Kal. vel Kal. Mai. an. 43

D. BRUTUS COS. DESIG. M. CICERONI S. D.

Parmensis miserrimos * * *

382 (X.11)

Scr. in Allobrogibus c. Kal. Mai an. 43

PLANCUS CICERONI

1   Immortalis ago tibi gratias agamque dum vivam; nam relaturum me adfirmare non possum. tantis enim tuis officiis non videor mi respondere posse, nisi forte, ut tu gravissime disertissimeque scripsisti, ita sensurus es ut me referre gratiam putes cum memoria tenebo. si de fili tui dignitate esset actum, amabilius certe nihil facere potuisses. primae tuae sententiae infinitis cum muneribus, posteriores ad tempus arbitriumque amicorum meorum compositae, oratio adsidua et perpetua de me, iurgia cum obtrectatoribus propter me notissima mihi sunt. non mediocris adhibenda mihi est cura ut rei publicae me civem

1 regii(s) *(Or.)*

---

1 The rest is lost. Parma, which must have passed into the

29 April, from camp at Regium.

381 (XI.13b)
D. BRUTUS TO CICERO

Camp at Parma, 30 April or 1 May 43

From D. Brutus, Consul-Elect, to M. Cicero greetings.
The unfortunate people of Parma * * *[1]

382 (X.11)
PLANCUS TO CICERO

Country of the Allobroges, ca. 1 May 43

From Plancus to Cicero.

Thank you a thousand, thousand times.[1] As long as I live I shall thank you—as for repaying you, I cannot promise. I feel incapable of matching such services as yours—unless, perchance, as you have so movingly and eloquently written, you will consider yourself repaid so long as I hold them in remembrance. If your own son's standing had been in question, assuredly you could have shown no warmer affection. Your earlier motions in the Senate heaping all imaginable favours on my head, those more recent adapted to the occasion and the wishes of my friends, your unremitting series of speeches concerning me, your altercations with detractors for my sake—how well I know it all! I must study, no light matter, to show myself a patriot

hands of the republicans (cf. Letter 365.2), had been captured and sacked by L. Antonius.   [1] Plancus is answering Letter 377.

CICERO'S LETTERS TO FRIENDS

dignum tuis laudibus praestem, in amicitia tua memorem atque gratum. quod reliquum est, tuum munus tuere et me, si quem esse voluisti eum exitu rebusque cognoscis, defende ac suscipe.

2 Cum Rhodanum copias omnis traiecissem fratremque cum tribus milibus equitum praemisissem, ipse iter ad Mutinam dirigerem, in itinere de proelio facto Brutoque et Mutina obsidione liberatis audivi. animadverti nullum alium receptum Antonium reliquiasque quae cum eo essent habere nisi in his partibus, duasque ei spes esse propositas, unam Lepidi ipsius, alteram exercitus, quod quaedam pars exercitus non minus furiosa est quam qui cum Antonio fuerunt. equitatum revocavi, ipse in Allobrogibus constiti, ut proinde ad omnia paratus essem ac res me moneret. si nudus hoc se Antonius confert, facile mi videor per me sustinere posse remque publicam ex vestra sententia administrare, quamvis ab exercitu Lepidi recipiatur. si vero copiarum aliquid secum adducet et si decima legio veterana, quae nostra opera revocata cum reliquis est, ad eundem furorem redierit, tamen ne quid detrimenti fiat dabitur opera a me, idque me praestaturum spero dum istinc copiae traiciantur coniunctaeque nobiscum facilius perditos opprimant.

3 Hoc tibi spondeo, mi Cicero, neque animum nec diligentiam mihi defuturam. cupio mehercules nullam residuam sollicitudinem esse; sed si fuerit, nec animo nec benevolentiae nec patientiae cuiusquam pro vobis cedam.

---

[2] Despite Appian's statement (*Civil Wars,* 3.83) that this famous legion was under Lepidus' command it seems to have been under Plancus. How otherwise could he have recalled it to its duty?

worthy of your eulogies and a friend whose gratitude is un-
dying. For the rest, act in the spirit of your bounty, and if in
the actual event you find me the man you wished me to be,
take me under your protection and patronage.

After taking all my forces across the Rhone, I sent my
brother ahead with 3,000 horse and myself advanced along
the road to Mutina. While on the march, I heard the news
of the battle and of Brutus' and Mutina's liberation from
siege. It was apparent to me that Antony and the remnants
accompanying him had no refuge except in these areas;
also that he had two hopes before him, one in Lepidus
himself, the other in Lepidus' army, since part of that army
is no less rabid than the men who were with Antony. I
recalled the cavalry and have myself halted in the Allobrogian country to be ready for anything as circumstances
may suggest. If Antony comes here without a following,
I believe I can easily cope with him by myself and handle
the situation to your and your friends' satisfaction, even
though Lepidus' army takes him in. On the other hand, if
he brings some force with him and if the veteran Tenth
Legion,[2] which I recalled to its duty along with the others,
reverts to its former infatuation, I shall still do my best (and
I hope with success) to see that no harm comes until forces
are sent over from Italy. United we shall have less difficulty
in crushing the desperados.

This I guarantee you, my dear Cicero, that neither
courage nor pains shall be lacking on my part. I most earnestly hope that there is no further reason for anxiety. But
if any there should be, my spirit, good will, and endurance
on your collective behalf shall be second to no man's. I am

do quidem ego operam ut etiam Lepidum ad huius rei societatem incitem, omniaque ei obsequia polliceor si modo
rem publicam respicere volet. utor in hac re adiutoribus
interpretibusque fratre meo et Laterense et Furnio nostro.
non me impedient privatae offensiones quo minus pro rei
publicae salute etiam cum inimicissimo consentiam. quod
si nihil profecero, nihilo minus maximo sum animo, et
maiore fortasse cum mea gloria vobis satis faciam.

Fac valeas meque mutuo diligas.

383 (XII.25a)

Scr. Romae in. m. Mai. an. 43

‹CICERO CORNIFICIO S.›

1   P. Luccium mihi meum commendas; quem quibuscumque rebus potero diligenter tuebor.

Hirtium quidem et Pansam, collegas nostros, homines
in consulatu rei publicae salutaris, alieno sane tempore
amisimus, re publica Antoniano quidem latrocinio liberata
sed nondum omnino explicata. quam nos, si licebit, more
nostro tuebimur, quamquam admodum sumus iam defati-
gati. sed nulla lassitudo impedire officium et fidem debet.
2   verum haec hactenus. ab aliis te de me quam a me ipso
malo cognoscere.

De te audiebamus ea quae maxime vellemus. de Cn.
Minucio, quem tu quibusdam litteris ad caelum laudibus
extulisti, rumores duriores erant. id quale sit omninoque
quid istic agatur facias me velim certiorem.

---

[3] If Lepidus took the wrong side after all, Plancus would not
have to share the credit of victory.   [1] As Augurs.

doing my best to urge Lepidus too to come into the fold, and am promising him all manner of compliance, if only he chooses to remember his patriotic duty. As coadjutors and intermediaries in this matter I am employing my brother, Laterensis, and our friend Furnius. No private quarrels shall prevent me from cooperating with my worst enemy for the safety of the commonwealth. If these efforts turn out fruitless, none the less I am in excellent heart and perhaps I shall content you all with greater glory to myself.[3]

Take care of your health and remember me kindly, as I do you.

383 (XII.25a)
CICERO TO CORNIFICIUS

Rome, May (beginning) 43

From Cicero to Cornificius greetings.

You recommend to me P. Luccius, one of my own circle. I shall spare no pains to help him in any way I can.

We have lost our colleagues[1] Hirtius and Pansa at a very unfortunate moment. In their Consulship they gave good service to the commonwealth, which is now rid of Antony's brigandage, but not yet completely out of the wood. If permitted, I shall fight the good fight as ever, though I am now very tired. But no weariness should stand in the way of duty and loyalty. Well, enough of that. I would rather you heard about me from others than from myself.

Of you we hear what we should most have wished to hear. There are some ugly rumours abroad about Cn. Minucius, whom you praised to the skies in one of your letters. I should be glad if you would let me know the facts, and how things are going over there in general.

384 (X.14)

Scr. Romae III *Non. Mai. an. 43*

CICERO PLANCO S.

1   O gratam famam biduo ante victoriam de subsidio tuo, de studio, de celeritate, de copiis! atque etiam hostibus fusis spes omnis est in te. fugisse enim ex proelio Mutinensi dicuntur notissimi latronum duces. est autem non minus gratum extrema delere quam prima depellere.

2   Equidem ‹ex›spectabam iam tuas litteras, idque cum multis, sperabamque etiam Lepidum rei publicae temporibus admonitum tecum e re publica[1] esse facturum. in illam igitur curam incumbe, mi Plance, ut ne quae scintilla taeterrimi belli relinquatur. quod si erit factum, et rem publicam divino beneficio adfeceris et ipse aeternam gloriam consequere.

D. III Non. Mai.

385 (XI.10)

Scr. in castris Dertonae III *Non. Mai. an. 43*

D. BRUTUS S. D. M. CICERONI

1   Non mihi rem publicam plus debere arbitror quam me tibi. gratiorem me esse in te posse quam isti perversi sint in me exploratum habe[s];[1] si ta‹me›n haec[2] temporis vi-

---

[1] et reip. *(Buecheler)*

[1] *(R. Klotz)*

[2] hoc *(Man.)*

384 (X.14)
CICERO TO PLANCUS

Rome, 5 May 43

From Cicero to Plancus greetings.

Most welcome the report that arrived two days before the victory about the aid you are bringing—your devotion, your speed, your forces! Even after the rout of the enemy all our hopes are pinned on you. The foremost rebel leaders are said to have escaped from the field of Mutina. Now to wipe out the last remnants of mischief is no less thankworthy an achievement than to drive off its beginnings.

For my part I am already awaiting a dispatch from you, as are many others. I hope that Lepidus too will pay heed to the national emergency and cooperate with you in the national interest. Therefore bend your energies, my dear Plancus, to the end that not a spark of this abominable war is left alive. If that is accomplished you will have conferred a superhuman benefit upon the state and will yourself reap immortal glory.

Dispatched 5 May.

385 (XI.10)
D. BRUTUS TO CICERO

Camp at Dertona, 5 May 43

From D. Brutus to M. Cicero greetings.

I think the country owes me no more than I owe you. Be sure that I can be more grateful to you than those ill-natured folk are to me. But if you should think I am saying this for expediency's sake, then have it that I prefer your

263

deantur dici causa, malle me tuum iudicium quam ex altera parte omnium istorum. tu enim a certo sensu et vero iu-
dicas de nobis; quod isti ne faciant summa malevolentia et
livore impediuntur. interpellent me quo minus honoratus
sim, dum ne interpellent quo minus res publica a me commode administrari possit. quae quanto sit in periculo quam
potero brevissime exponam.

2   Primum omnium quantam perturbationem rerum urbanarum adferat obitus consulum, quantamque cupiditatem hominibus honoris iniciat vacuitas non te fugit. satis
me multa scripsisse quae litteris commendari possint arbitror. scio enim cui scribam.

3   Revertor nunc ad Antonium. qui ex fuga cum parvulam
manum peditum haberet inermium, ergastula solvendo
omneque genus hominum abripiendo satis magnum nu-
merum videtur effecisse. hoc accessit manus Ventidi, quae
trans Appenninum itinere facto difficillimo ad Vada per-
venit atque ibi se cum Antonio coniunxit. est numerus
veteranorum et armatorum satis frequens cum Ventidio.

4   Consilia Antoni haec sint necesse est, aut ad Lepidum
ut se conferat, si recipitur, aut Appennino Alpibusque se
teneat et decursionibus per equites, quos habet multos,
vastet ea loca in quae incurrerit, aut rursus se in Etruriam
referat, quod ea pars Italiae sine exercitu est. quod si me
Caesar audisset atque Appenninum transisset, in tantas
angustias Antonium compulissem ut inopia potius quam
ferro conficeretur. sed neque Caesari imperari potest nec

---

[1] Octavian may already have given signs of his ambition to take
one of the vacant Consulships.

good opinion to that of the whole lot of them put together. For your judgement of me starts from a sure and true perception. *They* cannot judge so, because they are handicapped by vicious malice and jealousy. Let them interfere to block the conferment of honours upon me, so long as they do not interfere with my ability to do my job to the advantage of the country. Let me set out as briefly as I can the danger in which she stands.

To begin with, I do not have to tell you of the confusion into which the death of the Consuls has plunged affairs in Rome, or of the greedy spirit aroused by the official vacuum.[1] I think I have written enough—as much as can be committed to a letter. After all, I know to whom I am writing.

Now to come back to Antony. He fled with a petty little band of unarmed foot soldiers, but by throwing open the slave barracks and laying hands on every sort of manpower he seems to have made up a pretty sizable body. This has been joined by Ventidius' band, which after a very difficult march across the Apennines reached Vada and linked up with Antony there. There is a pretty considerable number of veterans and armed troops with Ventidius.

Antony must choose between the following plans: (a) He may go to Lepidus if Lepidus is receiving him. (b) He may keep to the Apennines and Alps and use his cavalry, with which he is well provided, in raids to devastate the areas he invades. (c) He may come back to Etruria, because there is no army in that part of Italy. If Caesar had listened to me and crossed the Apennines, I should have put Antony in so tight a corner that he would have been finished by lack of supplies rather than cold steel. But

265

Caesar exercitui suo, quod utrumque pessimum est.

Cum haec talia sint, quo minus quod ad me pertinebit homines interpellent, ut supra scripsi, non impedio. haec quem ad modum explicari possint aut, a te cum explica-
5 buntur, ne impediantur timeo. alere iam milites non possum. cum ad rem publicam liberandam accessi, HS mihi fuit pecuniae |CCCC| amplius. tantum abest ut meae rei familiaris liberum sit quicquam ut omnis iam meos amicos aere alieno obstrinxerim. septem numerum nunc legionum alo, qua difficultate tu arbitrare. non si Varronis thesauros haberem subsistere sumptui possem.

Cum primum de Antonio exploratum habuero, faciam te certiorem. tu me amabis ita si hoc idem me in te facere senseris.

III Non. Mai. ex castris Dertona.

386 (XI.11)

Scr. in castris in finibus Statiellensium prid. Non. Mai. an. 43

D. BRUTUS IMP. COS. DESIG. S. D. M. CICERONI
1   Eodem exemplo a te mi litterae redditae sunt quo pueri mei attulerunt. tantum me tibi debere existimo quantum persolvere difficile est.

Scripsi tibi quae hic gererentur. in itinere est Antonius,

---

2 Possibly with reference to a fragment of one of Varro's Menippean Satires (ed. Riese, p. 103): 'not by treasure vaults (*thesauris*) nor by gold is the heart freed of bondage; not the

there is no giving orders to Caesar, nor *by* Caesar to his army—both very bad things.

In this situation, as I have said above, if people want to interfere with what concerns me personally, let them. What alarms me is how this situation can be straightened out, or that, when you are in process of straightening it, others may tangle it up. I cannot any longer feed my men. When I put my hand to the work of liberation, I had a fortune of over HS40,000,000. Now my whole estate is encumbered; not only that, but I have involved all my friends in debt. I am maintaining seven legions, you may imagine with what difficulty. If I had Varro's treasure vaults,[2] I could not stand against the expense.

As soon as I know for certain about Antony I shall send you word. Let me have your kind regard, provided you find a corresponding sentiment on my side.

5 May, from camp at Dertona.

386 (XI.11)
D. BRUTUS TO CICERO

Borders of the Statiellenses, 6 May 43

From D. Brutus, Imperator, Consul-Elect, to M. Cicero, greetings.

A duplicate of the letter which my boys brought from you has been delivered to me. I consider that I owe you a great debt, which it is difficult to pay in full.

I am writing to tell you what is going on here. Antony is

mountains of Persia nor the halls of wealthy Crassus take care and superstition from men's minds.'

ad Lepidum proficiscitur. ne de Planco quidem spem adhuc abiecit, ut ex libellis eius animadverti qui in me inciderunt, in quibus quos ad Asinium, quos ad Lepidum, quos ad Plancum mitteret scribebat. Ego tamen non habui ambiguum et statim ad Plancum misi et biduo ab Allobrogibus et totius Galliae legatos exspecto; quos confirmatos domum remittam.

2 Tu, quae istic opus erunt administrari, prospicies ut ex tua voluntate reique publicae commodo fiant. malevolentiae hominum in me, si poteris, occurres; si non potueris, hoc consolabere, quod me de statu meo nullis contumeliis deterrere possunt.

Prid. Non. Mai. ex castris, ⟨ex⟩[1] finibus Statiellensium.

387 (XII.12)

Scr. in castris in Syria Non. Mai. an. 43

CASSIUS PRO COS. S. D. M. CICERONI SUO

1 S. v. b.; e. e. q. v.

Legi tuas litteras in quibus mirificum tuum erga me amorem recognovi. videbaris enim non solum favere nobis, id quod et nostra et rei publicae causa semper fecisti, sed etiam gravem curam suscepisse vehementerque esse de nobis sollicitus. itaque quod te primum existimare putabam nos oppressa re publica quiescere non posse, deinde,

[1] *(Wes.)*

---

[1] Doubtless Letter 367.

on the march, he is going to Lepidus. He has not yet given up hope even of Plancus, as I have perceived from some papers of his which have come my way, in which he entered the names of his various emissaries to Asinius, Lepidus, and Plancus. However, I entertained no misgivings, and sent word to Plancus straight away. And in a couple of days I expect envoys from the Allobroges and the whole of Gaul. I shall send them back home in good heart.

Please look to future action in Rome, so that any necessary steps may be taken in accordance with your views and the public interest. You will counter the world's malice towards me if you can. If that is beyond your power, you will have the consolation of knowing that they cannot by any indignities turn me away from the position I have taken up.

6 May, from camp on the borders of the Statiellenses.

387 (XII.12)
CASSIUS TO CICERO

In camp, Syria, 7 May 43

From Cassius, Proconsul, to his friend M. Cicero, greetings.

I trust you are well, as I am and my army.

I have read your letter,[1] in which I find evidence once again of your singular regard for me. You would appear not only to wish me well, as you have always done both for my sake and the country's, but to have taken a grave responsibility upon yourself and to be very anxious on my account. Because I felt you were persuaded that I could not stand idly by while freedom was stifled, and because I felt that, suspecting me to be at work, you were anxious about my

269

cum suspicarere nos moliri ⟨aliquid⟩,[1] quod te sollicitum
esse et de salute nostra et de rerum eventu putabam, simul
ac legiones accepi quas A. Allienus eduxerat ex Aegypto,
scripsi ad te tabellariosque compluris Romam misi. scripsi
etiam ad senatum litteras, quas reddi vetui prius quam tibi
recitatae essent, si forte mei obtemperare mihi voluerint.
quod si litterae perlatae non sunt, non dubito quin Dolabella, qui nefarie Trebonio occiso Asiam occupavit, tabellarios meos deprehenderit litterasque interceperit.

2   Exercitus omnis qui in Syria fuerunt teneo. habui pol-
lulum morae dum promissa militibus persolvo; nunc iam
sum expeditus. a te peto ut dignitatem meam commendatam tibi habeas si me intellegis nullum neque periculum
neque laborem patriae denegasse, si contra importunissi-
mos latrones arma cepi te hortante et auctore, si non solum
exercitus ad rem publicam libertatemque defendendam
comparavi sed etiam crudelissimis tyrannis eripui. quos
si occupasset Dolabella, non solum adventu sed etiam
opinione et exspectatione exercitus sui Antonium con-
firmasset.

3   Quas ob res milites tuere, si eos mirifice de re publica
meritos esse animadvertis, et effice ne quem paeniteat rem
publicam quam spem praedae et rapinarum sequi ma-
luisse. item Murci et Crispi imperatorum dignitatem,
quantum est in te, tuere. nam Bassus misere noluit mihi
legionem tradere. quod nisi milites invito eo legatos ad me

[1] *(SB,* duce Lamb.)*

270

safety and the outcome of the enterprise, I wrote to you
and sent a number of couriers to Rome as soon as I took
over the legions which A. Allienus had led from Egypt. I
also wrote a dispatch to the Senate, with orders that it
should not be delivered until it had been read to you—if
my people have seen fit to comply with my instructions. If
the letters have not been delivered, I can only suppose that
Dolabella, who has villainously put Trebonius to death and
seized Asia, has caught my couriers and intercepted the
letters.

All the armies that were in Syria are at my orders. I was
held up for a short time pending discharge of promises
given to the men. Now my hands are free. May I ask you to
regard my public standing as entrusted to your care, if you
recognize that I have declined no risk or labour for the
country's sake? On your encouragement and advice I have
taken up arms against a set of savage brigands, and have
not only raised armies for the defence of commonwealth
and liberty but wrested them from the grip of cruel ty-
rants. Had Dolabella seized upon these troops before me,
he would have strengthened Antony's hands, not only by
the arrival of his army on the scene but by the report and
expectation of it.

In view of these facts take the soldiers under your
protection, if you perceive that they have deserved won-
derfully well of the state, and see to it that no man of them
regrets having chosen to follow the national cause rather
than the hope of spoil and plunder. Likewise defend the
standing of Generals Murcus and Crispus, so far as in you
lies. As for Bassus, he was sorely reluctant to hand over his
legion to me, and if the troops had not sent me their repre-
sentatives against his will, he would have shut the gates and

misissent, clausam Apameam tenuisset quoad vi esset ex-
pugnata. haec a te peto non solum rei publicae, quae tibi
semper fuit carissima, sed etiam amicitiae nostrae nomine,
4   quam confido apud te plurimum posse. crede mihi hunc
exercitum quem habeo senatus atque optimi cuiusque esse
maximeque tuum, de cuius voluntate adsidue audiendo
mirifice te diligit carumque habet. qui si intellexerit com-
moda sua curae tibi esse, debere etiam se tibi omnia puta-
bit.
5   Litteris scriptis audivi Dolabellam in Ciliciam venisse
cum suis copiis. proficiscar in Ciliciam. quid egerim celeriter ut scias dabo operam. ac velim, ut meremur de re publica, sic felices simus.

Fac valeas meque ames.

Non. Mai. ex castris.

388 (XI.13)

Scr. in castris Pollentiae c. VII *Id. Mai. an 43*

D. BRUTUS IMP. COS. DESIG. S. D. M. CICERONI

1   Iam non ago tibi gratias; cui enim re vix referre possum,
huic verbis non patitur res satis fieri. attendere te volo
quae in manibus sunt. qua enim prudentia es, nihil te
fugiet, si meas litteras diligenter legeris.

Sequi confestim Antonium his de causis, Cicero, non
potui: eram sine equitibus, sine iumentis; Hirtium perisse

---

2 On the Orontes, south of Antioch.

held Apamea[2] until it was taken by storm. I make these requests of you not only for the sake of the commonwealth, which has always been most dear to your heart, but also in the name of our friendship, which I am confident counts for a great deal with you. Believe me, this army under my command is devoted to the Senate and the loyalists, and most of all to you. By dint of constantly hearing about your friendly sentiments they have developed an extraordinary regard and affection for you. Once they realize that you have their interests at heart, they will feel unbounded gratitude as well.

P.S. I hear that Dolabella has entered Cilicia with his force. I shall set out for Cilicia. I shall try to let you know quickly how I get on. And I hope that luck will be on my side in so far as I deserve well of the commonwealth.

Take care of yourself and your affection for me.

Nones of May, from camp.

388 (XI.13)
D. BRUTUS TO M. CICERO

Camp at Pollentia, ca. 9 May 43

From D. Brutus, Imperator, Consul-Elect, to M. Cicero, greetings.

I have given up thanking you. There is no making adequate return in words to one whom I can scarcely repay in deeds. I want you to concentrate on the matters in hand—nothing will escape your perspicacity if you read my letter carefully.

The reasons why I was unable to pursue Antony at once, my dear sir, were these: I had no cavalry, no pack

nesciebam, Aquilam perisse [ne]sciebam;[1] Caesari non credebam prius quam convenissem et collocutus essem.

2   hic dies hoc modo abiit. postero die mane a Pansa sum accersitus Bononiam. cum in itinere essem, nuntiatum mihi est eum mortuum esse. recurri ad meas copiolas; sic enim vere eas appellare possum. sunt extenuatissimae et inopia omnium rerum pessime acceptae. biduo me Antonius antecessit, itinera fecit multo maiora fugiens quam ego sequens. ille enim iit passim, ego ordinatim. quacumque iit, ergastula solvit, homines abripuit; constitit nusquam prius quam ad Vada venit. quem locum volo tibi esse notum. iacet inter Appenninum et Alpis, impeditissimus ad iter faciendum.

3   Cum abessem ab eo milia passuum XXX et se iam Ventidius coniunxisset, contio eius ad me est adlata in qua petere coepit a militibus ut se trans Alpis sequerentur; sibi cum M. Lepido convenire. succlamatum est ei[2] frequenter a militibus Ventidianis (nam suos valde quam paucos habet) sibi aut in Italia pereundum esse aut vincendum, et orare coeperunt ut Pollentiam iter facerent. cum sustinere eos non posset, in posterum diem iter suum contulit.

4   Hac re mihi nuntiata statim quinque cohortis Pollentiam praemisi meumque iter eo contuli. hora ante praesidium meum Pollentiam venit quam Trebellius cum equitibus. sane quam sum gavisus. in hoc enim victoriam puto consistere * * *[3]

[1] *(SB)*
[2] et *(Scheller)*
[3] *lac. agnovit Frey*

animals; I did not know of Hirtius' death, but I did know of
Aquila's; I did not trust Caesar until I had met and talked to
him. So the first day passed. Early on the next I had a message from Pansa summoning me to Bononia. As I was on
my way I received the report of his death. I hastened back
to my own apology for an army, as I can truly call it; it is
most sadly reduced, and in very bad shape through lack of
all things needful. Antony got two days' start of me and
made far longer marches as the pursued than I as the pur-
suer, for he went helter-skelter, while I moved in regular
order. Wherever he went he opened up slave barracks and
carried off the men, stopping nowhere until he reached
Vada. I want you to know this place. It lies between the
Apennines and the Alps, and its approach offers the greatest difficulties.

When I was thirty miles away from Antony and Ventidius had already joined up with him, a speech of his was
brought to me in which he now asked his troops to follow
him across the Alps and told them that he had an understanding with Lepidus. There was a shout (coming in vol-
ume from Ventidius' men, for Antony has precious few of
his own) of 'death or victory in Italy,' and they started begging him to let them march on Pollentia. Unable to hold
out against them, he fixed his march for the following day.

On receiving this report I immediately sent five cohorts
in advance to Pollentia, and myself set out for the town. My
detachment arrived there an hour ahead of Trebellius and
a squadron of horse.[1] I felt no small satisfaction, for I think
victory depends upon * * *.

[1] The evidence does not support the view that D. Brutus was
deceived by a feint.

389 (X.13)

Scr. Romae c. v Id. Mai. an. 43

CICERO PLANCO

1   Ut primum potestas data est augendae dignitatis tuae,
nihil praetermisi in te ornando quod positum esset aut in
praemio virtutis aut in honore verborum. id ex ipso senatus
consulto poteris cognoscere; ita enim est perscriptum ut a
me de scripto dicta sententia est. quam senatus frequens
2   secutus est summo studio magnoque consensu. ego quamquam ex tuis litteris quas mihi misisti perspexeram te
magis iudicio bonorum quam insignibus gloriae delectari,
tamen considerandum nobis existimavi, etiam si tu nihil
postulares, quantum tibi a re publica deberetur. tu con-
texes extrema cum primis. qui enim M. Antonium oppresserit, is bellum confecerit. itaque Homerus non Aiacem
nec Achillem sed Ulixem appellavit πτολιπόρθιον.

390 (X.15)

Scr. in castris in Gallia Narbonensi cis Isaram c. v Id. Mai.
an. 43

PLANCUS CICERONI

1   His litteris scriptis quae postea accidissent, scire te ad
rem publicam putavi pertinere. sedulitas mea, ut spero, et

---

[1] The passages in the *Iliad* in which Achilles is so called were
held by Aristarchus to be spurious.

389 (X.13)
CICERO TO PLANCUS

Rome, ca. 11 May 43

From Cicero to Plancus.

As soon as the opportunity to enhance your standing came my way, I left nothing undone to your honour—no recompense of merit, no verbal accolade. That you will be able to see from the terms of the Senate's decree. They are exactly those of my motion, which I delivered from a script and which a well-attended House adopted with remarkable enthusiasm and unanimity. It was indeed clear to me from the letter you sent me that you find greater satisfaction in the judgement of honest men than in badges of glory. None the less, I felt it incumbent upon us to consider what was due to you from the commonwealth, even though you asked for nothing. It is for you to match the end with the beginning. The man who crushes Mark Antony will have won the war. It was Ulysses whom Homer called 'sacker of cities,' not Ajax or Achilles.[1]

390 (X.15)
PLANCUS TO CICERO

Camp on the Isara, ca. 11 May 43

From Plancus to Cicero.

After writing the above,[1] I thought that in the public interest you should know the sequel. My assiduity has,

---

[1] The letter to which this is a postscript seems to have been lost (it can hardly be 382, written about thirteen days earlier).

mihi et rei publicae tulit fructum. namque adsiduis inter-
nuntiis cum Lepido egi ut omissa omni contentione recon-
ciliataque voluntate nostra communi consilio rei publicae
succurreret; se, liberos urbemque pluris quam unum perditum abiectumque latronem putaret obsequioque meo, si
ita faceret, ad omnis res abuteretur. profeci.

2   Itaque per Laterensem internuntium fidem mihi dedit
se Antonium, si prohibere provincia sua non potuisset, bello persecuturum; me ut venirem copiasque coniungerem
rogavit, eoque magis quod et Antonius ab equitatu firmus
esse dicebatur et Lepidus ne mediocrem quidem equitatum habebat. nam etiam ex paucitate eius non multis ante
diebus †decem†,[1] qui optimi fuerant, ad me transierunt.

Quibus rebus ego cognitis cunctatus non sum. in cursu
3   bonorum consiliorum Lepidum adiuvandum putavi. adventus meus quid profecturus esset vidi, vel quod equitatu
meo persequi[2] atque opprimere equitatum eius possem
vel quod exercitus Lepidi eam partem quae corrupta est et
ab re publica alienata et corrigere et coercere praesentia
mei exercitus possem. itaque in Isara, flumine maximo
quod in finibus est Allobrogum, ponte uno die facto exercitum a. d. VII[3] Id. Mai. traduxi. cum vero mihi nuntiatum
esset L. Antonium praemissum cum equitibus et cohortibus ad Forum Iuli venisse, fratrem cum equitum quattuor
milibus ut occurreret ei misi a. d. V Id. Mai. ipse maximis
itineribus cum IIII legionibus expeditis et reliquo equitatu
4   subsequar. si nos mediocris modo fortuna rei publicae

---

[1] DC *Schelle*
[2] ⟨Antonium⟩ persequi *Or.*
[3] IIII *(Nake)*

I hope, borne fruit both for the state and for myself. Through intermediaries frequently passing to and fro I urged Lepidus to lay aside all quarrel, be reconciled with me, and collaborate in aiding the commonwealth. I exhorted him to think more of himself, his children, and his country than of one ruined, desperate bandit, and told him that if he did so my compliance in all things was entirely his to command.

My representations took effect. Lepidus gave me his word through Laterensis to make war on Antony, if he was unable to bar him from his province. He requested me to come and join forces, particularly as Antony is said to be strong in cavalry, while Lepidus has not even a second-class cavalry force. Even of the few he had, six hundred (?), the pick of them, had come over to me not long beforehand.

On receiving this intelligence I lost no time, reckoning that Lepidus should be assisted in the flowing tide of his good intentions. I saw the salutary effects to be expected from my arrival on the scene. I should be able to pursue Antony and crush his cavalry with mine, and at the same time the presence of my troops would serve to reform and coerce that portion of Lepidus' army which is tainted with disaffection. I therefore constructed in one day a bridge across the great river Isara on the border of the Allobrogian territory, and led my army across on 9 May. On 11 May, receiving a report that L. Antonius had been sent ahead with some cavalry and cohorts and had reached Forum Julii, I dispatched my brother with 4,000 horse to block him. I shall follow myself by forced marches with four legions without baggage and my remaining horse. Aided, even to a moderate degree, by the Fortune of the

adiuverit, et audaciae perditorum et nostrae sollicitudinis hic finem reperiemus. quod si latro praecognito nostro adventu rursus in Italiam se recipere coeperit, Bruti erit officium occurrere ei; cui scio nec consilium nec animum defuturum. ego tamen, si id acciderit, fratrem cum equitatu mittam qui sequatur Italiamque a vastatione defendat.

Fac valeas meque mutuo diligas.

391 (X.21)

Scr. in castris ad Isaram III Id. Mai., ut vid., an. 43

PLANCUS CICERONI

1   Puderet me inconstantiae mearum litterarum si non haec ex aliena levitate penderent. omnia feci qua re Lepido coniuncto ad rem publicam defendendam minore sollicitudine vestra perditis resisterem. omnia ei et petenti recepi et ultro pollicitus sum, scripsique tibi biduo ante confidere me bono Lepido esse usurum communique consilio bellum administraturum. credidi chirographis eius, adfirmationi praesentis Laterensis, qui tum apud me erat reconciliaremque me Lepido fidemque haberem orabat. non licuit diutius bene de eo sperare. illud certe cavi et cavebo, ne mea credulitate rei publicae[1] summa fallatur.

[1] res p. *Lamb.*

commonwealth, we shall here find an end to the audacity of the desperados and our own anxiety. If, however, the bandit hears that I am on my way and beats a retreat back to Italy, it will be Brutus' duty to block him. I am sure that Brutus will lack neither skill nor courage. None the less, I shall in that event send my brother with the cavalry in pursuit and for the defence of Italy from devastation.

Take care of your health and remember me kindly, as I do you.

391 (X.21)
PLANCUS TO CICERO

Camp on the Isara, 13 (?) May 43

From Plancus to Cicero.

I should be ashamed to chop and change in my letters, were it not that these things depend on the fickleness of another person. I did everything in my power to combine with Lepidus for the defence of the commonwealth, so that I could oppose the desperados on terms which would leave you at home less cause for anxiety. I pledged myself to all he asked and made other promises voluntarily. The day before yesterday I wrote to you that I was confident of finding Lepidus amenable and of conducting the war in concert with him. I relied on letters in his handwriting and on the assurance given in person by Laterensis, who was with me at the time, begging me to make up my quarrel with Lepidus and to trust him. It is now no longer possible to augur well of him. But at least I have taken, and shall continue to take, good care that the supreme interests of the commonwealth are not betrayed by my credulity.

2   Cum Isaram flumen uno die ponte effecto exercitum
traduxissem pro magnitudine rei celeritatem adhibens,
quod petierat per litteras ipse ut maturarem venire, praesto mihi fuit stator eius cum litteris, quibus ne venirem de-
nuntiabat; se posse per se conficere negotium; interea ad
Isaram exspectarem. indicabo temerarium meum consilium tibi: nihilo minus ire decreram existimans eum socium gloriae vitare. putabam posse me nec de laude ieiuni
hominis delibare quicquam et subesse tamen propinquis
locis, ut, si durius aliquid esset, succurrere celeriter possem.

3   Ego non malus homo hoc suspicabar. at Laterensis, vir
sanctissimus, suo chirographo mittit mihi litteras nimis
quam[2] desperans de se, de exercitu, de Lepidi fide que-
rensque se destitutum, in quibus aperte denuntiat videam
ne fallar; suam fidem solutam esse; rei publicae ne desim.
exemplar eius chirographi Titio misi. ipsa chirographa
omnia, et ‹ea›[3] quibus credidi et ea quibus fidem non
habendam putavi, Laevo Cispio dabo perferenda, qui omnibus iis interfuit rebus.

4   Accessit eo ut milites eius, cum Lepidus contionaretur,
improbi per se, corrupti etiam per eos qui praesunt, Cani-
dios Rufrenosque et ceteros quos cum opus erit scietis,
conclamarent viri boni pacem se velle neque esse cum ullis
pugnaturos, duobus iam consulibus singularibus occisis,

[2] -isque *(Mend.)*
[3] *(Lamb.)*

---

[1] Probably Plancus' brother-in-law L. Titius, not the Tribune
mentioned in Letter 377.4.

After constructing in one day a bridge over the river Isara, I led my army across in all haste, as the importance of the emergency demanded, since Lepidus himself had requested me in writing to make all speed to go to him—only to be met by his orderly with a letter enjoining me not to come. He wrote that he could settle the business himself, and asked me in the meanwhile to wait on the Isara. I will tell you the rash plan I formed. I decided to go none the less, supposing that Lepidus did not want to share the glory. I reckoned that without in any way detracting from this paltry personage's credit I could be at hand somewhere in the vicinity, so as to come rapidly to the rescue if anything untoward should occur.

That was how in my innocence I gauged the situation. But Laterensis, who is a man of complete integrity, now sends me a letter in his own hand utterly despairing of himself, the army, and Lepidus' good faith, and complaining that he has been left in the lurch. He warns me in plain terms to beware of treachery, says that he himself has kept faith, and urges me not to fail the commonwealth. I am sending a copy of his letter to Titius.[1] All the autograph originals (both those which I believed and those which I considered untrustworthy) I shall give to Laevus Cispius, who has been privy to all these transactions, for him to take to Rome.

There is a further item. When Lepidus was addressing his soldiers, who are disloyal by inclination and have been further corrupted by their officers such as Canidius, Rufrenus, and others whose names you will know when the time comes, these honest patriots roared out that they wanted peace, that they would fight nobody now that two excellent Consuls had been killed and so many Romans

CICERO'S LETTERS TO FRIENDS

tot civibus [pro] patria‹e›[4] amissis, hostibus denique omnibus iudicatis bonisque publicatis; neque hoc aut vindicarat Lepidus aut sanarat.

5   Hoc me venire et duobus exercitibus coniunctis obicere exercitum fidelissimum, auxilia maxima, principes Galliae, provinciam cunctam summae dementiae et temeritatis esse vidi, mihique, si ita oppressus essem remque publicam mecum prodidissem, mortuo non modo honorem sed misericordiam quoque defuturum. itaque rediturus sum nec tanta munera perditis hominibus dari posse sinam.

6   Ut exercitum locis habeam opportunis, provinciam tuear, etiam si ille exercitus descierit, omniaque integra servem dabo operam, quoad exercitus hoc summittatis parique felicitate rem publicam hic vindicetis. nec depugnare, si occasio tulerit, nec obsideri, si necesse fuerit, nec mori, si casus inciderit, pro vobis paratior fuit quisquam. qua re hortor te, mi Cicero, exercitum hoc traiciendum quam primum cures et matures, prius quam hostes magis corroborentur et nostri perturbentur. in quo si celeritas erit adhibita, res publica in possessione victoriae deletis sceleratis permanebit.

Fac valeas meque diligas.

[4] pro patria *(SB)*

lost to the fatherland, branded wholesale moreover as public enemies and their goods confiscated. Lepidus neither punished this outburst nor remedied the mischief.

For me to go this way and expose my thoroughly loyal army with its auxiliaries and the Gaulish chiefs and the whole province to two combined armies, would clearly be the height of folly and temerity. If I was overwhelmed and had sacrificed the commonwealth along with myself, I could expect no pity, much less honour, for such a death. Therefore I intend to go back, and shall not let these desperate men be presented with the possibility of such advantages.

I shall take care to keep my army in suitable locations, to protect my province even if Lepidus' army defects, and to preserve the whole position uncompromised until you send armies to my support and defend the commonwealth here as successfully as you have done in Italy. On behalf of you all I am ready, no man has ever been more so, either to fight it out if I get a fair opportunity, or to stand a siege if it prove necessary, or to die if chance so fall. Therefore I urge you, my dear Cicero, to do your utmost to get an army across the Alps here as soon as possible, and to make haste before the enemy's strength grows further and our men become unsettled. If speed is used in this operation, the commonwealth will remain in possession of its victory and the criminals will be destroyed.

Take care of your health and remember me kindly.

392 (X.21a)

Scr. in castris ad Isaram c. Id. Mai. an. 43

‹PLANCUS CICERONI›

Fratrem meum tibi, fortissimum civem et ad omnia pa-
ratissimum, excusem litteris? qui ex labore in febriculam
incidit adsiduam et satis molestam. cum primum poterit,
istoc recurrere non dubitabit, ne quo loco rei publicae
desit.

Meam dignitatem commendatam habeas rogo. concupiscere me nihil oportet. habeo te et amantissimum mei et,
quod optavi, summae auctoritatis. tu videris quantum et
quando tuum munus apud me velis esse. tantum te rogo, in
Hirti locum me subdas et ad tuum amorem et ad meam
observantiam.

393 (X.19)

Scr. Romae med. m. Mai., ut vid., an. 43

CICERO PLANCO

1   Quamquam gratiarum actionem a te non desiderabam,
cum te re ipsa atque animo scirem esse gratissimum, tamen (fatendum est enim) fuit ea mihi periucunda. sic enim
vidi, quasi ea quae oculis cernuntur, me a te amari. dices
'quid antea?' semper equidem, sed numquam illustrius.

392 (X.21a)
PLANCUS TO CICERO

Camp on the Isara, ca. 15 May 43

Would you have me offer you apologies for my brother in a letter—the most gallant of gentlemen and the most forward in every patriotic endeavor? As a result of his exertions he has contracted a slight fever, continuous and pretty troublesome. As soon as he can manage it he will hasten back to Rome without question, so that the commonwealth may not lack his services wherever he may be.

Let me ask you to regard my public standing as entrusted to your care. There is no need for me to be covetous, for in you I have a most affectionate friend and (as I prayed you would be) a most influential one. The magnitude and timing of any benefaction you may wish me to owe you will be yours to determine. All I ask is that you take me as Hirtius' successor both in affection on your side and attention on mine.

393 (X.19)
CICERO TO PLANCUS

Rome, mid May (?) 43

From Cicero to Plancus.

I felt no need for words of thanks from you, knowing how grateful you are in truth and heart. But I must acknowledge that they gave me deep pleasure. I saw your affection for me plain as I see what is in front of my eyes. 'And before?' you may ask. Yes indeed, always, but never more clearly.

Litterae tuae mirabiliter gratae sunt senatui cum rebus ipsis, quae erant gravissimae et maximae, fortissimi animi summique consili, tum etiam gravitate sententiarum atque
2 verborum. sed, mi Plance, incumbe ut belli extrema perficias. in hoc erit summa et gratia et gloria. cupio omnia rei publicae causa; sed mehercules in ea conservanda iam defatigatus non multo plus patriae faveo quam tuae gloriae, cuius maximam facultatem tibi di immortales, ut spero, dederunt; quam complectere obsecro. qui enim Antonium oppresserit, is hoc bellum taeterrimum periculosissimumque confecerit.

394 (XI.12)

Scr. Romae c. III Id. Mai. an. 43

M. CICERO S. D. D. BRUTO IMP. COS. DESIG.
1 Tris uno die a te accepi epistulas, unam brevem, quam Flacco Volumnio dederas, duas pleniores, quarum alteram tabellarius T. Vibi attulit, alteram ad me misit Lupus.

Ex tuis litteris et ex Graecei oratione non modo non restinctum bellum sed etiam inflammatum videtur. non dubito autem pro tua singulari prudentia quin perspicias, si aliquid firmitatis nactus sit Antonius, omnia tua illa praeclara in rem publicam merita ad nihilum esse ventura. ita

---

1 Not preserved.
1 Letters 380, 385, and 386.

Your dispatch[1] made an extraordinarily favourable impression on the Senate, both from the great and momentous news it contained, magnificent evidence of your courage and judgement, and from the impressive quality of sentiments and style. Forward now, my dear Plancus, to finish the last remnants of the war! That will be a most grateful and glorious achievement. I am heart and soul devoted to the commonwealth; yet, truth to tell, I have grown weary in its preservation and my zeal for my country is not much greater than that which I feel for your glory. The Immortals have given you, as I trust, a golden opportunity to earn it. Grasp that opportunity, I beg of you. The man who crushes Antony will have finished this ghastly and perilous war.

394 (XI.12)
CICERO TO D. BRUTUS

Rome, ca. 13 May 43

From M. Cicero to D. Brutus, Imperator, Consul-Elect, greetings.

I have received three letters[1] from you on the same day: a short one, which you sent by Flaccus Volumnius, and two of more substance, one brought by T. Vibius' courier, the other sent to me by Lupus.

From what you write and from what Graeceius says, the flames of war, so far from having been extinguished, seem to be blazing higher. Knowing your exceptional perspicacity, I do not doubt you realize that if Antony acquires a position of any strength all your splendid services to the commonwealth will be brought to nothing, According to

enim Romam erat nuntiatum, ita persuasum omnibus,
cum paucis inermis, perterri⟨ti⟩s metu, fracto animo fu-
2   gisse Antonium. qui si ita se habet ut, quem ad modum audiebam de Graeceio, confligi cum eo sine periculo non
possit, non ille mihi fugisse a Mutina videtur sed locum
belli gerendi mutasse. itaque homines alii facti sunt. non
nulli etiam queruntur quod persecuti non sitis; opprimi
potuisse, si celeritas adhibita esset, existimant. omnino est
hoc populi maximeque nostri, in eo potissimum abuti
libertate per quem eam consecutus sit; sed tamen pro-
videndum est ne quae iusta querela esse possit. res se sic
habet: is bellum confecerit qui Antonium oppresserit. hoc
quam vim habeat te existimare malo quam me apertius
scribere.

395 (X.18)

Scr. in castris ad Isaram xv *Kal. Iun. an. 43*

PLANCUS CICERONI

1   Quid in animo habuerim cum Laevus Nervaque discesserunt a me et ex litteris quas iis dedi et ex ipsis cognoscere
potuisti, qui omnibus rebus consiliisque meis interfuerunt. accidit mihi quod homini pudenti et cupido satis faciendi rei publicae bonisque omnibus accidere solet, ut
consilium sequerer periculosum magis, dum me probarem, quam tutum, quod habere posset obtrectationem.
2   Itaque post discessum legatorum cum binis continuis

reports reaching Rome and to the universal persuasion
here Antony had fled in despair with a few unarmed and
demoralized followers. If in fact his condition is such that,
as I hear from Graeceius, a clash with him will be a dangerous matter, I do not regard him as having fled from Mutina
but as having shifted the war to another theatre. Accordingly, the public mood has changed. There are even those
who criticize you men in the field for having failed to pursue Antony. They think that with prompt action he might
have been overwhelmed. No doubt it is a characteristic of
the masses, those of Rome in particular, to exercise their
liberties upon the one person of all others through whose
agency they have gained them. Even so, care must be
taken not to give just grounds for complaint. The case
stands thus: the man who crushes Antony will have finished the war. What this means I would rather leave you to
consider than put it in plainer language myself.

395 (X.18)
PLANCUS TO CICERO

Camp on the Isara, 18 May 43

From Plancus to Cicero.

What I had in mind when Laevus and Nerva took their
leave you will have learned from the letter I gave them and
from their own report. They have been privy to all my actions and plans. I find myself, as a man of honour anxious to
do his duty to the state and all honest citizens is apt to find
himself, following a dangerous course in earning approval
rather than a safe one which might be censurable.

After the departure of my envoys I received two let-

litteris et Lepidus me ut venirem rogaret et Laterensis
multo etiam magis prope implorans obtestaretur, non
ullam rem aliam extimescens quam eandem quae mihi
quoque facit timorem, varietatem atque infidelitatem
exercitus eius, non dubitandum putavi quin succurrerem
meque communi periculo offerrem. sciebam enim, et⟨si⟩[1]
cautius illud erat consilium, exspectare me ad Isaram dum
Brutus traiceret exercitum et cum collega consentiente,
exercitu concordi ac bene de re publica sentiente, sicut milites faciunt, hostibus obviam ire, tamen, si quid Lepidus
bene sentiens detrimenti cepisset, hoc omne adsignatum
iri aut pertinaciae meae aut timori videbam, si aut hominem offensum mihi, coniunctum cum re publica non
sublevassem aut ipse a certamine belli tam necessari me
removissem.

3   Itaque potius periclitari volui si possem mea praesentia
et Lepidum tueri et exercitum facere meliorem quam
nimis cautus videri. sollicitiorem certe hominem non suis
contractis neminem puto fuisse. nam quae res nullam
habebat dubitationem si exercitus Lepidi absit, ea nunc
magnam adfert sollicitudinem magnumque habet casum.
mihi enim si contigisset ut prior occurrerem Antonio, non
mehercules horam constitisset; tantum ego et mihi confido
et sic perculsas illius copias Ventidique mulionis castra
despicio. sed non possum non exhorrescere si quid intra
cutem subest vulneris, quod prius nocere potest quam sciri curarique possit. sed certe, [ni]si[2] uno loco me tenerem,

[1] *(Lamb.)*
[2] *(Man.)*

ters in quick succession, one from Lepidus urging me to
go to him, the other in still more pressing terms from
Laterensis, almost begging and imploring me. His one fear
was exactly my own—the fickle and disloyal disposition of
Lepidus' troops. I felt I must not hesitate to go to his assistance and face the common peril. No doubt I should be
acting more cautiously if I waited on the Isara till Brutus
brought his army across the Alps, and then advanced
against the enemy with a like-minded colleague and a
united and patriotic army (as my men are). But I can see
that if Lepidus came to any harm in the right cause, all
would be blamed on my obstinacy in not going to the relief
of a friend to the public with whom I had a personal quarrel, or on my pusillanimity in deliberately withdrawing
myself from the clash in so necessary a conflict.

Accordingly, I have chosen to take a chance, in the hope
that my presence will bolster up Lepidus and improve the
morale of his army, rather than to be considered overcau-
tious. I really believe no man was ever in greater anxiety
through no fault of his own. If Lepidus' army were elsewhere, it would be plain sailing; but as matters stand, there
is great cause for anxiety and great risk. If I had had the
luck to meet Antony first, I give you my word he would
not have lasted an hour—I have enough self-confidence
and enough contempt for his battered forces and that
muleteer[1] Ventidius' army to say so much. But I cannot
help trembling at the thought of a wound beneath the skin
which may do mischief before it can be diagnosed and
treated. Yet if I stayed where I am, it is certain that Lepidus

[1] Ventidius had at one time made money by contracting for the
supply of mules and carts for provincial governors.

magnum periculum ipse Lepidus, magnum ea pars exercitus adiret quae bene de re publica sentit. magnam etiam perditi hostes accessionem sibi fecissent si quas copias a Lepido abstraxissent. quae si adventus meus represserit, agam gratias Fortunae constantiaeque meae, quae me ad hanc experientiam excitavit.

4   Itaque a. d. xv Kal. Iun. ab Isara castra movi: pontem tamen quem in Isara feceram castellis duobus ad capita positis reliqui praesidiaque ibi firma posui, ut venienti Bruto exercituique eius sine mora transitus esset paratus. ipse, ut spero, diebus VIII quibus has litteras dabam cum Lepidi copiis me coniungam.

396 (X.34)

Scr. in castris ad Pontem Argenteum xv Kal. Iun. vel paulo post an. 43

‹M.› LEPIDUS IMP. ITER. PONT. MAX. S. D. M. TULLIO CICERONI

1   S. v. b.; e. e. q.[1] v.

Cum audissem M. Antonium cum suis copiis praemisso L. Antonio cum parte equitatus in provinciam meam venire, cum exercitu meo ab confluente †ab Rhodano†[2] castra movi ac contra eos venire institui. itaque continuis itineribus ad Forum Vocon[t]ium[3] veni et ultra castra ad flumen Argenteum contra Antonios[4] feci. P. Ventidius suas legiones tris coniunxit cum eo et ultra me castra posuit. habebat antea legionem V et ex reliquis legionibus mag-

---

[1] q. DV*: *om.* MH   [2] ‹Durentiae› ac Rhodani *Wes.*
[3] *(Man.)*   [4] Antoni‹an›os ⛉

himself and the loyal section of his troops would be in deadly peril. The enemy ruffians too would have gained much in strength if they had drawn forces over from Lepidus. If my arrival dispels these threats, I shall thank my stars and my own resolution, which has spurred me on to this adventure.

Accordingly, this 18th of May I am striking camp on the Isara. I am, however, leaving the bridge which I constructed over the river and two forts at either bridgehead strongly garrisoned, so that when Brutus and his army arrive they will find free passage. I hope myself to effect a junction with Lepidus' forces within eight days of dispatching this letter.

396 (X.34)
LEPIDUS TO CICERO

Camp at Pons Argenteus, ca. 19 May 43

M. Lepidus, Imperator for the second time, Pontifex Maximus, to M. Tullius Cicero, greetings.

I trust you are well, as I am and my army.

On hearing that M. Antonius was on his way with his forces into my province and had sent L. Antonius ahead with part of his cavalry, I struck my camp at the confluence of the Rhone and the * and started to advance against them with my army. Marching every day, I reached Forum Voconium and took up a position against the Antonii east of the town on the River Argenteus. P. Ventidius joined him with his three legions, and pitched his camp to the east of me. Previously Antony had the Fifth Legion and a great number of men from his other legions, but these latter are

nam multitudinem, sed inermorum. equitatum habet magnum; nam omnis ex proelio integer discessit, ita ut sint amplius equitum milia quinque.[5] ad me complures milites et equites ab eo transierunt et in dies singulos eius copiae
2 minuuntur. Silanus et Culleo ab eo discesserunt. nos etsi graviter ab iis laesi eramus, quod contra nostram voluntatem ad Antonium ierant, tamen nostrae humanitatis et necessitudinis causa eorum salutis rationem habuimus; nec tamen eorum opera utimur neque in castris habemus neque ulli negotio praefecimus.

Quod ad bellum hoc attinet, nec senatui nec rei publicae deerimus. quae postea egerimus faciam te certiorem.

397 (XI.18)

Scr. Romae XIV *Kal. Iun. an.* 43

M. CICERO S. D. D. BRUTO IMP. COS. DESIG.
1 Etsi ex mandatis quae Galbae Volumnioque ad senatum dedisti quid timendum putares suspicabamur, tamen timidiora mandata videbantur quam erat dignum tua populique Romani victoria. senatus autem, mi Brute, fortis est et habet fortis duces. itaque moleste ferebat se a te, quem omnium quicumque fuissent fortissimum iudicaret,
2 timidum atque ignavum iudicari. etenim cum te incluso

---

[5] (m.) itaque (*Madvig:* VM *iam Schütz*)

---

[1] Perhaps son of Q. Terentius Culleo, Tribune in 58 (*Letters to*

unarmed. His cavalry is very strong; the whole of it withdrew without loss from the battle, amounting to more than
5,000 troopers. Numbers of foot and horse have deserted
him to join me, and his forces are dwindling every day.
Silanus and Culleo[1] have left him. Although they had committed a grave offence against me in going to Antony
against my will, yet for mercy and friendship's sake I have
spared their lives; but I do not employ them or have them
in camp, nor have I given them any charge.

As for this war, I shall not fail the Senate or the commonwealth. I shall keep you informed of my further activities.

397 (XI.18)
CICERO TO D. BRUTUS

Rome, 19 May 43

From M. Cicero to D. Brutus, Imperator, Consul-Elect,
greetings.

From the messages you sent to the Senate by Galba and
Volumnius we suspect the nature of the dangers you envis-
age; but those messages seem apprehensive to a degree
unworthy of your and the Roman People's victory. The
Senate, my dear Brutus, is brave and has brave leaders;
and so they are vexed to be set down by you, whom they
judge the bravest man that ever was, as a body of nervous
faint-hearts. And really, considering that when you were
shut up in the town everybody placed the highest hopes

Atticus 60 (III.15).5. He had let Antony through the Alpine passes
which he was supposed to guard (with Lepidus' connivance?).

spem maximam omnes habuissent in tua virtute florente
Antonio, quis erat qui quicquam timeret profligato illo, te
liberato? nec vero Lepidum timebamus. quis enim esset
qui illum tam furiosum arbitraretur ut, qui in maximo bello
pacem velle se dixisset, is in optatissima pace bellum rei
publicae indiceret?

3   Nec dubito quin tu plus providas. sed tamen tam recenti gratulatione, quam tuo nomine ad omnia deorum
templa fecimus, renovatio timoris magnam molestiam ad-
ferebat. quare velim equidem, id quod spero, ut plane
abiectus et fractus sit Antonius; sin aliquid virium forte
collegerit, sentiet nec senatui consilium nec populo Romano virtutem deesse nec rei publicae te vivo imperatorem.

     XIII Kal. Iun.

398 (X.17)

Scr. ex itinere ad Forum Voconi paulo post XV *Kal. Iun.
an. 43*

PLANCUS CICERONI

1   Antonius Id. Mai. ad Forum Iuli cum primis copiis
venit. Ventidius bidui spatio abest ab eo. Lepidus ad Forum Voconi castra habet, qui locus a Foro Iuli quattuor et
viginti millia passus abest, ibique me exspectare constituit,
quem ad modum ipse mihi scripsit. quod si omnia mihi
integra et ipse et Fortuna servarit, recipio vobis celeriter
me negotium ex sententia confecturum.

2   Fratrem meum adsiduis laboribus concursationibus-

upon your valour, though Antony was flourishing, who could be afraid of anything after his virtual overthrow and your liberation? Nor are we afraid of Lepidus. After declaring his desire for peace when the war was at its height, could anyone suppose him mad enough to declare war on the commonwealth when peace, the peace we prayed for, reigned?

At the same time I don't doubt that you see further than we. All the same, this renewal of alarm, following so swiftly upon the thanksgivings which we offered upon your account at every temple, is causing great vexation. So for my part, my wish and hope is that Antony is really down and out. If, however, he manages to collect some sort of power, he shall find that the Senate does not lack for counsel, nor the People of Rome for valour, nor the commonwealth, while you live, for a general.

19 May.

398 (X.17)
PLANCUS TO CICERO

En route to Forum Voconii, shortly after 18 May 43

From Plancus to Cicero.

On the Ides of May Antony arrived at Forum Julii with his advance guard. Ventidius is two days' march away from him. Lepidus is encamped at Forum Voconii, twenty-four miles from Forum Julii, and has decided to wait for me there, as he has written to me himself. If he and Fortune leave me a clear field, I guarantee that I shall quickly finish the job to your collective satisfaction.

I have already told you that my brother has been seri-

que confectum graviter se habuisse antea tibi scripsi. sed tamen, cum primum posse ingredi coepit, non magis sibi quam rei publicae se convaluisse existimans ad omnia pericula princeps esse non recusabat. sed ego eum non solum hortatus sum verum etiam coegi isto proficisci, quod et illa valetudine magis conficere se quam me iuvare posset in castris et quod acerbissimo interitu consulum rem publicam nudatam tali cive praetore in urbanis officiis indigere existimabam. quod si qui vestrum non probabit, mihi prudentiam in consilio defuisse sciat, non illi erga patriam fidelitatem.

3   Lepidus tamen quod ego desiderabam fecit, ut Apellam ad me mitteret, quo obside fidei illius et societatis in re publica administranda uterer. in ea re studium mihi suum L. Gellius †de tribus fratribus segaviano†[1] probavit, quo ego interprete novissime ad Lepidum sum usus. amicum eum rei publicae cognosse videor libenterque ei sum testimonio et omnibus ero qui bene merentur.

Fac valeas meque mutuo diligas dignitatemque meam, si mereor, tuearis, sicut adhuc singula<ri> cum benevolentia fecisti.

[1] Segovia *Or., sed vide comm.*

ously ill, worn out by the fatigue of continual hurrying to and fro. None the less, as soon as he was able to walk, he was ready to be foremost in every dangerous work, regarding his recovery as for the commonwealth's benefit as much as his own. However, I have urged, in fact compelled, him to leave for Rome, on the ground that in his present state of health he would be more likely to wear himself out than to help me in camp; and I thought that a man of his calibre would be needed as Praetor in city affairs, now that the state has been left denuded by the lamentable loss of the Consuls. If anyone at home disapproves of this, let him know that there has been a failure of judgement on my part, not any lack of patriotic loyalty on my brother's.

To resume, Lepidus has complied with my desire that he should send me Apella[1] as a hostage for his good faith and collaboration in the public service. In this connection, I have found L. Gellius, one of the three brothers from Segovia (?),[2] very ready to help. He has been my latest go-between with Lepidus. I think I can say that he has proved himself a good patriot and I am glad to testify accordingly, as I shall readily do for all who deserve it.

Take care of your health and remember me kindly, as I do you. Stand up for me in public (if I deserve it), as you have done hitherto with such notable good will.

[1] Presumably a confidential freedman of Lepidus.

[2] The reading is very doubtful. If 'Segovia' is wrong, this Gellius may be L. Gellius Poplicola, Consul in 36, who later served with Brutus and Cassius in the East.

Scr. Vercellis XII *Kal. Iun. an. 43*

D. BRUTUS IMP. COS. DESIG. S. D. M. CICERONI

1   Ad senatum quas litteras misi velim prius perlegas et si
qua tibi videbuntur commutes. necessario me scripsisse
ipse animadvertes. nam cum putarem quartam et Martiam
legiones mecum futuras, ut Druso Paulloque placuerat vobis adsentientibus, minus de reliquis rebus laborandum
existimavi. nunc vero, cum sim cum tironibus egentissi-
mis,[1] valde et meam et vestram vicem timeam necesse est.

2   Vicetini me et M. Brutum praecipue observant. his ne
quam patiare iniuriam fieri in senatu vernarum causa a te
peto. causam habent optimam, officium in re<m> publicam summum, genus hominum adversariorum seditiosum
et incertissimum.

XII Kal. Iun. Vercellis.

---

[1] recent- *Sedgwick*

302

399 (XI.19)
D. BRUTUS TO CICERO

Vercellae, 21 May 43

From D. Brutus, Imperator, Consul-Elect, to M. Cicero greetings.

Will you be good enough to read beforehand the dispatch I am sending to the Senate and make any alterations you think proper? You will see for yourself that I had no choice but to write it. When I thought I should have the Fourth and Martian Legions with me, as proposed by Drusus and Paullus with the assent of yourself and the rest, I saw less reason for anxiety as to future operations. But now that I am left with a body of very necessitous recruits, I must needs be gravely apprehensive on my own account and that of you all.

The Vicetini show myself and M. Brutus particular attention. May I beg of you not to let any injury come to them in the Senate for the sake of a pack of slaves?[1] They have an excellent case, and are eminently loyal to the commonwealth; and their opponents are a disorderly, thoroughly untrustworthy set.

21 May, from Vercellae.

[1] Perhaps contemptuously for freedmen. But they may have been slaves belonging to the municipality, which denied the validity of their manumission.

400 (X.34a)[1]

Scr. in castris ad Pontem Argenteum XI *Kal. Iun. an. 43*

‹LEPIDUS CICERONI›

1   Etsi omni tempore summa studia offici mutuo inter nos
certatim constiterunt pro nostra inter nos familiaritate et
proinde diligenter ab utroque conservata sunt, tamen non
dubito in tanto et tam repentino motu rei publicae quin
non nulla de me falsis rumoribus a meis obtrectatoribus
me indigna ad te delata sint, quae tuum animum magno
opere moverent pro tuo amore in rem publicam. ea te
moderate accepisse neque temere credendum iudicasse
a meis procuratoribus certior sum factus. quae mihi, ut
debent, gratissima sunt. memini enim et illa superiora
quae abs tua voluntate profecta sunt ad meam dignitatem
augendam et ornandam, quae perpetuo animo meo fixa
manebunt.

2   Abs te, mi Cicero, magno opere peto, si meam vitam,
studium, diligentiam, fidem[2] superioribus temporibus in
re publica administranda quae Lepido digna sunt perspec-
ta habes, ut paria aut eo ampliora reliquo tempore exspectes et proinde tua auctoritate me tuendum existimes quo
tibi plura tuo merito debeo.

Vale.

D. XI Kal. Iun. ex castris ex Ponte Argenteo.

[1] *novam ep. Vict.*
[2] diligentissime (*SB*.: -ntiam *Lamb.*)

400 (X.34a)
LEPIDUS TO CICERO

Camp at Pons Argenteus, 22 May 43

M. Lepidus, Imperator for the second time, Pontifex Maximus, to M. Tullius Cicero greetings.

You and I have always vied in the eagerness of our mutual zeal to do one another service in virtue of the friendship between us, and both of us have been careful to maintain our practice accordingly. At the same time I have no doubt that in the present violent and unexpected political disturbance my detractors have brought you false and unworthy reports concerning me, calculated to give your patriotic heart no small disquiet. My agents have informed me that you have not allowed these rumours to upset you or thought it right to give them hasty credence. For that I am deeply and duly grateful. I also remember your earlier friendly efforts to promote and enhance my standing; they will ever remain firmly rooted in my mind.

I have one earnest request to make of you, my dear Cicero. If in time past my life and endeavour, my diligence and good faith in the conduct of public affairs, have to your knowledge been worthy of the name I bear, I beg you to expect equal or greater things in time to come, and to regard me as deserving the protection of your public influence in proportion as your kindness places me further and further in your debt.

Good-bye.

Dispatched 22 May from camp, Pons Argenteus.

401 (XI.20)

Scr. Eporediae IX *Kal. Iun. an. 43*

D. BRUTUS S. D. M. CICERONI

1   Quod pro me non facio, id pro te facere amor meus in te tuaque officia cogunt, ut timeam. saepe enim mihi cum esset dictum neque a me contemptum, novissime Labeo Segulius, homo sui simillimus, narrat mihi apud Caesarem se fuisse multumque sermonem de te habitum esse; ipsum Caesarem nihil sane de te questum nisi dictum, quod diceret te dixisse laudandum adulescentem, ornandum, tollendum; se non esse commissurum ut tolli possit. hoc ego Labeonem credo illi rettulisse aut finxisse dictum, non ab adulescente prolatum. veteranos vero pessime loqui volebat Labeo me credere et tibi ab iis instare periculum, maximeque indignari quod in decem viris neque Caesar neque ego habiti essemus atque omnia ad vestrum arbitrium essent collata.

2   Haec cum audissem et iam in itinere essem, committendum nondum putavi prius ut Alpis transgrederer quam quid istic ageretur scirem. nam de tuo periculo, crede mihi iactatione verborum et denuntiatione periculi sperare eos te pertimefacto, adulescente impulso, posse magna consequi praemia, et totam istam cantilenam ex hoc pendere ut

---

[1] *Laudandum, ornandum, tollendum.* The last verb seems to be used with a double meaning, 'exalt' and 'get rid of.'

[2] Appointed by the Senate after the battle of Mutina to review Antony's 'acts' as Consul. Decimus seems to have thought that land and gratuities for the republican army were involved, but cf. Letter 411.5.

401 (XI.20)
D. BRUTUS TO CICERO

Eporedia, 24 May 43

From D. Brutus to M. Cicero greetings.

My affection for you and your services to me make me feel on your account what I do not feel on my own: fear. Here is something I have often been told and have not thought negligible—my latest informant is Labeo Segulius (he never acts out of character), who tells me that he has been with Caesar and that a good deal of talk about you took place. Caesar, he says, made no complaints about you to be sure, except for a remark which he attributed to you: 'the young man must get praises, honours, and—the push.'[1] He added that he had no intention of letting himself get the push. I believe that the remark was repeated to him (or invented) by Labeo, not produced by the young man. As for the veterans, Labeo would have me believe that they are grumbling viciously, and that you are in danger from them. He says they are particularly indignant that neither Caesar nor I have been put on the Commission of Ten,[2] and that everything has been placed in the hands of you gentlemen.

When I heard all this, though I was already on the march, I thought it would be wrong for me to cross the Alps yet, before I knew what was going on in Rome. As for the danger to yourself, believe me, they are hoping to gain larger gratuities by talking at large and threatening trouble. They mean to terrorize you and instigate the young man. This whole rigmarole has one origin: they want to make as much profit for themselves as possible. At the same time I don't want you to be other than circumspect

307

quam plurimum lucri faciant. neque tamen non te cautum
esse volo et insidias vitantem. nihil enim tua mihi vita
3   potest esse iucundius neque carius. illud vide, ne timendo
magis timere cogare, et ⟨tamen,⟩[1] quibus rebus potest
occurri veteranis, occurras: primum quod desiderant de
decem viris facias, deinde de praemiis, si tibi videtur, agros
eorum militum qui cum Antonio veterani fuerunt iis dandos censeas ab utrisque nobis. de nummis lente ac ratione
habita pecuniae; senatum de ea re constituturum. quattuor legionibus iis quibus agros dandos censuistis video
facultatem fore ex agris †silani†[2] et agro Campano. aequa-
liter aut sorte agros legionibus adsignari puto oportere.
4   Haec me tibi scribere non prudentia mea hortatur sed
amor in te et cupiditas oti, quod sine te consistere ⟨non⟩
potest. ego, nisi valde necesse fuerit, ex Italia non exce-
dam. legiones armo, paro. spero me non pessimum exercitum habiturum ad omnis casus et impetus hominum. de
exercitu quem Pansa habuit legionem mihi Caesar non
remittit.

     Ad has litteras statim mihi rescribe tuorumque aliquem
mitte, si quid reconditum magis erit meque scire opus esse
putaris.

     VIII⟨I⟩ Kal. Iun. Eporedia.

[1] (*SB, qui* idem *etiam coni.*)
[2] Sullanis ⌐

308

and wary of plots; I can have no greater source of pleasure, nothing more precious, than your life. Only you must be careful that fearing does not give you further cause for fear; and at the same time you should meet the veterans where you can. First, do what they want about the Commission of Ten. Second, with regard to gratuities, you should propose, if you think fit, that the lands of the veteran soldiers who were with Antony be assigned them by the two of us, and, as regards cash, say that the Senate will take time to decide in the light of the financial situation. It occurs to me that the four legions for whom the Senate has voted grants of land can be provided for out of the * lands and the Campanian land. I think the lands should be assigned to the legions in equal portions, or by lot.

It is not my perspicacity that impels me to write all this, but my affection for you and my desire for public tranquillity, which cannot subsist without you. Unless it is really necessary, I shall not leave Italy. I am arming and equipping my troops. I hope I shall have a not wholly contemptible army to meet all contingencies and attacks. Caesar is not sending me back the legion from Pansa's army.

Please answer this letter at once, and send one of your own people if there is anything especially confidential which you think I ought to know.

24 May, from Eporedia.

402 (XI.23)

Scr. Eporediae VIII *Kal. Iun. an. 43*

D. BRUTUS S. D. M. CICERONI

1 Nos hic valemus recte et quo melius valeamus operam
dabimus. Lepidus commode [de]¹ nobis sentire videtur.
omni timore deposito debemus libere rei publicae consulere. quod si omnia essent aliena, tamen tribus tantis exercitibus propriis rei publicae valentibus magnum animum
habere debebas; quem et semper habuisti et nunc Fortuna
2 adiuvante augere potes. quae tibi superioribus litteris mea
manu scripsi terrendi tui causa homines loquuntur. si frenum momorderis, peream si te omnes quot sunt conantem
loqui ferre poterint.

Ego, tibi ut antea scripsi, dum mihi a te litterae veniant,
in Italia morabor.

VIII Kal. Iun. Eporedia.

403 (X.25)

Scr. Romae m. Mai. an. 43

CICERO S. D. FURNIO

1 Si interest, id quod homines arbitrantur, rei publicae
te, ut instituisti atque fecisti, navare operam rebusque

¹ *(Man.)*

---

¹ Those of Decimus himself, Plancus, and Octavian.

402 (XI.23)
D. BRUTUS TO CICERO

Eporedia, 25 May 43

From D. Brutus to M. Cicero greetings.

We are in good shape here and shall try to be in better. Lepidus' sentiments seem to me satisfactory. We must put all fear aside and take measures for the public interest without inhibition. But even if everything were against us, with three such large and powerful armies[1] dedicated to the public service you ought to keep your spirit high—high you have always kept it, and now with Fortune's help you can raise it higher. As for what I wrote in my own hand in my earlier letter, people talk like this to scare you. Just take the bit between your teeth, and I'll be hanged if the whole pack of them will be able to stand against you when you open your mouth.[2]

As I wrote to you in my earlier letter, I shall stay in Italy till I hear from you.

25 May, from Eporedia.

403 (X.25)
CICERO TO FURNIUS

Rome, May 43

From Cicero to Furnius greetings.

If, as is generally supposed, it is in the public interest for you to continue as you have begun, still taking an active part in the vitally important operations directed to stamp-

---

[2] For the singular infelicity of the metaphor Decimus is responsible.

maximis quae ad exstinguendas reliquias belli pertinent
interesse, nihil videris melius neque laudabilius neque honestius facere posse, istamque operam tuam, navitatem,
animum in rem publicam celeritati praeturae anteponendam censeo. nolo enim te ignorare quantam laudem
consecutus sis; mihi crede, proximam Planco, idque ipsius
Planci testimonio, praeterea fama sententiaque omnium.
2 quam ob rem, si quid operis tibi etiam nunc restat, id maximo opere censeo persequendum; quid enim honestius, aut
quid honesto anteponendum? sin autem satis factum
officio, rei publicae satis factum putas, celeriter ad comitia,
quoniam mature futura sunt, veniendum censeo, dum
modo ne haec ambitiosa festinatio aliquid imminuat eius
gloriae quam consecuti sumus. multi clarissimi viri, cum
rei publicae darent operam, annum petitionis suae non
obierunt. quod eo facilius nobis est quod non est annus hic
tibi destinatus, ut, si aedilis fuisses, post biennium tuus
annus esset. nunc nihil praetermittere videbere usitati et
quasi legitimi temporis ad petendum. video autem Planco
consule, etsi etiam sine eo rationes expeditas haberes,
tamen splendidiorem petitionem tuam, si modo ista ex
sententia confecta essent.

---

1 As often, Cicero politely affects to consider his correspondent's affairs as his own.

2 Literally 'the year of their candidature,' i.e. in which they
attained the qualifying age for this or that office. Since Furnius
had been Tribune in 50 he will already have been past the normal
minimum age for praetorian candidacy.

3 In common parlance (though not technically) candidacy began long before the official declaration (*professio*). If Furnius

ing out the remnants of the war, I think that no course
could be better or redound more to your credit and honour; and I consider that your activity, energy, and patriotic
spirit should be of more account than a swift attainment of
the Praetorship. For I would not have you unaware how
much credit you have already won. Believe me, it is second
only to Plancus', and that by Plancus' own testimony as
well as by report and universal opinion. So if you have any
further work to do, I consider it most important that you
should go ahead with it. Surely that is the most honourable
course, and surely honour must come first. On the other
hand, if you think you have done enough for duty and
enough for your country, I advise you to lose no time in returning for the elections, since they will be held early; always provided that such haste in the furtherance of your
career does not in any degree detract from the reputation
we[1] have won. Many famous men, while engaged on public
service, have not stood for office in the normal year.[2] That
course is all the easier for us because this is not your appointed year in the way that, had you been Aedile, your
time would have come two years later. As things stand, you
will be looked upon as not letting slip any of the customary,
quasi-legal period of candidacy.[3] It also occurs to me that
your candidacy will have more éclat when Plancus is Consul (though you would have nothing to worry about even
without him), if only matters in Gaul have been brought to
a satisfactory conclusion.

stood in 43 he would be a candidate in this customary sense for a
much shorter time than was normal, whereas if he waited till the
following year he would be regarded as giving himself the benefit
of the full period.

3   Omnino plura me scribere, cum tuum tantum consilium iudiciumque sit, non ita necesse arbitrabar; sed tamen sententiam meam tibi ignotam esse nolebam. cuius
est haec summa, ut omnia te metiri dignitate malim quam
ambitione maioremque fructum ponere in perpetuitate
laudis quam in celeritate praeturae. haec eadem locutus
sum domi meae adhibito Quinto, fratre meo, et Caecina et
Calvisio, studiosissimis tui, cum Dardanus, libertus tuus,
interesset. omnibus probari videbatur oratio mea; sed tu
optime iudicabis.

404 (X.16)

Scr. Romae c. VIII *Kal. Iun. an.* 43

CICERO PLANCO

1   Nihil post hominum memoriam gloriosius, nihil gratius, ne tempore quidem ipso opportunius accidere vidi
quam tuas, Plance, litteras. redditae sunt enim frequenti
senatu Cornuto, cum is frigidas sane et inconstantis reci-
tasset litteras Lepidi. sub eas statim recitatae sunt tuae non
sine magnis quidem clamoribus. cum rebus enim ipsis
essent et studiis beneficiisque in re‹m› publicam gratissimae, tum erant gravissimis verbis ac sententiis. flagitare
senatus institit Cornutum ut referret statim de tuis litteris.
ille se considerare velle. cum ei magnum convicium fieret

---

4 Surely to be distinguished from the obnoxious C. Calvisius
Sabinus.

1 Its contents will have corresponded to Letter 390.

To be sure, I do not think there is much need for me to write at length to a man of such sense and judgement as yourself. However, I would not have you ignorant of my opinion, the long and short of which is that I should like you in all things to make prestige rather than ambition for office your criterion, and to look for reward in lasting reputation rather than swift attainment of the Praetorship. I asked your very good friends my brother Quintus, Caecina, and Calvisius[4] to my house, and said the same to them in the presence of your freedman Dardanus. My words seemed to find favour with them all. But you will judge best.

404 (X.16)
CICERO TO PLANCUS

Rome, ca. 25 May 43

From Cicero to Plancus.

I know of nothing in history, my dear Plancus, more glorious than your dispatch.[1] No happening in my experience has ever been more welcome, more fortunate too in its moment. It was delivered to Cornutus during a well-attended meeting of the Senate, after he had read out a distinctly cold, shuffling communication from Lepidus. Yours was read immediately after, and to loud cheers. The facts themselves and your patriotic zeal and services gave the most lively satisfaction; and furthermore, words and sentiments alike were deeply impressive. The House began to importune Cornutus for an immediate debate on your dispatch. He said he wanted time to consider. There was a great outcry from the entire House, and finally five

cuncto a senatu, quinque tribuni pl. rettulerunt. Servilius
rogatus rem distulit. ego eam sententiam dixi cui sunt
adsensi ad unum. ea quae fuerit ex senatus consulto cognosces.

2   Tu, quamquam consilio non eges, vel abundas potius,
tamen hoc animo esse debes ut nihil huc reicias neve in
rebus tam subitis tamque angustis a senatu consilium petendum putes, ipse tibi sis senatus; quocumque te ratio rei
publicae ducet, sequare; cures ut ante factum aliquid a te
egregium audiamus quam futurum putarimus. illud tibi
promitto, quicquid erit a te factum, id senatum non modo
ut fideliter sed etiam ut sapienter factum comprobaturum.

405 (XII.14)

Scr. Pergae IV *Kal. Iun. an. 43*

LENTULUS CICERONI SUO S. P. D.

1   Cum Brutum nostrum convenissem eumque tardius in
Asiam venturum animadverterem, in Asiam redii, ut reliquias mei laboris colligerem et pecuniam quam primum
Romam mitterem. interim cognovi in Lycia esse classem
Dolabellae ampliusque centum navis onerarias, in quas
exercitus eius imponi posset, idque Dolabellam ea mente
comparasse ut, si Syriae spes eum frustrata esset, conscen-
deret in navis et Italiam peteret seque cum Antoniis et reliquis latronibus coniungeret.

---

[1] I.e. tax collecting.

Tribunes put the question. Servilius, when called upon, proposed an adjournment. I put forward a motion which received unanimous assent. You will learn its terms from the Senate's decree.

You stand in no need of counsel, or rather you have it in abundance. Still, you should make up your mind not to refer any decision to Rome and not to consider yourself obliged to seek the Senate's advice in a situation so fraught with surprises and with so little margin for error. You must be your own Senate, and follow wherever the public interest leads you. Let us hear of some fine achievement on your part before we think that it is coming. One thing I promise you: whatever you do will meet with the Senate's approval as not only loyally, but wisely done.

405 (XII.14)

LENTULUS SPINTHER THE YOUNGER TO CICERO

Perge, 29 May 43

Lentulus to his friend Cicero cordial greetings.

After meeting our friend Brutus and perceiving that his arrival in Asia was likely to be somewhat delayed, I returned to the province to tie up the loose ends of my work[1] and dispatch the money to Rome at the earliest possible moment. Meanwhile I learned that Dolabella's fleet was in Lycia together with more than a hundred freighters in which his army might be embarked. He was reported to have got them together in case his hopes of Syria were disappointed, with a view to going aboard and making for Italy, there to join forces with the Antonii and the other bandits.

317

Cuius rei tanto in timore fui ut omnibus rebus relictis cum paucioribus et minoribus navibus ad illas ire conatus 2 sim. quae res, si a Rhodiis non essem interpellatus, fortasse tota sublata esset, tamen magna ex parte profligata est, quoniam quidem classis dissipata est adventus nostri timore, milites ducesque effugerunt, onerariae omnes ad unam a nobis sunt exceptae. certe, quod maxime timui, videor esse consecutus ut non possit Dolabella in Italiam pervenire nec suis sociis firmatis durius vobis efficere negotium.

3 Rhodii nos et rem publicam quam valde spreverint[1] ex litteris quas publice misi cognosces. et quidem multo parcius scripsi quam re vera furere eos inveni. quod vero aliquid de iis scripsi mirari noli; mira est eorum amentia. nec me meae ullae privatim iniuriae umquam ⟨moverunt⟩;[2] malus animus eorum in nostra⟨m⟩ salute⟨m⟩, cupiditas partium aliarum, perseverantia in contemptione optimi cuiusque ferenda mihi non fuit. nec tamen omnis perditos esse puto. sed idem illi qui tum fugientem patrem meum, qui L. Lentulum, qui Pompeium, qui ceteros viros clarissimos non receperunt, idem tamquam aliquo fato et nunc aut magistratum gerunt aut eos qui sunt in magistratu in sua habent potestate. itaque eadem superbia in pravitate utuntur. quorum improbitatem aliquando retundi et non perpetua[3] impunitate augeri non solum utile est rei publicae nostrae sed etiam necessarium.

4 De nostra dignitate velim tibi, ut semper, curae sit et,

---

[1] desperaverint *(Kleyn)*
[2] *SB: ante* umq- ⟨ς⟩)
[3] putati *vel* -ari *(Watt)*

LETTER 405 (XII.14)

This news alarmed me so much that I dropped all else and set out to meet them with a squadron of vessels inferior in number and size. Had I not been obstructed by the Rhodians, perhaps the whole business would be out of the way. Even as it is, the back of it has been nearly broken. Their fleet scattered in alarm at my coming, commanders and men took to flight, and all the freighters without exception fell into our hands. I think I can at least say that I have prevented Dolabella from getting to Italy and reinforcing his associates, so as to make your task the harder—which was my principal fear.

The contempt which the Rhodians have displayed for me and for the commonwealth you will see from my official dispatch. Actually I wrote in terms much less emphatic than their infatuation, as I found it, really warranted. That I *did* write something about them you must not be surprised. Their folly is extraordinary. My private injuries have at no time influenced me, but their hostility to our welfare, their partiality to the other side, their obstinate contempt for our leading men, were more than I could tolerate. Not that I regard the whole community as hopelessly depraved. But by a strange fatality the same individuals who formerly refused to admit my father in his flight, and L. Lentulus, Pompey, and other exalted personages likewise, now again either hold magistracies themselves or have the magistrates under their thumb. Accordingly they are behaving with the same arrogant perversity. It is not only desirable in our public interest, it is necessary that their evil disposition should at last be checked and not allowed to wax with impunity.

As for my own standing, I hope you will always make it your concern, and lend your support to anything tending to

quocumque tempore occasionem habueris, et in senatu et
ceteris rebus laudi nostrae suffragere. quoniam consulibus
decreta est Asia et permissum est iis ut, dum ipsi venirent,
darent negotium qui Asiam obtinea[n]t, rogo te petas ab iis
ut hanc dignitatem potissimum nobis tribuant et mihi dent
negotium ut Asiam obtineam dum ipsorum alter uter venit;[4] nam quod hoc properent in magistratu venire aut
exercitum mittere causam non habent. Dolabella enim in
Syria est et, ut tu divina tua mente prospexisti et praedicas-
ti, dum isti veniunt, Cassius eum opprimet. exclusus enim
ab Antiochea Dolabella et in oppugnando male acceptus,
nulla alia confisus urbe, Laodiceam, quae est in Syria ad
mare, se contulit. ibi spero celeriter eum poenas daturum.
nam neque quo refugiat habet neque diutius ibi poterit
tantum exercitum Cassi sustinere. spero etiam confectum
esse iam et oppressum Dolabellam.

5   Qua re non puto Pansam et Hirtium in consulatu pro-
peraturos in provincias exire sed Romae acturos[5] consula-
tum. itaque, si ab iis petieris ut interea nobis procuratio-
nem Asiae dent, spero te posse impetrare. praeterea mihi
promiserunt Pansa et Hirtius coram et absenti mihi scripserunt, Verrioque nostro Pansa adfirmavit se daturum
operam ne in suo consulatu mihi succedatur. ego porro
non me dius fidius cupiditate provinciae produci longius
spatium mihi volo; nam mihi fuit ista provincia plena laboris, periculi, detrimenti. quae ego ne frustra subierim nive,
prius quam reliquias meae diligentiae consequar, decedere cogar valde laboro. nam si potuissem quam exegeram

[4] venerit *Ern.*: veniat *Wes.*
[5] perac- χ

my credit whenever you find occasion, both in the Senate
and in other contexts. Since Asia has been assigned by
decree to the Consuls with licence to appoint a deputy to
govern the province pending their arrival, I would ask you
to request them to confer this distinction upon me rather
than another, and to appoint me as their deputy to govern
Asia until one or other of them arrives. They have no cause
to hurry out here during their term of office or to send an
army. Dolabella is in Syria, and, as you with your prophetic
instinct foresaw and publicly foretold, Cassius will crush
him while these gentlemen are still on their way. Antioch
shut its gates against him and gave him a rough reception
when he tried an assault; so, having no other town he could
rely on, he betook himself to Laodicea on the Syrian coast.
There I trust he will soon be brought to book. He has nowhere to retreat, and he cannot hold out there for long
against an army the size of Cassius'. Indeed I trust that
Dolabella has already been finally crushed.

Thus I do not expect Pansa and Hirtius to leave Rome
and hurry to their provinces during their Consulship, but
rather to serve their term of office in Rome. And so, if you
ask them to put me in charge of Asia in the meantime, I
imagine you can gain your point. Furthermore, Pansa and
Hirtius promised me in person and wrote to me after I left,
and Pansa confirmed to our friend Verrius, that he would
see that I was not relieved during their Consulship. As for
myself, I do assure you that I don't want my tenure extended because I covet provincial office; it has brought me
abundance of work, risk, and financial loss. I *am* much concerned that I shall not have undergone all this for nothing,
nor be compelled to leave before I have reaped the remaining harvest of my efforts. Had I been able to send the

pecuniam universam mittere, postularem ut mihi succederetur. nunc, quod Cassio dedi, quod Treboni morte amisimus, quod etiam crudelitate Dolabellae aut perfidia eorum qui fidem mihi reique publicae non praestiterunt, id consequi et reficere volo. quod aliter non potest fieri nisi spatium habuero. id ut per te consequar velim, ut solet, tibi curae sit.

6 Ego me de re publica puto esse meritum ut non provinciae istius beneficium exspectare debeam sed tantum quantum Cassius et Bruti, non solum illius facti periculique societate sed etiam huius temporis studio et virtute. primus enim ego leges Antonias fregi, primus equitatum Dolabellae ad rem publicam traduxi Cassioque tradidi, primus dilectus habui pro salute omnium contra coniurationem sceleratissimam, solus Cassio et rei publicae Syriam exercitusque qui ibi erant coniunxi; nam nisi ego tantam pecuniam tantaque praesidia et tam celeriter Cassio dedissem, ne ausus quidem esset ire in Syriam, et nunc non minora pericula rei publicae a Dolabella instarent
7 quam ab Antonio. atque haec omnia is feci qui sodalis et familiarissimus Dolabellae eram, coniunctissimus sanguine Antoniis, provinciam quoque illorum beneficio habebam; sed 'πατρίδα ἐμὴν μᾶλλον φιλῶν' omnibus meis bellum primus indixi. haec etsi adhuc non magno opere mihi tulisse fructum animadverto, tamen non despero nec defatigabor permanere non solum in studio libertatis sed etiam

[2] Lentulus was one of several who, though not party to the plot against Caesar, joined the assassins immediately and claimed to have been of their number.

whole of the money I raised, I should be asking to be relieved. As it is, I want to collect and make good the sums I gave Cassius and lost by Trebonius' death, also by Dolabella's ruthlessness or the bad faith of those who broke their word to me and to the commonwealth. This cannot be done unless I have time. I hope you will gain it for me, with your usual solicitude.

I conceive my public deserts to be such that I may legitimately expect not only the favour of this assignment but as much as Cassius and the two Bruti, in virtue both of my association in the great deed and danger[2] and of my current zeal and activity. After all, I was the first to break Antony's enactments, the first to bring Dolabella's cavalry over to the national cause and hand them over to Cassius, the first to levy troops for the defence of the whole community against a criminal conspiracy. I alone brought Syria and the armies there to Cassius' side; for if I had not so promptly furnished Cassius with money and troops on so considerable a scale, he would not even have ventured to go to Syria, and Dolabella would now constitute no less serious a threat to the commonwealth than Antony. And I, who have done all this, was Dolabella's familiar friend and companion, closely related by blood to the Antonii, to whose favour moreover I owed my provincial post. But, 'loving my country more,'[3] I took the lead in declaring war on all those near to me. Although I do not observe that my conduct has so far brought me any very notable return, I do not give up hope, nor shall I grow tired of persevering in zeal for lib-

[3] Perhaps from Euripides' *Erechtheus* (Nauck, p. 918).

323

in labore et periculis. ac tamen,[6] si etiam aliqua gloria iusta
et merita provocabimur senatus et optimi cuiusque officiis,
maiore cum auctoritate apud ceteros erimus et eo plus
prodesse rei publicae poterimus.

8   Filium tuum, ad Brutum cum veni, videre non potui
ideo quod iam in hiberna cum equitibus erat profectus,
sed me dius fidius ea esse eum opinione et tua et ipsius et
in primis mea causa gaudeo. fratris enim loco mihi est qui
ex te natus teque dignus est.

Vale.

D. IIII Kal. Iun. Pergae.

406 (XII.15)

Scr. Pergae IV Kal. Iun. et IV Non. Iun. an. 43

P. LENTULUS P. F. PRO Q. PRO PR. S. D. COSS. PR. TR. PL.
SENATUI POPULO PLEBIQUE ROMANAE

1   S. v. l. ⟨q⟩[1] v. v. b.; e. v.

Scelere Dolabellae oppressa Asia in proximam provinciam Macedoniam praesidiaque rei publicae quae M. Brutus, v. c., tenebat, me contuli et id egi ut per quos celerrime
possent Asia provincia vectigaliaque in vestram potesta-
tem redigerentur. quod cum pertimuisset Dolabella, vas-
tata provincia, correptis vectigalibus, praecipuis[2] civibus

erty and in toil and danger as well. At the same time, if I am challenged to further effort by some just and well-merited distinction through the good offices of the Senate and leading loyalists, I shall carry more weight with others and my power to serve the state will be all the greater.

I was unable to see your son when I visited Brutus, because he had already left for winter quarters with the cavalry. But upon my word I am delighted both for your sake and his, and not least for my own, that he should be so well thought of. As a son of yours, and worthy of you, he is like a brother to me.

Good-bye.

Dispatched 29 May, at Perge.

406 (XII.15)

LENTULUS SPINTHER THE YOUNGER TO THE MAGISTRATES, SENATE, AND PEOPLE

Perge, 29 May and 2 June 43

From P. Lentulus, son of Publius, Proquaestor *pro praetore,* to the Consuls, Praetors, Tribunes of the Plebs, Senate, and People and Plebs of Rome greetings.

I trust you and your children are well, as I am.

After Dolabella's criminal seizure of Asia I made my way to the adjacent province of Macedonia and the national forces under our illustrious fellow citizen, M. Brutus. From there I worked for the restoration of your authority over the province of Asia and its revenues through the agency of those best able to achieve the same with speed. Dolabella took alarm at this prospect, and evacuated the province before troops could be brought

Romanis omnibus crudelissime denudatis ac divenditis, celeriusque Asia excessisset quam eo praesidium adduci potuisset, diutius morari aut exspectare praesidium non necesse habui et quam primum ad meum officium revertendum mihi esse existimavi, ut et reliqua vectigalia exigerem et quam deposui pecuniam colligerem, quidque[3] ex ea correptum esset aut quorum id culpa accidisset cognoscerem quam primum et vos de omni re facerem certiores.

2   Interim cum per insulas in Asiam naviganti mihi nuntiatum est classem Dolabellae in Lycia esse Rhodiosque navis compluris instructas et paratas in aqua habere, cum iis navibus quas aut mecum adduxeram aut comparaverat Patiscus pro q., homo mihi cum familiaritate tum etiam sen‹s›ibus in re publica coniunctissimus, Rhodum deverti[4] confisus auctoritate vestra senatusque consulto quo hostem Dolabellam iudicaratis, foedere quoque quod cum iis M. Marcello Ser. Sulpicio ‹coss.› renovatum erat, quo iuraverant Rhodii eosdem hostis se habituros quos senatus populusque Romanus.

Quae res nos vehementer fefellit. tantum enim afuit ut illorum praesidio nostram firmaremus classem ut etiam a Rhodiis urbe, portu, statione quae extra urbem est, commeatu, aqua denique prohiberentur nostri milites, nos vix ipsi singulis cum navigiolis reciperemur. quam indignitatem deminutionemque maiestatis non solum iuris nostri sed etiam imperi populique Romani idcirco tulimus quod interceptis litteris cognoramus Dolabellam, si desperasset

3 quicquid *(Wes.)*
4 reverti *(Wes.)*

against him, having laid it waste, seized the revenues, and ruthlessly stripped and sold the goods of all outstanding Roman citizens. It appeared to me unnecessary to delay any longer or to wait for troops; and I considered it my duty to return to my post as soon as possible in order to levy the remaining taxes and collect the money I had deposited, also to discover as soon as possible how much of it had been carried off and by whose fault this had occurred, and to inform you of the whole transaction.

Meanwhile, as I was sailing through the islands to Asia, it was reported to me that Dolabella's fleet was in Lycia and that the Rhodians had a number of ships afloat equipped and ready. With a squadron consisting of the vessels which I had brought with me and those collected by Proquaestor Patiscus (an officer with whom I have close ties of political sentiment as well as of personal friendship) I changed course and made for Rhodes. In so doing I relied upon your authority and the Senate's decree pronouncing Dolabella a public enemy, as well as the treaty with Rhodes renewed in the Consulship of M. Marcellus and Servius Sulpicius, under which the people of that island bound themselves to regard as enemies the enemies of the Senate and People of Rome.

I was much deceived in my expectation. So far from our reinforcing our fleet with a Rhodian contingent, our troops were actually refused access to the town, the harbour, and the roadstead outside the town, as also supplies and even water. I myself gained admittance with difficulty, in one little boat on each occasion. I put up with this unseemly treatment and the derogation to the majesty, not merely of my official prerogative, but of the Empire and People of Rome, because an intercepted letter had apprised me that,

de Syria Aegyptoque, quod necesse erat fieri, in navis cum omnibus suis latronibus atque omni pecunia conscendere esse paratum Italiamque petere; idcirco etiam navis onerarias, quarum minor nulla erat duum milium amphorum,[1] contractas in Lycia a classe eius obsideri.

3 Huius rei timore, p. c., percitus iniurias perpeti et cum contumelia etiam nostra omnia prius experiri malui. itaque ad illorum voluntatem introductus in urbem et in senatum eorum, quam diligentissime potui, causam rei publicae egi periculumque omne quod instaret, si ille latro cum suis omnibus navis conscendisset, exposui. Rhodios autem tanta in pravitate animadverti ut omnis firmiores putarent quam bonos, ut hanc concordiam et conspirationem omnium ordinum ad defendendam libertatem propense non crederent esse factam, ut patientiam senatus et optimi cuiusque manere etiam nunc confiderent nec potuisse audere quemquam Dolabellam hostem iudicare, ut denique omnia quae improbi fingebant magis vera existimarent quam quae vere facta erant et a nobis docebantur.

4 Qua mente etiam ante nostrum adventum post Treboni indignissimam caedem ceteraque tot tamque nefaria facinora binae profectae erant ad Dolabellam legationes eorum et quidem novo exemplo, contra leges ipsorum, prohibentibus iis qui tum magistratus gerebant. haec sive timore, ut dictitant, de agris quos in continenti habent sive furore sive potentia paucorum, qui et antea pari contumelia viros clarissimos adfecerant et nunc maximos magistratus gerentes, nullo exemplo neque nostra ex parte

---

[1] About 52.4 tons.

if Dolabella gave up hope of Syria and Egypt (as he must), he was ready to embark with his entire band of ruffians and all his money, and make for Italy; for which purpose he had requisitioned freighters, none of less than 2,000 amphorae,[1] and kept them in Lycia under guard with his fleet.

Alarmed at such a prospect, Fathers Conscript, I preferred to swallow insults and try every means of prevention, even at the cost of my dignity. I was accordingly admitted into their town and Senate in the manner of their choice, and there I pleaded the public cause to the best of my ability, and gave a full exposition of the impending danger, should that bandit embark with all his following. But I found the Rhodians utterly wrongheaded, convinced that preponderance of force lay anywhere but with the honest men, refusing to believe that the present union and concert of all classes for the defence of freedom had come about spontaneously, confident that the apathy of the Senate and its supporters still continued and that nobody could have dared to pronounce Dolabella a public enemy. In short, they gave more credence to every rascally fabrication than to the true facts as presented by myself.

This attitude had been in evidence even before my arrival. After the shocking murder of Trebonius and all his other heinous crimes a couple of Rhodian delegations set out to meet Dolabella—contrary to precedent, moreover, and their own laws, and against the orders of the magistrates then in office. Whether their conduct is due to apprehensions for their possessions on the mainland, as they like to allege, or to mental aberration, or to the domination of a clique who similarly insulted exalted personages on a former occasion and hold the principal offices just at this time, the fact is that, without precedent and with no provo-

‹provocati›[5] neque nostro praesentium neque imminenti Italiae urbique nostrae periculo, si ille parricida cum suis latronibus navibus ex Asia Syriaque expulsus Italiam petisset, mederi, cum facile possent, voluerunt.

5   Non nullis etiam ipsi magistratus veniebant in suspicionem detinuisse nos et demorati esse, dum classis Dolabellae certior fieret de adventu nostro. quam suspicionem consecutae res aliquot auxerunt, maxime quod subito ex Lycia Sex. Marius et C. Titius, legati Dolabellae, a classe discesserunt navique longa profugerunt onerariis relictis, in quibus colligendis non minimum temporis laborisque consumpserant. itaque cum ab Rhodo cum iis quas habueramus navibus in Lyciam venissemus, navis onerarias recepimus dominisque restituimus idemque, quod maxime verebamur, ne posset Dolabella cum suis latronibus in Italiam venire, timere desiimus; classem fugientem persecuti sumus usque Sidam, quae extrema regio est provinciae meae.

6   Ibi cognovi partem navium Dolabellae diffugisse, reliquas Syriam Cyprumque petisse. quibus disiectis, cum scirem C. Cassi, singularis civis et ducis, classem maximam fore praesto in Syria, ad meum officium reverti, daboque operam ut meum studium diligentiam vobis, p. c., reique publicae praestem pecuniamque quam maximam potero et quam celerrime cogam omnibusque ‹cum›[6] rationibus ad vos mittam. si percurrero provinciam et cognovero qui nobis et rei publicae fidem praestiterunt in conservanda pecunia a me deposita quique scelere ultro deferentes pecuniam publicam hoc munere societatem facinorum cum

5 *(Wes.)*
6 *(Man.)*

cation on my part, they have refused the assistance they might easily have rendered in my own immediate danger and in that which hung over Italy and Rome, should the traitor and his rebel following have sailed for Italy after his expulsion from Asia and Syria.

In some quarters the magistrates themselves were suspected of having deliberately detained us so as to give time for news of our approach to reach Dolabella's fleet. Some subsequent events lent colour to this suspicion, especially the fact that Dolabella's Legates, Sex. Marius and C. Titius, suddenly left the fleet and took flight from Lycia in a warship, abandoning the freighters which they had collected at no small expense of time and trouble. Accordingly, when I arrived in Lycia from Rhodes with the squadron I already had, I took over the freighters and returned them to their owners. My principal fear, that Dolabella and his ruffians might get to Italy, was thus at an end. I pursued the fleet in its flight as far as Side, which district forms the border of my province.

There I learned that part of Dolabella's ships had fled in various directions and the remainder made for Syria and Cyprus. After their dispersal, knowing that a very large naval force under the orders of our distinguished fellow citizen and general C. Cassius would be to hand in Syria, I returned to my post. I shall take good care that my zeal and diligence shall be forthcoming in your service, Fathers Conscript, and the commonwealth's, and shall collect as large a sum as I can with all possible speed, and forward it to you with complete accounts. As soon as I have made a rapid tour of the province and found out who has kept faith with me and the state in preserving intact the funds I deposited, as well as the villains who went to Dolabella with

Dolabella inierunt, faciam vos certiores. de quibus, si vobis videbitur, si, ut meriti sunt, graviter constitueritis nosque vestra auctoritate firmaveritis, facilius et reliqua exigere vectigalia et exacta servare poterimus. interea quo commodius vectigalia tueri provinciamque ab iniuria defendere possim, praesidium voluntarium necessariumque comparavi.

7   His litteris scriptis milites circiter XXX, quos Dolabella ex Asia conscripserat, ex[7] Syria fugientes in Pamphyliam venerunt. hi nuntiaverunt Dolabellam Antiocheam quae in Syria est venisse, non receptum conatum esse aliquotiens vi introire; repulsum semper esse cum magno suo detrimento; itaque DC circiter amissis, aegris relictis, noctu Antiochea profugisse Laodiceam versus; ea nocte omnis fere Asiaticos milites ab eo discessisse; ex his ad octingentos Antiocheam redisse et se iis tradidisse qui a Cassio relicti urbi illi praeerant, ceteros per ‹A›manum in Ciliciam descendisse, quo ex numero se quoque esse dicebant; Cassium autem cum suis omnibus copiis nuntiatum esse quadridui iter Laodicea afuisse tum cum Dolabella eo tenderet.

Quam ob rem opinione celerius confido sceleratissimum latronem poenas daturum.

IIII Non. Iun. Pergae.

[7] et (*Benedict*)

the public money in their hands as an offering with which to buy their way into a partnership of crime, I shall apprise you accordingly. If of your good pleasure you take drastic measures with the latter as they have deserved and strengthen my position by your authority, it will be easier for me to levy the taxes still due and to keep safe those levied already. In the meanwhile, I have raised a necessary guard on a voluntary basis, thus enabling myself to look after the revenues with less trouble and to defend the province from any harm.

After this dispatch was written, about thirty soldiers recruited by Dolabella in Asia arrived in Pamphylia in flight from Syria. They reported as follows: Dolabella went to Antioch in Syria. Refused admittance, he made several attempts to enter by force, but was repulsed every time with heavy casualties. After losing about 600 men and abandoning his disabled, he fled from Antioch at night in the direction of Laodicea. Almost all his Asiatic troops deserted that night. About 800 of them returned to Antioch and surrendered to the officers left by Cassius in charge of the city, while the rest crossed the Amanus into Cilicia (they themselves claimed to be part of this body). Cassius and his entire force were reported to be four days' march from Laodicea when Dolabella was moving towards the place.

In the light of this news I am confident that the nefarious bandit will be brought to book sooner than was anticipated.

2 June, Perge.

407 (X.20)

Scr. Romae IV *Kal. Iun. an.* 43

CICERO PLANCO

1 Ita erant omnia quae istim adferebantur incerta ut quid ad te scriberem non occurreret. modo enim quae vellemus de Lepido, modo contra nuntiabantur. de te tamen fama constans, nec decipi posse nec vinci. quorum alterius Fortuna partem habet quandam, alterum proprium est prudentiae tuae.

2 Sed accepi litteras a collega tuo datas Id. Mai. in quibus erat te ad se scripsisse a Lepido non recipi Antonium; quod erit certius si tu ad nos idem scripseris. sed minus audes fortasse propter inanem laetitiam litterarum superiorum. verum ut errare, mi Plance, potuisti[1] (quis enim id effugerit?), sic decipi te non potuisse quis non videt? nunc vero etiam [iam][2] erroris causa sublata est; culpa enim illa 'bis ad eundem' vulgari reprehensa proverbio est. sin ut scripsisti ad collegam ita se res habet, omni cura liberati sumus; nec tamen erimus prius quam ita esse tu nos feceris certiores.

3 Mea quidem, ut ad te saepius scripsi, haec sententia est, qui reliquias huius belli oppresserit, eum totius belli confectorem fore; quem te et opto esse et confido futurum. studia mea erga te, quibus certe nulla esse maiora potuerunt, tibi tam grata esse quam ego putavi fore minime

[1] voluisti *(Man.)*
[2] *(Man.)*

[1] Letter 390.

407 (X.20)
CICERO TO PLANCUS

Rome, 29 May 43

From Cicero to Plancus.

Reports coming in from Gaul are so uncertain that what to write to you I cannot tell. Sometimes we get satisfactory accounts of Lepidus, sometimes the reverse. As for yourself, rumour speaks with one tongue to the effect that you can be neither tricked nor overcome. Fortune has some part in the latter; for the former your own prudence is alone responsible.

However, I have received a letter from your colleague dispatched on the Ides of May in which be says you have written to him that Lepidus is not letting Antony in. I shall be better assured of that if you write the same to me. Perhaps you do not much care to do so because the optimism of your earlier letter[1] turned out to be unfounded. My dear Plancus, you could make a mistake like everybody else, but anyone can see that you were not to be tricked. But now there can be no excuse even for a mistake. There's a common proverb scolding people who trip twice over the same stone. If, however, the fact is as you have written to your colleague, then all our worries are over; but they will not be until you have told us that it is so.

My view is, as I have often told you, that the man who crushes its remnants will be the winner of the entire war. I pray you are that man, and believe you will be. That you appreciate my efforts on your behalf (which certainly could not have been greater) as highly as I expected you would does not in the least surprise me, but makes me very

miror vehementerque laetor. quae quidem tu, si recte istic erit, maiora et graviora cognosces.

IIII Kal. Iun.

408 (X.35)

Scr. a Ponte Argenteo III Kal. Iun. an. 43

M. LEPIDUS IMP. ITER. PONT. MAX. S. D. PR. TR. PL. SENATUI POPULO PLEBIQUE ROMANAE

1   Si v. liberique vestri v. b.; e. e. q. v.

Deos hominesque testor, p. c., qua mente et quo animo semper in rem publicam fuerim et quam nihil antiquius communi salute ac libertate iudicarim. quod vobis brevi probassem, nisi mihi Fortuna proprium consilium extorsisset. nam exercitus cunctus consuetudine⟨m⟩ sua⟨m⟩ in civibus conservandis communique pace seditione facta retinuit meque tantae multitudinis civium Romanorum salutis atque incolumitatis causam suscipere, ut vere dicam, coegit.

2   In qua re ego vos, p. c., oro atque obsecro ut privatis offensionibus omissis summae rei publicae consulatis neve misericordiam nostram exercitusque nostri in civili dissensione sceleris loco ponatis. quod si salutis omnium ac dignitatis rationem habueritis, melius et vobis et rei publicae consuletis.

D. III Kal. ⟨Iun.⟩[1] a Ponte Argenteo.

[1] *(Man.)*

happy. If all goes well in your quarter, you will find them greater and more effective.

29 May.

408 (X.35)

LEPIDUS TO THE MAGISTRATES, SENATE, AND PEOPLE

Pons Argenteus, 30 May 43

M. Lepidus, Imperator for the second time, Pontifex Maximus, to the Praetors, Tribunes of the Plebs, Senate, and People and Plebs of Rome greetings.

I trust you and your children are well, as I am and my army.

I call Gods and men to witness, Fathers Conscript, how my heart and mind have ever been disposed towards the commonwealth, how in my eyes nothing has taken precedence of the general welfare and freedom. Of this I should shortly have given you proof, had not Fortune wrested my decision out of my hands. My entire army, faithful to its inveterate tendency to conserve Roman lives and the general peace, has mutinied; and, truth to tell, has compelled me to champion the preservation in life and estate of so vast a number of Roman citizens.

Herein, Fathers Conscript, I beg and implore you to put private quarrels aside and to consult the supreme interests of the commonwealth. Do not treat the compassion shown by myself and my army in a conflict between fellow countrymen as a crime. If you take account of the welfare and dignity of all, you will better consult your own interests and those of the state.

Dispatched 30 May from Pons Argenteus.

409 (X.33)

Scr. Cordubae parte priore m. Iun. an. 43

POLLIO CICERONI S.P.

S. v. b.; e. e. q. v.

1   Quo tardius certior fierem de proeliis apud Mutinam factis Lepidus effecit, qui meos tabellarios novem dies retinuit; tametsi tantam calamitatem rei publicae quam tardissime audire optandum est, sed illis qui prodesse nihil possunt neque mederi. atque utinam eodem senatus consulto quo Plancum et Lepidum in Italiam arcessistis me quoque iussissetis venire! profecto non accepisset res publica hoc vulnus. quo si qui laetantur in praesentia quia videntur et duces et veterani Caesaris partium interisse, tamen postmodo necesse est doleant cum vastitatem Italiae respexerint. nam et robur et suboles militum interiit, si quidem quae nuntiantur ulla ex parte vera sunt.

2   Neque ego non videbam quanto usui rei publicae essem futurus si ad Lepidum venissem. omnem enim cunctationem eius discussissem, praesertim adiutore Planco. sed scribenti ad me eius modi litteras quas leges et contionibus videlicet quas Narbone habuisse dicitur similis palparer necesse erat si vellem commeatus per provinciam eius iter faciens habere. praeterea verebar ne, si ante quam ego incepta perficerem proelium confectum esset, pium consilium meum raperent in contrariam partem obtrectatores mei propter amicitiam quae mihi cum Antonio, non maior tamen quam Planco, fuit.

409 (X.33)
POLLIO TO CICERO

Corduba, early June 43

From Pollio to Cicero best greetings.

I trust you are well, as I am and my army.

News of the battles at Mutina reached me later than it should thanks to Lepidus, who held up my couriers for nine days; albeit, it is desirable to hear of so grievous a public calamity as late as may be; that is to say, for those who can do nothing to help or remedy. I only wish you and your colleagues had ordered me back to Italy in the same decree in which you summoned Plancus and Lepidus. Surely the commonwealth would not then have suffered this blow. Some may be rejoicing at the moment, because the leaders and veterans of Caesar's party appear to have perished, but they must needs be sorry ere long, when they contemplate the desolation of Italy. For the flower of our soldiers, present and to come, has perished, if there is any truth in the reports.

I did not fail to realize how useful I could have been to the commonwealth if I had joined Lepidus. I should have dispelled all his hesitation, especially with Plancus to help me. But when he wrote me letters of the kind you will read, similar no doubt to the speeches which he is said to have delivered at Narbo, I had to stroke him the right way if I wanted to get provisions on my way through his province. I was also afraid that if the decisive battle took place before I had completed my intention, detractors of mine might put the opposite construction on my patriotic purpose, because of my former friendship with Antony—though no closer than Plancus had with him.

339

3   Itaque a Gadibus mense Aprili binis tabellariis in duas navis impositis et tibi et consulibus et Octaviano scripsi ut me faceretis certiorem quonam modo plurimum possem prodesse rei publicae. sed, ut rationem ineo, quo die proelium Pansa commisit eodem a Gadibus naves profectae sunt; nulla enim post hiemem fuit ante eam diem navigatio. et hercules longe remotus ab omni suspicione futuri civilis tumultus penitus in Lusitania legiones in hibernis collocaram. ita porro festinavit uterque confligere tamquam nihil peius timerent quam ne sine maximo rei publicae detrimento bellum componeretur. sed si properandum fuit, nihil non summi ducis consilio gessisse Hirtium video.

4   Nunc haec mihi scribuntur ex Gallia Lepidi et nuntiantur: Pansae exercitum concisum esse, Pansam ex vulneribus mortuum, eodem proelio Martiam legionem interisse et L. Fabatum et C. Peducaeum et D. Carfulenum; Hirtino[1] autem proelio et quartam legionem et omnis peraeque Antoni caesas, item Hirti, quartam vero, cum castra quoque Antoni cepisset, a quinta legione concisam esse; ibi Hirtium quoque perisse et Pontium Aquilam; dici etiam Octavianum cecidisse (quae si, quod di prohibeant, vera sunt, non mediocriter doleo); Antonium turpiter Mutinae obsessionem reliquisse, sed habere equitum ⟨v̄⟩,[2] legiones sub signis armatas tris et P. Bagienni unam, inermis bene multos; Ventidium quoque se cum legione VII, VIII, VIIII coniunxisse; si nihil in Lepido spei sit, descensurum ad extrema et non modo nationes sed etiam servitia conci-

---

[1] Hirtiano ⟨   [2] (Man.)

[1] Narbonensis.

Accordingly, in April I dispatched two couriers in two ships from Gades with letters to yourself, to the Consuls, and to Octavian, asking to be informed how I could best help the commonwealth. But according to my reckoning the ship left Gades on the same day that Pansa joined battle; for before that day there had been no navigation since last winter. Far removed as I certainly was from any suspicion of a coming civil upheaval, I had stationed my legions in winter quarters in the interior of Lusitania. And both sides were in such a hurry to come to grips, one might think their worst fear was of a settlement to the war without maximum loss to the commonwealth. However, if haste was called for, Hirtius evidently showed the highest qualities of generalship throughout.

According to letters and reports coming in to me from Lepidus' part of Gaul,[1] Pansa's army has been cut to pieces, Pansa is dead of his wounds, the Martian Legion has been destroyed in the same battle together with L. Fabatus, C. Peducaeus, and D. Carfulenus. In Hirtius' battle I hear that the Fourth Legion and all Antony's legions alike have suffered severely, as also Hirtius', and that the Fourth was cut to pieces by the Fifth after capturing Antony's camp; that Hirtius too lost his life there, and Pontius Aquila; and that Octavian also is said to have fallen. If these reports are true, which heaven forfend, I am sorry indeed. I further hear that Antony has ignominiously abandoned the siege of Mutina, but that he has 5,000 horse and three well-armed legions under the standards and one under P. Bagiennus, along with a considerable number of unarmed men; that Ventidius too has joined him with the Seventh, Eighth, and Ninth Legions; that, if he has nothing to hope for from Lepidus, he will go to all lengths and stir up the

taturum; Parmam direptam; L. Antonium Alpis occupasse.

5   Quae si vera sunt, nemini nostrum cessandum est nec exspectandum quid decernat senatus. res enim cogit huic tanto incendio succurrere omnis qui aut imperium aut nomen denique populi Romani salvum volunt esse. Brutum enim cohortis xvii et duas non frequentis tironum legiones, quas conscripserat Antonius, habere audio; neque tamen dubito quin omnes qui supersint de Hirti exercitu confluant ad eum. nam in dilectu non multum spei puto esse, praesertim cum nihil sit periculosius quam spatium confirmandi sese Antonio dari. anni autem tempus libertatem maiorem mihi dat propterea quia frumenta aut in agris aut in villis sunt. itaque proximis litteris consilium meum expedietur. nam neque deesse neque superesse rei publicae volo. maxime tamen doleo adeo et longo et infesto itinere ad me veniri ut die quadragesimo post aut ultra etiam quam facta sunt omnia nuntientur.

410 (XI.26)

Scr. in castris in Alpibus III *Non. Iun. an. 43*

D. BRUTUS S. D. M. CICERONI

    Maximo meo dolore hoc solacio utor quod intellegunt homines non sine causa me timuisse ista quae acciderunt. deliberent utrum traiciant legiones ex Africa necne et ex

---

    [2] I.e. D. Brutus.   [3] That Antony's recruits joined D. Brutus before or after the flight from Mutina is otherwise unrecorded and inherently unlikely. But after Pansa's death three of his recruited legions *were* taken over by Brutus. Pollio's report apparently had the two confused.

native tribes, even the slaves; that Parma has been sacked; and that L. Antonius has occupied the Alps.

If these reports are true, then none of us must lose time or wait for what the Senate decrees. The nature of the case compels all who wish the survival of the empire, or even the very name, of the Roman People to rush to quench the devouring flames. I hear that Brutus[2] has seventeen cohorts and two legions of recruits, not up to strength, which Antony had raised;[3] though I make no doubt that all the survivors of Hirtius' army will flock to join him. I see little hope in a levy, especially as the most dangerous thing of all would be to give Antony time to recover. The season of the year, moreover, gives me greater freedom of action because the grain is now in the fields or on the farms. So I shall explain my plans in my next letter. I do not wish to fail the commonwealth, nor to survive it. But what irks me most is that the distance to my whereabouts is so long and the route so unsafe that all news reaches me forty days, if not more, after it has happened.

410 (XI.26)

D. BRUTUS TO CICERO

Camp in the Alps, 3 June 43

From D. Brutus to M. Cicero greetings.

Greatly as I am distressed by what has happened, I take some comfort in the general realization that my fears of it were not idle. Let them deliberate whether to bring over the legions from Africa and Sardinia or not, whether to

Sardinia, et Brutum accersant necne, et mihi stipendium dent an decernant![1] ad senatum litteras misi. crede mihi, nisi ista omnia fiunt quem ad modum scribo, magnum nos omnis adituros periculum. rogo te, videte quibus hominibus negotium detis qui ad me legiones adducant. et fide opus est et celeritate.

III Non. Iun. ex castris.

411 (XI.21)

Scr. Romae prid. Non. Iun. an. 43

M. CICERO S. D. D. BRUTO IMP. COS. DESIG.

1   Di isti Segulio male faciant, homini nequissimo omnium qui sunt, qui fuerunt, qui futuri sunt! quid? tu illum tecum solum aut cum Caesare? qui neminem praetermiserit quicum loqui potuerit cui non eadem ista dixerit. te tamen, mi Brute, sic amo ut debeo quod istud quicquid esset nugarum me scire voluisti. signum enim magnum amoris dedisti.

2   Nam quod idem Segulius veteranos queri quod tu et Caesar in decem viris non essetis, utinam ne ego quidem essem! quid enim molestius? sed tamen, cum ego sensissem de iis qui exercitus haberent sententiam ferri oportere, idem illi qui solent reclamarunt. itaque excepti etiam estis, me vehementer repugnante. quocirca Segulium neglegamus; qui res novas quaerit, non quo veterem come-

---

[1] denegent *coni. SB* (*pro* dent *Mend.*)

---

[1] Cf. Letter 401.1.

summon Brutus or not, whether to give me pay for my troops or decree it! I am sending a dispatch to the Senate. Believe me unless all these steps are taken as I say, we shall all find ourselves in great danger. I beg of you, let the Senate be careful in choosing the men for the job of conducting the legions to me. Both loyalty and speed are needful.

3 June, from camp.

411 (XI.21)
CICERO TO D. BRUTUS

Rome, 4 June 43

From M. Cicero to D. Brutus, Imperator, Consul-Elect, greetings.

Confound that Segulius,[1] the most arrant scoundrel alive or dead or yet to be! Do you really suppose that he talks only to you or to Caesar? He has told the same tale to every person he could find to listen to him. But I am properly grateful to you, my dear Brutus, for wanting me to know of this piece of tittle-tattle, such as it is—a notable mark of your affection.

As for this same Segulius' story that the veterans are grumbling because you and Caesar are not on the Commission of Ten, I only wish *I* was not on it! A most tiresome business! However, I did move that a vote should be taken on generals in command of armies, but was met by an outcry from the usual quarters. So you two were actually excluded specifically, against my strong opposition. Let us then pay no attention to Segulius. He's out for news and a new deal—not that he squandered his share (which was

derit (nullam enim habuit), sed hanc ipsam recentem novam devoravit.

3 Quod autem scribis te, quod pro te ipso non facias, id pro me ⟨facere⟩,[1] ut de me timeas aliquid, omni te, vir optime mihique carissime, Brute, de me metu libero. ego enim quae provideri poterunt non fallar in iis; quae cautionem non habebunt de iis non ita valde laboro. sim enim impudens si plus postulem quam homini a Rerum Natura tribui potest.

4 Quod mihi praecipis ut caveam ne timendo magis timere cogar, et sapienter et amicissime praecipis, sed velim tibi persuadeas, cum te constet excellere hoc genere virtutis ut numquam extimescas, numquam perturbere, me huic tuae virtuti proxime accedere. quam ob rem nec metuo quicquam et cavebo omnia. sed vide ne tua iam, mi Brute, culpa futura sit si ego quicquam timeam. tuis enim opibus et consulatu tuo, etiam si timidi essemus, tamen omnem timorem abiceremus, praesertim cum persuasum omnibus esset mihique maxime a te nos unice diligi.

5 Consiliis tuis, quae scribis de quattuor legionibus deque agris adsignandis ab utroque[2] vestrum, vehementer adsentior. itaque cum quidam de collegis nostris agrariam curationem ligurrirent, disturbavi rem totamque vobis[3] integram reservavi.

Si quid erit occultius et, ut scribis, reconditum, meo-

1 ⊊*
2 utrisque (*Lamb.*)
3 nobis

nil) in the old deal, but he *has* wolfed down what he got out of this latest new one![2]

You say that you have some fears on my account, feeling for me what you do not feel for yourself. Excellent and dearest Brutus, I hereby absolve you of all fear concerning me. As regards foreseeable dangers, I shall not be caught napping; and as for those which will not admit of precaution, I am not worrying so very much about them. After all, I should be presumptuous if I claimed more than can be granted to humanity by the Nature of Things.

You advise me to have a care lest fearing give me further cause for fear, a wise and friendly precept. But as you are generally admitted to be an outstanding example of the courage that is never frightened or discomposed, I should like you to believe that I am not far your inferior in this quality. Therefore I fear nothing and shall beware of everything. But you must take care, my dear Brutus, that the fault be not yours in future, if I should have any fears. Even if I were a timid man, I should cast all fear aside when I thought of your resources and your Consulship, especially as everyone (and I myself above all) is persuaded that you have a singular regard for me.

I emphatically agree with your advice in what you write about the four legions and the assignment of lands by the two of you. For that reason, when certain of my colleagues were nibbling at the agrarian business, I thwarted it and reserved the whole matter for your two selves.

If anything of a secret and, as you say, 'recondite' nature

[2] I.e. Segulius, a poor man before the Civil War, had profited from the Caesarian victory, but squandered his gains. See my Commentary.

rum aliquem mittam, quo fidelius ad te litterae perferan-
tur.

Prid. Non. Iun.

412 (XI.24)

Scr. Romae VIII *Id. Iun. an. 43*

M. CICERO S. D. D. BRUTO IMP. COS. DESIG.

1   Narro tibi: antea subirascebar brevitati tuarum litterarum, nunc mihi loquax esse videor. te igitur imitabor.
quam multa quam paucis! te recte valere operamque dare
ut cottidie melius; Lepidum commode sentire; tribus exercitibus quidvis nos oportere confidere. si timidus essem,
tamen ista epistula mi omnem metum abstersisses. sed ut
mones, frenum momordi. etenim, qui te incluso omnem
spem habuerim in te, quid nunc putas? cupio iam vigiliam
meam, Brute, tibi tradere, sed ita ut ne desim constantiae
meae.

2   Quod scribis in Italia te moraturum dum tibi litterae
meae veniant, si per hostem licet, non erraris; multa enim
Romae. sin[1] adventu tuo bellum confici potest, nihil sit
antiquius. pecunia expeditissima quae erat tibi decreta est.
habes amantissimum Servium. nos non desumus.

VIII Id. Iun.

[1] si in *(Man.)*

---

[1] In Letter 402.
[2] Ser. Sulpicius Rufus, son of the Consul of 51. He was D.
Brutus' cousin.

arises, I shall send you a letter by one of my own people for more trustworthy delivery.

4 June.

412 (XI.24)
CICERO TO D. BRUTUS

Rome, 6 June 43

From M. Cicero to D. Brutus, Imperator, Consul-Elect, greetings.

Take note: I used to be a trifle irritated by the brevity of your letters. Now I look upon myself as a chatterbox, so I shall follow your example. How much you have said in a few words![1]—that you are in good shape and trying to be in better every day, that Lepidus' sentiments are satisfactory, that we ought to place unlimited confidence in the three armies. Even if I were a timid man, this epistle of yours would have swept all apprehensions out of my mind; but, as you advise, I have taken the bit between my teeth. After all, I placed my entire hopes in you when you were a prisoner, so you can imagine my feelings now. I long to hand over my patrol to you, dear sir, but only if I can do so while remaining true to my own resolution.

You say you will stay in Italy until you hear from me, if the enemy allows. You will not be doing wrong, for there is much afoot in Rome. But if the war can be finished by your advent, let nothing come before that. You have been decreed the funds most immediately available. Servius[2] is devoted to you. I am not behind.

6 June.

413 (XI.14)

Scr. Romae VII *Id. Iun. an. 43*

M. CICERO D. BRUTO COS. DESIG. S. D.

1   Mirabiliter, mi Brute, laetor mea consilia measque sententias a te probari de decem viris, de ornando adulescente. sed quid refert? mihi crede, homini non ⟨parum⟩[1]
glorioso, plane iam, Brute, frigeo. ὄργανον enim erat
meum senatus; id iam est dissolutum. tantam spem attulerat exploratae victoriae tua praeclara Mutina eruptio, fuga
Antoni conciso exercitu ut omnium animi relaxati sint
meaeque illae vehementes contentiones tamquam σκια-
μαχίαι esse videantur.

2   Sed ut ad rem redeam, legionem Martiam et quartam
negant qui illas norunt ulla condicione ad te posse perduci.
pecuniae quam desideras ratio potest haberi eaque habe-
bitur. de Bruto arcessendo Caesareque ad Italiae praesidium tenendo valde tibi adsentior. sed, ut scribis, habes
obtrectatores; quos equidem facillime sustineo, sed impe-
diunt tamen. ex Africa legiones exspectantur.

3   Sed bellum istuc renatum mirantur homines. nihil tam
praeter spem umquam; nam die tuo natali victoria nuntiata in multa saecula videbamus rem publicam liberatam. hi
novi timores retexunt superiora. scripsisti autem ad me
litteris iis quas Id. Mai. dedisti modo te accepisse a Planco
litteras non recipi Antonium a Lepido.[2] id si ita est, omnia

¹ *(SB)*

---

[1] Octavian. D. Brutus' letter to which Cicero refers is lost.
[2] They put themselves under Octavian.

413 (XI.14)
CICERO TO D. BRUTUS

Rome, 7 June 43

From M. Cicero to D. Brutus, Consul-Elect, greetings.

I am wholeheartedly delighted, my dear Brutus, that you approve of my views and proposals on the Commission of Ten and the honours for the young man.[1] And yet, what is the use? Believe me, Brutus, as one not given to self-depreciation, I am a spent force. The Senate was my right hand, and it has lost its cunning. Your splendid breakout from Mutina and Antony's flight with his army cut to pieces had brought such high hopes of assured victory that there was a universal slackening of energy, and those vehement harangues of mine look like so much shadowboxing.

However, to come back to the business in hand, those who know the Martian and Fourth Legions say that they cannot be brought to join you on any terms.[2] The money you require can be looked to, and will be. As regards sending for Brutus and keeping Caesar to protect Italy, I entirely agree with you. But, as you say, you have your detractors—I withstand them very easily, but still they hold things up. The legions from Africa are expected.

But there is general amazement at the revival of the war in the north. Nothing was ever so unexpected. When the victory was announced on your birthday,[3] we looked to the reestablishment of freedom for centuries to come. Now these new alarms undo all that was done. You wrote to me in the letter you dispatched on the Ides of May that you had recently heard from Plancus that Lepidus is not

---

[3] The date is uncertain, perhaps 26 April.

faciliora; sin aliter, magnum negotium. cuius exitum non extimesco. tuae partes sunt. ego plus quam feci facere non possum. te tamen, id quod spero, omnium maximum et clarissimum videre cupio.

414 (X.23)

Scr. Cularone VIII *Id. Iun. an. 43*

PLANCUS CICERONI

1   Numquam mehercules, mi Cicero, me paenitebit maxima pericula pro patria subire dum, si quid acciderit mihi, a reprehensione temeritatis absim. confiterer imprudentia me lapsum si umquam Lepido ex animo credidissem; credulitas enim error est magis quam culpa, et quidem in optimi cuiusque mentem facillime irrepit. sed ego non hoc vitio paene sum deceptus; Lepidum enim pulchre noram. quid ergo est? pudor me, qui in bello maxime est periculosus, hunc casum co<e>git subire. nam si uno loco essem, verebar ne cui obtrectatorum viderer et nimium pertinaciter Lepido offensus et mea patientia etiam alere bellum.

2   Itaque copias prope in conspectum Lepidi Antonique adduxi quadragintaque milium passuum spatio relicto consedi, eo consilio ut vel celeriter accedere vel salutariter recipere me possem. adiunxi haec in loco eligendo, flumen oppositum ut haberem in quo mora transitus esset, Vocon-

4 Cf. Letter 407.2.

harbouring Antony.[4] If that is so, all will be easier; if otherwise, we have a big job on our hands, but I am not afraid of the outcome. That is your part. I can do no more than I have done. But I am anxious to see you the greatest and most famous of us all, as I expect I shall.

414 (X.23)
PLANCUS TO CICERO

Cularo, 6 June 43

From Plancus to Cicero.

Never, my dear Cicero, shall I regret the grave risks I am taking for my country's sake, provided that I am free of the reproach of rashness if anything happens to me. I should confess to a mistake due to imprudence if I had ever in my heart trusted Lepidus. After all, credulity is an error rather than a sin, and one which slides into an honourable mind with peculiar ease. But it was not through any such tendency that I was almost hoodwinked, for I knew Lepidus only too well. The truth is that sensitivity to criticism, a most dangerous proclivity in military operations, impelled me to take this chance. I was afraid that, if I stayed where I was, some detractor might think I was too obstinately holding a grudge against Lepidus, and even that my inertia was responsible for the enlargement of the conflict.

Accordingly, I led my forces almost within sight of Lepidus and Antony, and took up a position at a distance of forty miles from which I could either make a rapid approach or a successful retreat. Further, I chose a position with a river to my front which would take time to cross,

CICERO'S LETTERS TO FRIENDS

tii sub manu ut essent, per quorum loca fideliter mihi
pateret iter. Lepidus desperato adventu meo, quem non
mediocriter captabat, se cum Antonio coniunxit a.d. IIII
Kal. Iun., eodemque die ad me castra moverunt. viginti
3 milia passuum cum abessent, res mihi nuntiata est. dedi
operam deum benignitate ut et celeriter me reciperem et
hic discessus nihil fugae simile haberet, non miles ullus,
non eques, non quicquam impedimentorum amitteretur
aut ab illis ferventibus latronibus interciperetur. itaque
prid. Non. Iun. omnis copias Isaram traieci pontisque quos
feceram interrupi, ut spatium ad colligendum se homines
haberent et ego me interea cum collega coniungerem;
quem triduo, cum has dabam litteras, exspectabam.
4   Laterensis nostri et fidem et animum singularem in
re<m> publicam semper fatebor. sed certe nimia eius in-
dulgentia in Lepidum ad haec pericula perspicienda fecit
eum minus sagacem. qui quidem, cum in fraudem se de-
ductum videret, manus, quas iustius in Lepidi perniciem
armasset, sibi adferre conatus est. in quo casu tamen interpellatus et adhuc vivit et dicitur victurus; sed tamen de hoc
parum mihi certum est.
5   Magno cum dolore parricidarum elapsus sum iis. veniebant enim eodem furore in me quo in patriam incitati,
iracundias autem harum rerum recentis habebant, quod
Lepidum castigare non destiteram ut exstingueret bellum,
quod colloquia facta improbabam, quod legatos fide Lepi-

---

[1] He died.

354

hard by the Vocontii, through whose territory I could count on a free and trustworthy passage. Lepidus made strenuous efforts to lure me on, but finally giving up hope of success he joined forces with Antony on 29 May, and they advanced against me on the same day. This intelligence reached me when they were twenty miles away. I took good care, under providence, to retreat rapidly, but without letting my departure look in any way like a flight, so that not a soldier nor a trooper nor an item of baggage was lost or intercepted by those red-hot rebels. So on 4 June I recrossed the Isara with my entire force and broke the bridge which I had constructed, so as to give people time to readjust while I myself effect a junction with my colleague. I am expecting him three days after the dispatch of this letter.

I shall always acknowledge the good faith and conspicuously patriotic spirit of our friend Laterensis. But his overtenderness towards Lepidus undeniably made him less alert to perceive the dangers in which we stood. When he saw that he had been the victim of a deception, he tried to turn against himself the hands which he might with greater justice have armed to destroy Lepidus, but he was interrupted in the act. He is still alive, and is said to be likely to live.[1] However, I have no certain information on the latter score.

The traitors are deeply chagrined at my escape from their clutches. They came at me with the same fury that stirred them against their country, angry besides on several recent counts arising from these transactions: namely, that I had continually taken Lepidus to task and urged him to stamp out the war, that I censured the talks that were going on, that I refused to allow envoys sent to me under safe

di missos ad me in conspectum venire vetueram, quod C. Catium Vestinum, tribunum militum, missum ab Antonio ad me cum litteris exceperam numeroque hostis habueram. in quo hanc capio voluptatem quod certe, quo magis me petiverunt, tanto maiorem iis frustratio dolorem attulit.

6   Tu, mi Cicero, quod adhuc fecisti, idem praesta ut vigilanter nervoseque nos qui stamus in acie subornes. veniat Caesar cum copiis quas habet firmissimas, aut, si ipsum aliqua res impedit, exercitus mittatur; cuius ipsius magnum periculum agitur. quicquid aliquando futurum fuit in castris perditorum contra patriam, hoc omne iam convenit. pro urbis vero salute cur non omnibus facultatibus quas habemus utamur? quod si vos istic non defueritis, profecto, quod ad me attinet, omnibus rebus abunde rei publicae satis faciam.

7   Te quidem, mi Cicero, in dies mehercules habeo cariorem sollicitudinesque meas cottidie magis tua merita exacuunt, ne quid aut ex amore aut ex iudicio tuo perdam. opto ut mihi liceat iam praesenti pietate meorum officiorum tua beneficia tibi facere iucundiora.

VIII Id. Iun. Cularone ex finibus Allobrogum.

conduct from Lepidus into my sight, that I arrested C. Catius Vestinus, Military Tribune, carrying a letter to me from Antony, and treated him as an enemy. It gives me some satisfaction to think that at any rate their disappointment will annoy them in proportion to the viciousness with which they attacked me.

For your part, my dear Cicero, continue as hitherto to furnish us here in the front line with vigilant and energetic support. Let Caesar come with the very dependable force under his command, or, if he is personally prevented for some reason, let his army be sent. He is himself perilously[2] involved. All the elements that were ever likely to appear in the camp of the desperados to fight against their country have now joined forces. Why should we not use every means we possess to save Rome? As for me, if you at home do not fail me, I need hardly say that I shall do my patriotic duty to the very uttermost.

Of yourself, my dear Cicero, I do assure you I grow fonder daily; and every day your good offices sharpen my anxiety not to forfeit one jot of your affection or esteem. I pray that I may be able in person to add by my devoted services to the pleasure you take in your benefactions.

6 June, from Cularo, on the border of the Allobrogian territory.

---

[2] This can hardly refer to plots by Antony against Octavian's life. Plancus is merely pointing out incidentally that Octavian had a vital interest in doing everything possible to achieve victory.

415 (X.32)

Scr. Cordubae VI *Id. Iun. an. 43*

C. ASINIUS POLLIO CICERONI

1   Balbus quaestor magna numerata pecunia, magno pondere auri, maiore argenti coacto de publicis exactionibus, ne stipendio quidem militibus reddito duxit se a Gadibus et triduum tempestate retentus ad Calpen Kal. Iun. traiecit sese in regnum Bogudis plane bene peculiatus. his rumoribus utrum Gadis referatur an Romam (ad singulos enim nuntios turpissime consilia mutat) nondum scio.

2   Sed praeter furta et rapinas et virgis caesos socios haec quoque fecit, ut ipse gloriari solet, eadem quae C. Caesar: ludis, quos Gadibus fecit, Herennium Gallum histrionem summo ludorum die anulo aureo donatum in XIIII sessum deduxit (tot enim fecerat ordines equestris loci); quattuorviratum sibi prorogavit; comitia bienni biduo habuit, hoc est renuntiavit quos ei visum est; exsules reduxit, non horum temporum sed illorum quibus a seditiosis senatus trucidatus aut expulsus est Sex. Varo pro consule.

3   Illa vero iam ne Caesaris quidem exemplo, quod ludis praetextam de suo itinere ad L. Lentulum pro consule sollicitandum posuit, et quidem, cum ageretur, flevit memoria rerum gestarum commotus; gladiatoribus autem

---

   1 Mauretania.

   2 The badge of a Knight.

   3 The governing magistrates of the town.

   4 In 56 or 55. Nothing is known of this incident.

   5 Shortly before the battle of Pharsalia the younger Balbus secretly entered Pompey's camp and talked to Lentulus Crus.

415 (X.32)
POLLIO TO CICERO

Corduba, 8 June 43

From C. Asinius Pollio to Cicero.

My Quaestor Balbus has taken himself off from Gades, and after three days' hold-up off Calpe due to weather has crossed over into King Bogud's territory[1] with his pockets very nicely lined—a large sum in cash, a mass of gold, and a bigger mass of silver, all collected from the public revenues—without even giving the troops their pay. With the rumours that are coming in, I don't yet know whether he will be returning to Gades or going to Rome—he changes his plans on every new report in the most contemptible fashion.

The following exploits, on the model of C. Caesar as he himself boasts, are in addition to his pilferings and robberies and floggings of provincials: At the games which he gave at Gades he presented a gold ring[2] to an actor, one Herennius Gallus, on the last day of the show, and led him to a seat in the fourteen rows (that being the number he had assigned to the Knights). He extended his own term of office on the Board of Four.[3] He held elections, that is to say he returned his own nominees, for two years in two days. He brought back exiles, not those of recent years but agitators responsible for the massacre or expulsion of the Senate during Sex. Varus' Proconsulate.[4]

For other proceedings he could not even quote Caesar's precedent. He put on a play at the show about the journey he made to persuade Proconsul L. Lentulus to change sides,[5] and what is more, burst into tears during the performance at the poignant memory of his adventures. At

Fadium quendam, militem Pompeianum, quia, cum depressus in ludum bis gratis depugnasset, auctor⟨ar⟩e[1] sese nolebat et ad populum confugerat, primum Gallos equites immisit in populum (coniecti enim lapides sunt in eum cum abriperetur Fadius), deinde abstractum defodit in ludo et vivum combussit, cum quidem pransus nudis pedibus, tunica soluta, manibus ad tergum reiectis inambularet et illi misero quiritanti 'c. R. natus sum' responderet 'abi nunc, populi fidem implora'; bestiis vero civis Romanos, in iis circulatorem quendam auctionum, notissimum hominem Hispali, quia deformis erat, obiecit. cum huiusce modi portento res mihi fuit.

4   Sed de illo plura coram, nunc, quod praestat, quid me velitis facere constituite. tris legiones firmas habeo, quarum unam, XXVIII, cum ad se initio belli arcessisset Antonius hac pollicitatione, quo die in castra venisset denarios quingenos singulis militibus daturum, in victoria vero eadem praemia quae suis legionibus (quorum quis ullam finem aut modum futurum putavit?), incitatissimam retinui aegre mehercules, nec retinuissem si uno loco habuissem, utpote cum singulae quaedam cohortes seditionem fecerint; reliquas quoque legiones non destitit litteris atque infinitis pollicitationibus incitare. nec vero minus

1 (Rut.)

---

6 A Roman citizen had the right of appeal to the People against a sentence of death or flogging.

the gladiators a Pompeian soldier called Fadius, who had been forced to join the troop, twice fought to a finish without pay. Being unwilling to bind himself over as a gladiator, he besought the people to protect him. Balbus had his Gaulish horse charge the crowd (some stones had been flung at him when Fadius was being hauled off), and then carried the man off to the Gladiator School, where he had him buried in the ground and burned alive. While this was going on, Balbus walked up and down after lunch barefoot, his tunic loose and his hands behind his back. The poor fellow kept crying out pitifully that he was a Roman citizen born. 'Off you go then!' said Balbus. 'Appeal to the People!'[6] He even threw Roman citizens to the wild beasts, among them a certain peddler who went round auction sales, a very well-known character in Hispalis—because he had a deformity! Such is the monster I have had to deal with!

More of him, however, when we meet. What is of greater importance at the moment, you gentlemen must decide what you want me to do. I have three reliable legions. One of them, the Twenty-Eighth, was summoned by Antony at the start of the war with a promise that the day they arrived in his camp he would give them 500 denarii per man; further, that when he had won, they should have the same bounties as his own legions—and these, as anyone may guess, would be absolutely unbounded. The men were much excited, and I give you my word I had a hard job of it to hold them in check. I should not have succeeded if I had kept them together—certain cohorts mutinied individually. He has been continually inciting the other legions too with letters and unlimited promises. Lepidus has been

Lepidus ursit me et suis et Antoni litteris ut legionem xxx mitterem sibi.

5   Itaque quem exercitum neque vendere ullis praemiis volui nec eorum periculorum metu quae victoribus illis portendebantur deminuere, debetis existimare retentum et conservatum rei publicae esse atque ita credere, quodcumque imperassetis facturum fuisse, si quod iussistis feci. nam et provinciam in otio et exercitum in mea potestate tenui, finibus meae provinciae nusquam excessi, militem non modo legionarium sed ne auxiliarium quidem ullum quoquam misi et, si quos equites decedentis nactus sum, supplicio adfeci. quarum rerum fructum satis magnum re publica salva tulisse me putabo. sed res publica si me satis novisset et maior pars senatus, maiores ex me fructus tulisset.

    Epistulam quam Balbo, cum etiam nunc in provincia esset, scripsi, legendam tibi misi. etiam praetextam si voles legere, Gallum Cornelium, familiarem meum, poscito.

    vi Id. Iun. Corduba.

416 (XII.8)

Scr. Romae paulo post v *Id. Iun. an. 43*

CICERO CASSIO S.

1   Scelus adfinis tui Lepidi summamque levitatem et inconstantiam ex actis, quae ad te mitti certo scio, cognosse te arbitror. itaque nos confecto bello, ut arbitrabamur, re-

no less insistent, urging me by letters (his own and Antony's) to send him the Thirtieth.

You must then consider this army, which I have refused
to sell for any rewards or to reduce out of fear of the
dangers held over my head in the event of these people
winning the war, as kept and preserved for the commonwealth. On the evidence of my obedience to the orders you
have actually given you must believe that I should have
obeyed any I had received. I have kept this province free of
disturbance and the army under my control, I have not
stirred outside my province borders, have dispatched not a
single legionary or even auxiliary to any destination, and
have punished any troopers I found leaving. For all of
which I shall feel sufficiently recompensed if the commonwealth is saved. But had the commonwealth and the majority of the Senate known me better, they would have
gained more from me.

I am sending you for your perusal a letter I wrote to
Balbus when he was still in the province. If you want to
read the play too, ask my friend Gallus Cornelius for it.

8 June, from Corduba.

416 (XII.8)
CICERO TO CASSIUS

Rome, shortly after 9 June 43

From Cicero to Cassius greetings.

I expect you have learned from the city news, which I
am sure is sent to you regularly, of the criminal behaviour
of your relative Lepidus, his egregious faithlessness and
fickleness. After the war had been finished, as we thought,

novatum bellum gerimus spemque omnem in D. Bruto et
Planco habemus, ⟨vel⟩,[1] si verum quaeris, in te et in M.[2]
Bruto, non solum ad praesens perfugium si, quod nolim,
adversi quid acciderit sed etiam ad confirmationem perpetuae libertatis.

2   Nos hic de Dolabella audiebamus quae vellemus, sed
certos auctores non habebamus. te quidem magnum hominem et praesenti iudicio et reliqui temporis exspectatione scito esse. hoc tibi proposito fac ut ad summa
contendas. nihil est tantum quod non populus Romanus a
te perfici atque obtineri posse iudicet.

Vale.

417 (XII.30)

Scr. Romae c. v Id. Iun. an 43

⟨CICERO CORNIFICIO S.⟩

1   Itane? praeter litigatores nemo ad te meas litteras?
multae istae quidem; tu enim perfecisti ut nemo sine litteris meis tibi se commendatum putaret. sed quis umquam
tuorum mihi dixit esse cui darem quin dederim? aut quid
mi iucundius quam, cum coram tecum loqui non possim,
aut scribere ad te aut tuas legere litteras? illud magis mihi
solet esse molestum, tantis me impediri occupationibus ut
ad te scribendi meo arbitratu facultas nulla detur. non
enim te epistulis sed voluminibus lacesserem; quibus quidem me a te provocari oportebat. quamvis enim occupatus

[1] *(SB)*
[2] meo *(Gron.)*

we find ourselves waging it afresh, and pin all our hopes on D. Brutus and Plancus, or, if you will have the truth, on you and M. Brutus, not only for immediate refuge, should some reverse unfortunately occur, but for the assurance of freedom in perpetuity.

Satisfactory reports concerning Dolabella are reaching us here, but without reliable authority. You are in grand repute, let me tell you, both on present estimate and in expectation of things to come. Set that thought before you, and strive on to the heights! There is nothing that the People of Rome does not judge you capable of achieving and maintaining.

Good-bye.

417 (XII.30)
CICERO TO CORNIFICIUS

Rome, ca. 9 June 43

From Cicero to Cornificius greetings.

So! Nobody brings you a letter of mine except people with lawsuits! Such letters, to be sure, you get in plenty—it is your own doing that nobody thinks himself recommended to you without a letter from me. But has there been a single occasion when one of your people told me of a bearer and I did not write? Now that I cannot talk to you face to face, what could I like better than writing to you or reading your letters? My trouble is rather that I have such a press of matters to keep me occupied that I am given no chance of writing to you at will, or I should be bombarding you with letters, or rather with pamphlets. *You* should be the challenger, for, busy as you are, you have more time to

sis, oti tamen plus habes; aut si ne tu quidem vacas, noli impudens esse nec mihi molestiam exhibere et a me litteras
2 crebriores, cum tu mihi raro mittas, flagitare. nam cum antea distinebar maximis occupationibus propterea quod omnibus curis mihi tuendam ⟨rem publicam⟩[1] putabam, tum hoc tempore multo distineor vehementius. ut enim gravius aegrotant ii qui, cum levati morbo videntur, in eum de integro inciderunt, sic vehementius nos laboramus, qui profligato bello ac paene sublato renovatum bellum gerere cogamur.[2]

3 Sed haec hactenus. tu tibi, mi Cornifici, fac ut persuadeas non esse me tam imbecillo animo, ne dicam inhumano, ut a te vinci possim aut officiis aut amore. non dubitabam equidem, verum tamen multo mihi notiorem amorem tuum effecit C⟨h⟩aerippus. o hominem semper illum quidem mihi aptum, nunc vero etiam suavem! vultus mehercule tuos mihi expressit omnis, non solum animum ac verba pertulit. itaque noli vereri ne tibi suscensuerim quod eodem exemplo ad me quo ad ceteros. requisivi equidem proprias ad me unum litteras, sed neque vehementer et amanter.

4 De sumptu quem te in rem militarem facere et fecisse dicis nihil sane possum tibi opitulari, propterea quod et orbus senatus consulibus amissis et incredibiles angustiae pecuniae publicae; quae conquiritur undique, ut optime meritis militibus promissa solvantur. quod quidem fieri sine tributo posse non arbitror.

5 De Attio Dionysio nihil puto esse, quoniam mihi nihil

_____

[1] (*hic Castiglioni, ante vel post* mihi ⊊)
[2] conamur *(Man.)**

call your own than I—or if you too have none, don't have
the effrontery to nag me and dun me for letters when you
write so few yourself. Even earlier on I was under very
heavy pressure of work, because I felt it my duty to give my
whole mind to protecting the commonwealth, but at the
present time the pressure is far greater. We are like re-
lapsed invalids, who get much worse after an apparent recovery. Our troubles weigh heavier now that we have to set
about fighting a resurrected war after the old one had been
all but finished and done with.

Well, so much for that. Now please assure yourself, my
dear Cornificius, that I am not so poor-spirited, not to say
unfeeling, as to be capable of letting you outmatch me
either in friendly services or in affection. Of your affection
I had no doubts before, but thanks to Chaerippus I know it
far better than I did. What a good fellow he is! I always
liked him, but now I find him absolutely charming. Upon
my word, he made me see your every look to the life, let
alone conveying your mind and words. So don't be in any
apprehension as to my feeling irritated at your sending me
the same letter you sent to others. True, I should have liked
a special letter to myself individually, but it was not a very
strong reaction and it was an affectionate one.

As regards the expenses to which you say you are being
put, and have already been put, for military purposes, I am
afraid I cannot help you. The Senate is bereaved, both
Consuls lost; and the Treasury is in terribly low water.
Efforts are being made to raise money from all sources in
order to discharge promises given to the soldiers who have
deserved so well. I don't think it can be done without a special levy.

With regard to Attius Dionysius, I imagine there is

dixit Tratorius. de P. Luccio nihil tibi concedo quo studiosior eius sis quam ego sum; est enim nobis necessarius. sed a magistris cum contenderem de proferendo die, probarunt mihi sese quo minus id facerent et compromisso et iure iurando impediri. qua re veniendum arbitror Luccio. quamquam, si meis litteris obtemperavit, cum tu haec leges illum Romae esse oportebit.

6   Ceteris de rebus maximeque de pecunia, cum Pansae mortem ignorares, scripsisti quae per nos ab eo consequi te posse arbitrarere. quae te non fefellissent si viveret; nam te diligebat. post mortem autem eius quid fieri posset non videbamus.

7   De Venuleio, Latino,[3] Horatio valde laudo. illud non nimium probo, quod scribis, quo illi animo aequiore ferrent, te tuis etiam legatis lictores ademisse (honore enim[4] cum ignominia dignis non erant comparandi), eosque, ex senatus consulto si non decedunt, cogendos ut decedant existimo.

Haec fere ad eas litteras quas eodem exemplo binas accepi. de reliquo velim tibi persuadeas non esse mihi meam dignitatem tua cariorem.

---

3 Latinio *coni. SB*
4 enim ⟨digni⟩ *Man*

nothing in it since Tratorius said nothing to me about it. As for P. Luccius, I won't allow that you are any more anxious to help him than I am—he is a friend of mine. But when I pressed the receivers for a postponement, they explained to my satisfaction that the arbitration agreement and their oath would not allow them to do it. So I think Luccius had better come over. To be sure, if he has paid attention to my letter, he should be in Rome by the time you read this.

You write on other points, especially money, which you thought you might be able to obtain from Pansa (not knowing of his death) through my mediation. Had he lived, you would not have been disappointed, for he had a high regard for you. But now that he is dead, I do not see what can be done.

As regards Venuleius, Latinus, and Horatius,[1] I emphatically approve of your decision. On one point I am not too happy—you say that to spare these people's feelings you have also withdrawn lictors from your own Legates. Persons deserving respect ought not to have been put on a par with those deserving the opposite. And I think that if the latter do not leave the province in accordance with the Senate's decree, they should be compelled to do so.

The above more or less answers the letter which I have received in two copies. As for all else, please rest assured that my own public standing is not more precious to me than yours.

[1] Apparently three Legates left in the province by the previous governor Calvisius Sabinus. Perhaps 'Latinus' should be 'Latinius,' a *gentilicium* like the other two.

418 (XI.13a)

Scr. Cularone c. IV *Id. Iun. an. 43*

‹PLANCUS IMP. COS. DESIG. ET D. BRUTUS IMP. COS.
DESIG. S. D. PR. TR. PL. SENATUI POPULO PLEBIQUE
ROMANAE›

1 * * * in spem venerant, quod neque Planci quattuor legiones omnibus suis copiis paris arbitrabantur neque ex
Italia tam celeriter exercitum traici posse credebant. quos
ipsi adhuc satis adroganter Allobroges equitatusque omnis, qui eo praemissus erat a nobis, sustinebant, nostroque
adventu sustineri facilius posse confidimus. tamen, si quo
etiam casu Isaram se traiecerint, ne quod detrimentum rei
publicae iniungant summa a nobis dabitur opera.

2 Vos magnum animum optimamque spem de summa re
publica habere volumus, cum et nos et exercitus nostros
singulari concordia coniunctos ad omnia pro vobis videatis
paratos. sed tamen nihil de diligentia remittere debetis
dareque operam ut quam paratissimi et ab exercitu reliquisque rebus pro vestra salute contra sceleratissimam
conspirationem hostium confligamus. qui quidem eas copias quas diu simulatione rei publicae compararant[1] subito
ad patriae periculum converterunt.

---

[1] comparabunt M: -rarunt D: -rare V: -ratur H *(Man.)*

418 (XI.13a)

D. BRUTUS AND PLANCUS TO THE MAGISTRATES, SENATE, AND PEOPLE

Cularo, ca. 10 June 43

* * * had come to hope, thinking Plancus' four legions no match for their total force and not believing that an army could be brought over from Italy at such speed. But so far the Allobroges and our entire cavalry, which we had sent there in advance, are holding them saucily enough, and we are confident that they can be held more easily when we arrive. All the same, even if by some chance they cross the Isara, we shall take very good care that they do the commonwealth no damage.

We would have you be of good courage and in the highest hopes for the national cause, seeing as you do that we and our armies stand shoulder to shoulder, notably united and ready for anything on your behalf. Even so, you should by no means relax your efforts, and should take care that in military force and all other respects we are as well equipped as possible to join battle in your defence against a criminal combination of enemies, who have suddenly turned the forces which they have for long been assembling under cover of the public interest into a national threat.

419 (XII.13)

Scr. in Cypro Crommyacride Id. Iun. an. 43

C. CASSIUS Q. S. D. M. CICERONI

1   S. v. b.; e. v.

Cum rei publicae vel salute vel victoria gaudemus tum instauratione tuarum laudum, quod maximus consularis maximum consulem te ipse vicisti, et laetamur et mirari satis non possumus. fatale nescio quid tuae virtuti datum, id quod saepe iam experti sumus. est enim tua toga omnium armis felicior; quae nunc quoque nobis paene victam rem publicam ex manibus hostium eripuit ac reddidit. nunc ergo vivemus liberi, nunc te, omnium maxime civis et mihi carissime, id quod maximis[1] rei publicae tenebris comperisti, nunc te habebimus testem nostri et in te et in coniunctissimam tibi rem publicam amoris, et, quae saepe pollicitus es te et taciturum dum serviremus[2] et dicturum de me tum cum mihi profutura essent, nunc illa non ego quidem dici tanto opere desiderabo quam sentiri a te ipso. neque enim omnium iudicio malim me a te commendari quam ipse tuo iudicio digne ac mereor commendatus esse, ut haec novissima nostra facta non subita nec convenientia sed similia illis cogitationibus quarum tu testis es fuisse iudices meque ad optimam spem patriae, non minimam[3] tibi

---

[1] maxime *(Graevius)*
[2] servis eremus *(Man.)*
[3] minimum *(Gron.)*

419 (XII.13)
CASSIUS PARMENSIS TO CICERO

Crommyacris, 13 June 43

C. Cassius, Quaestor, to M. Cicero greetings.

I trust you are well, as I am.

I am rejoicing not only at the national salvation and victory, but at the renewal of your glory. You have excelled yourself; Rome's greatest Consular has surpassed her greatest Consul. My joy and admiration know no bounds. Surely a mysterious blessing of providence rests upon your valour, as we have often found; your gown is more fortunate than the arms of any other man—the gown that once again has snatched our almost vanquished country from the hands of her enemies and restored her to us. So now we shall live as free men. I shall now have your testimony— the word of the greatest of Romans and to me (as you came to know in our country's darkest hours) the dearest—your testimony to my affection for yourself and for the commonwealth, with which you are identified. There are words concerning me which you often promised not to say while our bondage continued, but to pronounce when they should be to my benefit. For my part, I do not so much desire to have them now spoken aloud as to know that you feel them in your heart. I would rather myself be recommended to your good opinion according to my just deserts than be recommended by you to the good opinion of the world. I want you to set down my latest actions as no sudden or incongruous departure, but as conformable to the ideas which you are witness that I entertained; and to think me deserving of advancement to a fine prospect of service

ipsi, producendum putes.

2   Sunt tibi, M. Tulli, liberi propinquique digni quidem te et merito tibi carissimi; esse etiam debent in re publica[4] proxime hos cari qui studiorum tuorum sunt aemuli, quorum esse cupio tibi copiam. sed tamen non maxima me turba puto excludi quo minus tibi vacet me excipere et ad omnia quae velis et probes producere. animum tibi nostrum fortasse probavimus; ingenium diutina servitus certe, qualecumque est, minus tamen quam erat passa est videri.

3   Nos ex ora maritima Asiae provinciae et ex insulis quas potuimus navis deduximus, dilectum remigum magna contumacia civitatum tamen satis celeriter habuimus, secuti sumus classem Dolabellae, cui L. Figulus[5] praeerat. qui spem saepe transitionis praebendo neque umquam non decedendo novissime Corycum se contulit et clauso portu se tenere coepit. nos illa relicta, quod et in castra pervenire satius esse putabamus et sequebatur classis altera, quam anno priore in Bithynia Tillius Cimber compararat, Turullius quaestor praeerat, Cyprum petivimus. ibi quae cognovimus scribere ad vos quam celerrime voluimus.

4   Dolabellam ut Tarsenses, pessimi socii, ita Laodiceni multo amentiores ultro arcessierunt; ex quibus utrisque civitatibus Graecorum militum numero speciem exercitus

---

[4] *anne* in rem publicam, *post* tuorum *transferendum?*
[5] lucilius (*Schütz*)

---

[1] In fact only one, but the plural is often so used.

374

to my country and a prospect not negligible of service to you.

You have children,[1] dear sir, and blood relations who do you credit and of whom you are deservedly very fond. Next to them in your affections should stand those who emulate your patriotic ideals. I wish you to have many such, and yet I do not think I am shut out by a vast crowd. You will, I trust, find time to take my outstretched hand and advance me to such stations as you may wish and think proper. My spirit you have perhaps seen reason to approve. As for my talents, however humble, it can at least be claimed that the long years of servitude let them seem less than they really were.

Having launched all available ships from the coast of the province of Asia and the islands, and held a levy of rowers fairly quickly despite the stubbornly uncooperative attitude of the communes, I went in pursuit of Dolabella's fleet, which was under the command of L. Figulus. While often holding out hopes that he might change sides, he kept drawing away all the time until he finally betook himself to Corycus, where he blocked the harbour and shut himself inside. I left them there, because I thought it better to join the land army, and because another fleet, raised in Bithynia last year by Tillius Cimber, was sailing up behind me under the command of Quaestor Turullius. I therefore made for Cyprus, and have thought proper to write to Rome as soon as possible with information of what I learned there.

Like our treacherous allies the people of Tarsus, the Laodiceans, who are far more wrongheaded than they, have called in Dolabella of their own motion. From these two communes he has raised the semblance of an army

375

effecit. castra habet ante oppidum Laodiceam posita et
partem muri demolitus est et castra oppido coniunxit.
Cassius noster cum decem legionibus et cohortibus xx
auxiliariis et quattuor milium equitatu a milibus passuum
xx castra habet posita Πάλτῳ et existimat se sine proelio
posse vincere. nam iam ternis tetrachmis triticum apud
Dolabellam est. nisi quid navibus Laodicenorum suppor-
tarit, cito fame pereat necesse est; ne supportare possit et
Cassi classis bene magna cui praeest Sextilius Rufus et tres
quas nos adduximus, ego, Turullius, Patiscus, facile prae-
stabunt. te volo bene sperare et rem publicam, ut vos istic
expedistis, ita pro nostra parte celeriter [iter] nobis expedi-
ri posse confidere.

Vale.

D. Id. Iun. Cypro a Crommyacride.[6]

420 (XI.25)

Scr. Romae xiv *Kal. Quint. an.* 43

M. CICERO S. D. D. BRUTO

1   Exspectanti mihi tuas cottidie litteras Lupus noster
subito denuntiavit ut ad te scriberem si quid vellem. ego
autem, etsi quid scriberem non habebam (acta enim ad
te mitti sciebam, inanem autem sermonem litterarum
tibi iniucundum esse audiebam), ‹nihil tamen scribere
nolebam›,[1] brevitatem secutus sum te magistro.

2   Scito igitur in te et in collega spem omnem esse. de

[6] acromamyac- *(Man.)*
[1] *(SB; lac. agnoverat Baiter)*

with a quantity of native troops. He is encamped in front of the city of Laodicea, and has demolished part of the wall, thus joining camp and town. Our friend Cassius has pitched camp with ten legions, twenty auxiliary cohorts, and 4,000 horse about twenty miles away at Paltus. He reckons to win a bloodless victory, for the price of grain with Dolabella has gone up to twelve drachmae. Unless he brings in a supply in Laodicean ships, he must starve to death before long; and Cassius' very sizable fleet, commanded by Sextilius Rufus, and the three others which I myself, Turullius, and Patiscus have brought to join him, will have no trouble in preventing Dolabella from importing. So you may be of good cheer, confident that, following your example in Italy, we for our part shall soon succeed in solving the commonwealth's problems.

Good-bye.

Dispatched Ides of June, from Crommyacris, Cyprus.

420 (XI.25)
CICERO TO D. BRUTUS

Rome, 18 June 43

From M. Cicero to D. Brutus greetings.

I have been waiting to hear from you every day. All of a sudden our friend Lupus has given me notice to write to you if I have anything I want to say. In point of fact I haven't—I know that the news of the day is sent to you, and am told that empty chat in correspondence is not to your liking—but I did not want to write nothing at all. But I study to be brief, as your pupil.

Let me tell you then that all hopes rest on you and your

Bruto autem nihil adhuc certi; quem ego, quem ad modum praecipis, privatis litteris ad bellum commune vocare non desino. qui utinam iam adesset! intestinum urbis malum, quod est non mediocre, minus timeremus. sed quid ago? non imitor λακωνισμὸν tuum; altera iam pagella procedit.

Vince et vale.

XIIII Kal. Quint.

421 (XII.9)

Scr. Romae med. vel ex. m. Iun. an. 43

CICERO CASSIO S.

1   Brevitas tuarum litterarum me quoque breviorem in scribendo facit et, vere ut dicam, non satis occurrit quid scribam. nostras enim res in actis perferri ad te certo scio, tuas autem ignoramus. tamquam enim clausa sit Asia, sic nihil perfertur ad nos praeter rumores de oppresso Dolabella, satis illos quidem constantis, sed adhuc sine auctore.

2   Nos, confectum bellum cum putaremus, repente a Lepido tuo in summam sollicitudinem sumus adducti. itaque tibi persuade maximam rei publicae spem in te et in tuis copiis esse. firmos omnino exercitus habemus; sed tamen, ut omnia, ut spero, prospere procedant, multum interest te venire. exigua enim spes est rei publicae (nam nullam non libet dicere), sed, quaecumque est, ea despondetur anno consulatus tui.

Vale.

---

[1] 41, when, as Cicero assumes, Cassius and M. Brutus would hold the office.

colleague. Of Brutus there is no certain news as yet. As you recommend, I am continually urging him in private letters to join the common fight. I only wish he were here now. I should then be less apprehensive about the internal mischief in Rome, which is no light matter. But what am I doing? I am not copying your laconism—here is the second little page on its way!

Victory and good-bye!

18 June.

421 (XII.9)
CICERO TO CASSIUS

Rome, June (middle or end) 43

From Cicero to Cassius greetings.

The brevity of your letters makes me too write more briefly; and, to tell the truth, nothing very much occurs to me to write about. I am sure our news reaches you in the city news, and of yours I know nothing. It is as though Asia were sealed off. Nothing gets through to us except rumours that Dolabella has been crushed—consistent enough, but so far unvouched for.

As for us, just when we thought the war was finished, we have suddenly been plunged into grave anxiety by your connection Lepidus. You must therefore realize that the state's best hope lies in you and your men. True, we have strong armies, but though all goes well, as I trust it may, it is highly important that you should come. The hope for a free constitution is meagre (I do not like to say nonexistent), but, such as it is, it is bound up with the year of your Consulship.[1]

Good-bye.

422 (XI.15)

Scr. Romae ex. m. Iun. an. 43

M. CICERO D. BRUTO COS. DESIG. S. D.

1   Etsi mihi tuae litterae iucundissimae sunt, tamen iucundius fuit quod in summa occupatione tua Planco collegae mandasti ut te mihi per litteras excusaret; quod fecit
ille diligenter. mihi autem nihil amabilius officio tuo et diligentia. coniunctio tua cum collega concordiaque vestra,
quae litteris communibus declarata est, senatui populoque
Romano gratissima accidit.

2   Quod superest, perge, mi Brute, et iam non cum aliis
sed tecum ipse certa. plura scribere non debeo, praesertim
ad te, quo magistro brevitatis uti cogito. litteras tuas vehementer exspecto, et quidem talis qualis maxime opto.

Vale.

423 (X.22)

Scr. Romae ex. m. Iun, ut vid., an. 43

CICERO PLANCO

In te et in collega omnis spes est dis approbantibus.
1   concordia vestra, quae senatui declarata litteris vestris est,
mirifice et senatus et cuncta civitas delectata est.

---

[1] The distribution of land to Plancus' troops. His letter on the
subject has not survived.

422 (XI.15)
CICERO TO D. BRUTUS

Rome, late June 43

From M. Cicero to D. Brutus, Consul-Elect, greetings.

Although your letters give me great pleasure, your asking your colleague Plancus to write to me and make your excuses in the midst of your heavy preoccupations gave me more. He did so faithfully. I am deeply touched by your attention and thoughtfulness. The full and friendly cooperation between you and your colleague, as declared in your joint dispatch, has been warmly welcomed by the Senate and People of Rome.

As for the future—carry on, my dear Brutus, and try now to excel, not others, but yourself. I ought not to write any more, especially to you from whom I plan to take lessons in brevity. I eagerly await a letter from you—one such as I must pray for.

Good-bye.

423 (X.22)
CICERO TO PLANCUS

Rome, late June 43

From Cicero to Plancus.

In you and your colleague lie all our hopes, with the favour of heaven. Your concert, declared to the Senate in your joint letters, has given the liveliest pleasure both to the Senate and the community at large.

As for what you wrote to me with reference to the agrarian matter,[1] if the Senate had been consulted, it

2   Quod ad me scripseras de re agraria, si consultus senatus esset, ut quisque honorificentissimam de te sententiam
dixisset, eam secutus esset;[1] qui certe ego fuissem. sed
propter tarditatem sententiarum moramque rerum cum
ea quae consulebantur ad exitum non pervenirent, com-
modissimum mihi Plancoque fratri visum est uti eo ‹senatus consulto›[2] quod ne nostro arbitratu componeretur quis
fuerit impedimento arbitror te ex Planci litteris cogno-
visse.

3   Sed sive in senatus consulto sive in ceteris rebus desideras aliquid, sic tibi persuade, tantam esse apud omnis
bonos tui caritatem ut nullum genus amplissimae dignitatis excogitari possit quod tibi non paratum sit.

Litteras tuas vehementer exspecto, et quidem talis qualis maxime opto.

Vale.

424 (X.26)

Scr. Romae fort. ex. m. Iun. an. 43

M. CICERO S. D. C. FURNIO

1   Lectis tuis litteris, quibus declarabas aut omittendos
Narbonensis aut cum periculo dimicandum, illud magis
timui; quod vitatum non moleste fero. quod de Planci et
Bruti concordia scribis, in eo vel maximam spem pono vic-

1 essem (*Graevius*)
2 (*Man.* (s.c.))

---

2 Perhaps Servilius Isauricus; cf. Letter 377.3f.

would have followed the proposer of the motion most complimentary to you—and no doubt he would have been none other than I myself. But the speeches dragged on and business was held up, so that the matters submitted to the House never came to an issue. Therefore your brother Plancus and I think it best to make do with the Senate's decree as it stands. Who[2] prevented its being drafted as we desired, you will, I suppose, have learned from your brother's letter.

However, if you have any further desires in respect to the Senate's decree or any other matter, the attachment which all honest men feel for you is such (rest assured of it) that every conceivable distinction, of whatever type or eminence, is yours for the asking.

I eagerly await a letter from you—one such as I most pray for.

Good-bye.

424 (X.26)
CICERO TO FURNIUS

Rome, end of June (?) 43

M. Cicero to C. Furnius greetings.

When I read your letter in which you declared that the choice lay between giving up Narbonese Gaul and fighting a risky battle, I found the former alternative the more alarming. I am not sorry it has been avoided. You write of the good understanding between Plancus and Brutus; therein lies my greatest hope of victory. As for the loyal spirit of the Gauls, we shall know one day, as you say, who

toriae. de Gallorum studio, nos aliquando cognoscemus, ut scribis, cuius id opera maxime excitatum sit; sed iam, mihi crede, cognovimus. itaque iucundissimis tuis litteris stomachatus sum in extremo. scribis enim, si in Sextilem comitia, cito te, sin iam confecta, citius, ne diutius cum periculo fatuus sis.

2   O mi Furni, quam tu tuam causam non nosti, qui alienas tam facile discas! tu nunc candidatum te putas et id cogitas ut aut ad comitia curras aut, si iam confecta, domi tuae sis, ne cum maximo periculo, ut scribis, stultissimus sis? non arbitror te ita sentire; omnis enim tuos ad laudem impetus novi. quod si ut scribis ita sentis, non magis te quam de te iudicium reprehendo meum. te adipiscendi magistratus levissimi et divulgatissimi, si ita adipiscare ut plerique, praepropera festinatio abducet a tantis laudibus, quibus te omnes in caelum iure et vere ferunt? scilicet id agitur, utrum hac petitione an proxima praetor fias, non ut ita de re publica mereare omni honore ut dignissimus iudicere. utrum nescis quam alte ascenderis an pro nihilo id 3   putas? si nescis, tibi ignosco, nos in culpa sumus; sin intellegis, ulla tibi est praetura vel officio, quod pauci, vel gloria, quam omnes sequuntur, dulcior? hac de re et ego et Calvisius, homo magni iudici tuique amantissimus, te accusamus cottidie. comitia tamen, quoniam ex iis pendes,

---

[1] Presumably Furnius himself.

[2] Caesar had increased the number of Praetors from eight to sixteen. The competition in 43 was keen, however (cf. Letter 435.1).

[3] Cf. Letter 403, n. 4.

has done most to evoke it[1] but, take my word for it, we know already. And so the final passage in your most agreeable letter put me out of humour. You write that if the elections are put off till August, you will soon be here, and if they have already taken place, sooner still, since you have been a fool at the risk of your neck long enough.

Oh my dear Furnius, for one so adept in getting up other people's cases, how little you know of your own! Do you at this moment regard yourself as a candidate? Are you thinking of hurrying back for the elections, or staying in your own house if they have taken place already, so as not to be an idiot and risk your life into the bargain, as you put it? I do not believe that these are your true sentiments. I know all your impulses to glory. But if you really feel as you write, then I do not blame you so much as the opinion I formed of you. Will you allow precipitate impatience to gain an insignificant office (if you were to come by it in the ordinary way), vulgarized as it is,[2] to draw you away from the shining honour with which all men are rightly and properly gilding your name? As though what signifies is whether you become Praetor this year or next, not that you should deserve so well of the commonwealth as to be judged most worthy of every distinction! Don't you know how high you have climbed or don't you think it of any consequence? If you don't know, I forgive you, the fault is ours. But if you do realize it, is any Praetorship sweeter to you than duty, the goal of the few, or glory, the goal of all mankind? I and Calvisius,[3] a man of the soundest judgement with a great affection for you, scold you every day over this. However, since the elections are keeping you on tenterhooks, we are doing our utmost to stave them off till

quantum facere possumus, quod multis de causis rei publicae arbitramur conducere, in Ianuarium mensem pro-
trudimus.

Vince igitur et vale.

425 (XII.10)

Scr. Romae c. Kal. Quint. an. 43

CICERO CASSIO S.

1   Lepidus, tuus adfinis, meus familiaris, prid. Kal. Quint.
sententiis omnibus hostis a senatu iudicatus est ceterique
qui una cum illo a re publica defecerunt; quibus tamen ad
sanitatem redeundi ante Kal. Sept. potestas facta est. fortis
sane senatus, sed maxime spe subsidi tui. bellum quidem
cum haec scribebam sane magnum erat scelere et levitate
Lepidi.

2   Nos de Dolabella cottidie quae volumus audimus, sed
adhuc sine capite, sine auctore, rumore nuntio. quod cum
ita esset, tamen litteris tuis quas Non. Mai. ex castris datas
acceperamus, ita persuasum erat civitati ut illum iam oppressum omnes arbitrarentur, te autem in Italiam venire
cum exercitu, ut, si haec ex sententia confecta essent,
consilio atque auctoritate tua, sin quid forte titubatum, ut
fit in bello, exercitu tuo niteremur. quem quidem ego exercitum quibuscumque potuero rebus ornabo. cuius rei tum
tempus erit cum quid opis rei publicae laturus is exercitus
sit aut quid iam tulerit notum esse coeperit. nam adhuc

---

[1] The wives of Lepidus and Cassius were sisters, half-sisters to
M. Brutus.   [2] Letter 387.

January, which we consider would be in the public interest for many reasons.

I wish you victory then, and good-bye.

425 (XII.10)
CICERO TO CASSIUS

Rome, ca. 1 July 43

From Cicero to Cassius greetings.

Lepidus, your relation[1] and my friend, was declared a public enemy by unanimous vote of the Senate on 30 June, as also those who defected from the commonwealth along with him. They have, however, been given until the Kalends of September to come to their senses. The Senate is in stout heart to be sure, but principally because they expect succour from you. At the time of writing we have a major war on our hands through Lepidus' criminality and fickleness.

Satisfactory reports come in every day about Dolabella, but still without known source or authority, just hearsay. Even so, your letter[2] dispatched from camp on the Nones of May has produced a universal conviction in the community that he has already been crushed, and that you are on your way to Italy with your army, so that we shall rely upon your advice and prestige, if operations here have by then been satisfactorily concluded, or upon your army, if anything goes awry, as is apt to happen in war. As for that army, I shall give it every subvention I can. The time for that will arrive when it becomes clear to what extent this army will assist the national cause, or has already done so. Hitherto we hear only of enterprises—fine and splendid to be sure,

simi; sed gesta res exspectatur, quam quidem aut iam esse
3   aliquam aut appropinquare confido. tua virtute ‹et›[1] magnitudine animi nihil est nobilius. itaque optamus ut quam
primum te in Italia videamus; rem publicam nos habere
arbitrabimur si vos habebimus.

Praeclare viceramus nisi spoliatum, inermem, fugientem Lepidus recepisset Antonium. itaque numquam tanto
odio civitati Antonius fuit quanto est Lepidus. ille enim ex
turbulenta re publica, hic ex pace et victoria bellum excitavit. huic oppositos consules designatos habemus, in quibus
est magna illa quidem spes sed anceps cura propter incer-
tos exitus proeliorum.
4   Persuade tibi igitur in te et in Bruto tuo esse omnia, vos
exspectari, Brutum quidem iam iamque. quod si, ut spero,
victis hostibus nostris veneritis, tamen auctoritate vestra
res publica exsurget et in aliquo statu tolerabili consistet.
sunt enim permulta quibus erit medendum, etiam si res
publica satis esse videbitur sceleribus hostium liberata.

Vale.

426 (X.29)

Scr. Romae prid. Non. Quint. an. 43
CICERO APPIO SAL.

De meo studio erga salutem et incolumitatem tuam
credo te cognosse ex litteris tuorum. quibus me cumulatis-

---

[1] *(Man.)**

but we are waiting for results; some I am confident have already materialized or soon will. Your vigour and generous courage are indeed admirable. We pray therefore to see you in Italy as soon as possible. We shall think we have a free constitution, if we have you two.

We had won a splendid victory, if Lepidus had not harboured Antony as he fled, stripped of his power and unarmed. Hence Lepidus is more hated in the community than ever Antony was; for whereas Antony stirred up war in a country that was already in turmoil, Lepidus has done so in time of peace and victory. Our Consuls-Elect stand against him, and we have great hopes of them, but suspense and anxiety too, since the results of a battle are never certain beforehand.

Believe then that all depends on you and your brother-in-law, that you are expected—Brutus indeed from day to day. Even if, as I hope, you arrive after our enemies have been defeated, the commonwealth will rise again and settle down in some tolerable shape under your leadership. There are a great many evils that will call for remedy, even if the commonwealth shall come to seem pretty well emancipated from the villainies of its enemies.

Good-bye.

426 (X.29)
CICERO TO APPIUS PULCHER MAJOR

Rome, 6 July 43

Cicero to Appius greetings.

Of my zeal for your welfare and restitution I believe your relatives' letters will have told you. I am sure that I

sime satis fecisse certo scio, nec iis concedo, quamquam
sunt singulari in te benevolentia, ut te salvum malint quam
ego; illi mihi necesse est concedant ut tibi plus quam ipsi
hoc tempore prodesse possim. quod quidem nec destiti facere nec desistam, et iam in maxima re feci et fundamenta
ieci salutis tuae. tu fac bono animo magnoque sis meque
tibi nulla re defuturum esse confidas.

Prid. Non. Quint.

427 (XI.22)

Scr. Romae in. m. Quint. (?) an. 43

M. CICERO S. D. D. BRUTO

1   Cum Appio Claudio C. f. summa mihi necessitudo est
multis eius officiis et meis mutuis constituta. peto a te
maiorem in modum vel humanitatis tuae vel mea causa ut
eum auctoritate tua, quae plurimum valet, conservatum
velis. volo te, cum fortissimus vir cognitus sis, etiam cle-
mentissimum existimari. magno tibi erit ornamento nobi-
lissimum adulescentem beneficio tuo esse salvum. cuius
quidem causa hoc melior debet esse quod pietate adductus propter patris restitutionem se cum Antonio coniunxit.
2   qua re etsi minus veram causam habebis, tamen †vel pro-
babilem†[1] aliquam poteris inducere.

Nu⟨tus⟩ tuus potest hominem summo loco natum,
summo ingenio, summa virtute, officiosissimum praeterea

---

[1] *del. SB olim*

---

[1] What this was cannot be determined.

have more than contented them; and signal as is their good will towards you, I cannot admit that any one of them is more anxious for your welfare than I. *They* must grant that at the present time I have more power than themselves to serve you, as I have never ceased and shall continue to do, and have already done in a matter of the greatest consequence[1] thereby laying the foundations of your welfare. On your side, be of good cheer and courage, and be confident that you may count on me in all matters.

6 July.

427 (XI.22)
CICERO TO D. BRUTUS

Rome, early July (?) 43

From M. Cicero to D. Brutus greetings.

I have the closest relations with Appius Claudius, son of Gaius, established by our many services to one another, rendered and received. May I particularly request you, whether for the sake of your own kindly nature or for my sake, to use your weighty public influence for his preservation? You are well known as a very brave man, and I want you to be considered a very merciful one. It will be a fine feather in your cap that a young man of the highest family should owe his civic existence to your kindness. His case ought to be improved by the fact that he joined Antony from a motive of filial affection on account of his father's restoration. So you will be able to put forward *some* excuse, even if you do not think it entirely convincing.

A nod from you can retain in the community a man of the highest birth, abilities, and character, one moreover

et gratissimum, incolumem in civitate retinere. quod ut facias ita a te peto ut maiore studio magisve ex animo petere
non possim.

428 (X.24)

Scr. in castris v Kal. Sext. an. 43

PLANCUS IMP. COS. DESIG. S. D. CICERONI

1   Facere non possum quin in singulas res meritaque tua
tibi gratias agam, sed mehercules facio cum pudore. neque
enim tanta necessitudo quantam tu mihi tecum esse voluisti desiderare videtur gratiarum actionem neque ego
libenter pro maximis tuis beneficiis tam vili munere de-
fungor orationis et malo praesens observantia, diligentia,
adsiduitate memorem me tibi probare. quod si mihi vita
contigerit, omnis gratas amicitias atque etiam pias propin-
quitates in tua observantia [indulgentia adsiduitate][1] vin-
cam; amor enim tuus ac iudicium de me utrum mihi plus
dignitatis in perpetuum an voluptatis cottidie sit adlaturus
non facile dixerim.

2   De militum commodis fuit tibi curae. quos ego non po-
tentiae meae causa (nihil enim me non salutariter cogitare
scio) ornari volui a senatu, sed primum quod ita meritos
iudicabam, deinde quod ad omnis casus coniunctiores rei
publicae esse volebam, novissime ut ab omni omnium sol-
licitatione aversos eos talis vobis praestare possem quales
adhuc fuerunt.

3   Nos adhuc hic omnia integra sustinuimus. quod consi-

[1] *(Or.)*

with a strong sense of obligation and gratitude. Let me request you to do so in all possible earnestness and sincerity.

428 (X.24)
PLANCUS TO CICERO

Camp in Gaul, 28 July 43

Plancus, Imperator, Consul-Elect, to Cicero greetings.

I cannot refrain from thanking you with respect to your services in this matter or that, but I assure you I do so with embarrassment. The intimate friendship which by your choice binds you and me does not seem to require expressions of gratitude. And it goes against the grain to acquit myself of your splendid benefactions with so cheap a commodity as words. I prefer to prove myself grateful in person by diligent and assiduous observance. If life is granted me, my devotion to you will transcend all gratitude of friends, all duteous observance of kin. For I should be hard put to it to say whether your affection and esteem will tend more to my lasting honour or to my pleasure from day to day.

You have been attending to my soldiers' interests. It was not for the sake of personal power (for I know that none but patriotic thoughts are in my mind) that I wished them to be provided for by the Senate, but, firstly, because I considered they deserved it; secondly, because I wished to strengthen their attachment to the commonwealth against all contingencies; and lastly, to enable me to guarantee you that their future behaviour will correspond to their past, proof against all solicitations from any quarter.

So far we have maintained the situation here entirely

lium nostrum, etsi quanta sit aviditas hominum non sine
causa ta‹m optabi›lis[2] victoriae scio, tamen vobis probari
spero. non enim, si quid in his exercitibus sit offensum,
magna subsidia res publica habet expedita quibus subito
impetu ac latrocinio parricidarum resistat. copias vero nostras notas tibi esse arbitror. in castris meis legiones sunt
veteranae tres, tironum vel luculentissima ex omnibus
una, in castris Bruti una veterana legio, altera bima, octo
tironum. ita universus exercitus numero amplissimus est,
firmitate exiguus. quantum autem in acie tironi sit committendum nimium saepe expertum habemus.

4   Ad hoc robur nostrorum exercituum sive Africanus
exercitus, qui est veteranus, sive Caesaris accessisset, ae-
quo animo summam rem publicam in discrimen deduce-
remus; aliquanto autem propius esse quod ad Caesarem
attinet videbamus. nihil destiti eum litteris hortari neque
ille intermisit adfirmare se sine mora venire, cum interim
aversum illum ab hac cogitatione ad alia consilia video se
contulisse. ego tamen ad eum Furnium nostrum cum mandatis litterisque misi, si quid forte proficere posset.

5   Scis tu, mi Cicero, quod ad Caesaris amorem attinet,
societatem mihi esse tecum, vel quod in familiaritate Caesaris vivo illo iam tueri eum et diligere fuit mihi necesse,
vel quod ipse, quoad ego nosse potui, moderatissimi atque
humanissimi fuit sensus, vel quod ex tam insigni amicitia

2 (SB)

---

[1] I.e. of the recently recruited legions.

uncompromised. I trust that this course meets with approval from you and your fellows, although I know the general and understandable impatience for a victory so much to be prayed for. If these armies meet with a reverse, the state has no large reserves in readiness to withstand a sudden brigand onslaught by these traitors. I think you know our forces. There are three veteran legions in my camp and one of recruits—a very fine one, the best of the lot.[1] In Brutus' camp there is one veteran legion, one of two years' service, and eight of recruits. The combined army is therefore very strong numerically, but meagre from the standpoint of reliability. We have seen only too often how much reliance can be placed on raw troops in battle.

If the power of our armies were augmented by the veteran African army or by Caesar's army, we should have no misgivings in staking the fate of the commonwealth on a decision. And we observe that in Caesar's case the distance is considerably less. I have continually urged him by letter, and he has never stopped affirming that he is coming without delay; but in the meanwhile I perceive that his mind has been diverted from that intention and shifted to other projects. However, I have sent our friend Furnius to him with a letter and an oral message in the hope that he may possibly be able to achieve something.

You are well aware, my dear Cicero, that so far as affection for Caesar is concerned you and I are partners. Even during the late Caesar's lifetime, as an intimate of his, I was bound to have a care and regard for the young man. So far as I could tell, his disposition was eminently moderate and gentle. By Caesar's decision and that of you all he has been given the place of Caesar's son, and I think it would be to

mea atque Caesaris hunc fili loco et illius et vestro iudicio
6 substitutum non proinde habere turpe mihi videtur. sed
(quicquid tibi scribo dolenter mehercules magis quam ini-
mice facio) quod vivit Antonius hodie, quod Lepidus una
est, quod exercitus habent non contemnendos [habent],
quod sperant, quod audent, omne Caesari acceptum referre possunt. neque ego superiora repetam; sed ex eo
tempore quo ipse mihi professus est se venire si venire vo-
luisset, aut oppressum iam bellum esset aut in aversissi-
mam illi⟨s⟩[3] Hispaniam cum detrimento eorum maximo
extrusum. quae mens eum aut quorum consilia a tanta
gloria, sibi vero etiam necessaria ac salutari, avocarit et ad
cogitationem consulatus semestris[4] summo cum terrore
hominum et insulsa cum efflagitatione transtulerit, ex-
7 putare non possum. multum in hac re mihi videntur necessarii eius et rei publicae et ipsius causa proficere posse,
plurimum, ut puto, tu quoque, cuius ille tanta merita habet
quanta nemo praeter me; numquam enim obliviscar maxima ac plurima me tibi debere. de his rebus ut exigeret cum
eo Furnio mandavi. quod si, quantam debeo, habuero
apud eum auctoritatem, plurimum ipsum iuvero.
8   Nos interea duriore condicione bellum sustinemus,
quod neque expeditissimam dimicationem putamus neque tamen refugiendo commissuri sumus ut maius detrimentum res publica accipere possit. quod si aut Caesar se
respexerit aut Africanae legiones celeriter venerint, secu-

[3] *(Man.)*
[4] bimes- *(Schütz)*

my discredit, considering the conspicuously friendly relations between Caesar and myself, if I did not look upon him as such. At the same time (and whatever I write to you, believe me, is written more in sorrow than in any spirit of ill will), the fact that Antony is alive today, that Lepidus is with him, that they have armies by no means contemptible, that their hopes and audacity run high—for all this they can thank Caesar. I will go no further back than the time when he himself professed to me to be coming: if he *had* chosen to come, the war would by now have been either quashed altogether or thrust back into Spain (a province thoroughly unfriendly to them) with heavy loss on their side. What he can be thinking of or whose advice has turned him away from so glorious a course, so necessary moreover and salutary to himself, and diverted him to this notion of a six-months' Consulship, which to the general consternation he is pushing with such tasteless persistence, is more than I can fathom. I imagine his connections can do a good deal in this matter, for the commonwealth's sake and his own; but you too, I think, can do most of all, since you have done more for him than for anyone in the world except myself—for I shall never forget the magnitude and number of my obligations to you. I have charged Furnius to go into these matters with him. If he pays as much attention to me as he ought, I shall have done him a great service.

Meanwhile we are bearing the brunt of the war in a situation of considerable difficulty. We do not see our way quite clear to a decisive engagement, and on the other hand we have no intention of risking further damage to the national cause by taking to our heels. If Caesar considers his own best interests, or if the African legions come up

ros vos ab hac parte reddemus.

Tu, ut instituisti, me diligas rogo proprieque tuum esse tibi persuadeas.

v Kal. Sext. ex castris.

429 (XII.21)

Scr. Romae an. 44 vel 43

CICERO CORNIFICIO

C. Anicius, familiaris meus, vir omnibus rebus ornatus, negotiorum suorum causa legatus est in Africam legatione libera. eum velim rebus omnibus adiuves operamque des ut quam commodissime sua negotia conficiat, in primisque, quod ei carissimum est, dignitatem eius tibi commendo idque a te peto quod ipse in provincia facere sum solitus non rogatus, ut omnibus senatoribus lictores darem; quod idem acceperam et id cognoveram a summis viris factitatum. hoc igitur, mi Cornifici, facies ceterisque rebus omnibus eius dignitati reique, si me amas, consules. erit mihi gratissimum.

Da operam ut valeas.

quickly, we shall free you from anxiety on this side.

Please maintain your regard for me, and be sure that I am thoroughly yours.

28 July, from camp.

429 (XII.21)
CICERO TO CORNIFICIUS

Rome, 44 or 43

From Cicero to Cornificius.

My friend C. Anicius, a man of quality in every sense of the word, has been appointed to a Free Commissionership to Africa for purposes of private business. I shall be grateful if you will give him every assistance, and do all you can to facilitate the smooth transaction of his affairs. In particular (something he has very much at heart) I would ask you to look after his personal dignity, and to do for him what I myself used to do for all Senators in my province without being asked: I granted them lictors, having received the same privilege myself and knowing it had been commonly done by persons of the highest eminence. So please do this as a friend, my dear Cornificius, and have regard for his prestige and material interests in all other respects. I shall take it very kindly.

Take care of your health.

430 (XII.24a)

Scr. Romae an. 44 vel 43

\<CICERO CORNIFICIO S.\>

T. Pinarium, familiarissimum meum, tanto tibi studio commendo ut maiore non possim. cui cum propter omnis virtutes tum etiam propter studia communia sum amicissimus. is procurat rationes negotiaque Dionysi nostri, quem et tu multum amas et ego omnium plurimum. ea tibi ego non debeo commendare, sed commendo tamen. facies igitur ut ex Pinari, gratissimi hominis, litteris tuum et erga illum et erga Dionysium studium perspiciamus.

431 (XII.26)

Scr. Romae an. 44 vel 43

\<CICERO CORNIFICIO S.\>

1   Q. Turius, qui in Africa negotiatus est, vir bonus et honestus, heredes fecit similis sui: Cn. Saturninum, Sex. Aufidium, C. Anneum, Q. Considium Gallum, L. Servilium Postumum, C. Rubellinum. ex eorum oratione intellexi gratiarum actione eos magis egere quam commendatione. tanta enim liberalitate se tua usos praedicabant ut iis plus a te tributum intellegerem quam ego te auderem ro-
2   gare. audebo tamen; scio enim quantum ponderis mea

---

[1] Cf. Letter 417.5.

430 (XII.24.A)
CICERO TO CORNIFICIUS

Rome, 44 or 43

I should like to recommend to you in the strongest possible way a very good friend of mine, T. Pinarius. I have a very warm regard for him, both for his generally admirable character and because of the pursuits we have in common. He is acting as accountant and general agent for our friend Dionysius,[1] for whom you have a considerable, and I a very special, affection. I ought not to recommend his affairs to *you,* but I do. So please see that Pinarius' letters (he is a very grateful sort of person) give me evidence of your interest both in him and in Dionysius.

431 (XII.26)
CICERO TO CORNIFICIUS

Rome, 44 or 43

From Cicero to Cornificius greetings.

Q. Turius, an honest and respectable gentleman who had business affairs in Africa, left as his heirs Cn. Saturninus, Sex. Aufidius, C. Anneus, Q. Considius Gallus, L. Servilius Postumus, and C. Rubellinus—men of his own stamp. From what they tell me I gather that an expression of thanks would be more to their purpose than a recommendation. They are so loud in praise of the handsome way you have treated them as to make it evident to me that you have done more for them than I should dare to ask. Dare, however, I shall, knowing how much weight my recommendation will carry. Let me therefore request of you

commendatio sit habitura. qua re a te peto ut ad eam liberalitatem qua sine meis litteris usus es quam maximus his
litteris cumulus accedat.

Caput autem est meae commendationis ne patiare Ero-
tem Turium, Q. Turi libertum, ut adhuc fecit, hereditatem
Turianam avertere ceterisque omnibus rebus habeas eos a
me commendatissimos. magnam ex eorum splendore et
observantia capies voluptatem. quod ut velis te vehementer etiam atque etiam rogo.

432 (XII.27)

Scr. Romae an. 44 vel 43

‹CICERO CORNIFICIO S.›

Sex. Aufidius et observantia qua me colit accedit ad
proximos et splendore equiti Romano nemini cedit. est autem ita temperatis moderatisque moribus ut summa severitas summa cum humanitate iungatur. cuius tibi negotia
quae sunt in Africa ita commendo ut maiore studio magisve ex animo commendare non possim. pergratum mihi
feceris si dederis operam ut is intellegat meas apud te litteras maximum pondus habuisse. hoc te vehementer, mi
Cornifici, rogo.

that your generosity, shown in ample measure without any letter of mine, may be increased as substantially as possible by what I now write.

The main point of my recommendation is that you should not allow Q. Turius' freedman Eros Turius to appropriate the estate, as he has done hitherto, and that in all other respects you regard the heirs as specially recommended by me. You may expect much gratification from the attentions of such distinguished persons. Let me again ask you very particularly to be good enough to act accordingly.

432 (XII.27)
CICERO TO CORNIFICIUS

Rome, 44 or 43

From Cicero to Cornificius greetings.

Sex. Aufidius is most attentive to me—my nearest intimates hardly more so—and there is no more distinguished member of the equestrian order. His personality is a singularly judicious blend of moral strictness and warm kindliness. Let me recommend to you his affairs in Africa in all earnestness and sincerity. I shall be deeply obliged if you make it apparent to him that my letter has carried great weight with you. My dear Cornificius, I ask this as a particular favour.

433 (XII.29)

Scr. Romae priore parte an. 43

CICERO CORNIFICIO SAL.

1   Non modo tibi, cui nostra omnia notissima sunt, sed neminem in populo Romano arbitror esse cui sit ignota ea familiaritas quae mihi cum L. Lamia est. etenim magno theatro spectata est tum cum est ab A. Gabinio consule relegatus quod libere et fortiter salutem meam defendisset. nec ex eo amor inter nos natus est, sed quod erat vetus et magnus, propterea nullum periculum pro me adire dubitavit. ad haec officia, vel merita potius, iucundissima consuetudo accedit, ut nullo prorsus plus homine delecter.

      Non puto te iam exspectare quibus eum tibi verbis commendem. causa enim tanti amoris intellegis quae ver-
2   ba desideret. iis me omnibus usum putato. tantum velim existimes, si negotia Lamiae, procuratores, libertos, familiam quibuscumque rebus opus erit defenderis, gratius mihi futurum quam si ea tua liberalitas pertinuisset ad rem familiarem meam. nec dubito quin sine mea commendatione, quod tuum est iudicium de hominibus, ipsius Lamiae causa studiose omnia facturus sis. quamquam erat nobis dictum te existimare alicui senatus consulto quod contra dignitatem tuam fieret scribendo Lamiam adfuisse; qui omnino consulibus illis numquam fuit ad scribendum; deinde omnia tum falsa senatus consulta deferebantur. nisi

---

[1] Literally 'when they (i.e. Antony and Dolabella) were Consuls,' i.e. in 44 after Caesar's death.

433 (XII.29)
CICERO TO CORNIFICIUS

Rome, spring (?) of 43

From Cicero to Cornificius greetings.

To say nothing of yourself, who are thoroughly familiar with all that concerns me, I suppose there is no man in all Rome who is ignorant of my friendship with L. Lamia. It came before the public eye on a grand stage when he was banished from Rome by Consul A. Gabinius for his free and intrepid defence of my status as a citizen. That was not the origin of our affection; on the contrary, he was ready to face any risk on my behalf just because of its strength and long standing. Besides these acts of friendship, or rather these benefactions, a most agreeable intimacy exists between us, and Lamia's society really gives me as much pleasure as that of anyone in the world.

After all this you will not be waiting to see what terms I use in recommending him. Where such affection exists, you know what terms are appropriate, and you are to suppose that I have used them all. I would only ask you to believe that if you protect Lamia's interests and assist his agents, freedmen, and household as occasion may require, I shall be more beholden to you than if your generosity had to do with my own finances. Knowing what a good judge of men you are, I do not doubt that you would do your utmost for Lamia's own sake without any recommendation from me. To be sure, I have been told that you are under the impression that Lamia witnessed the drafting of a certain decree derogatory to yourself. In fact, he never on any occasion witnessed a drafting that year;[1] furthermore, all manner of forged decrees were registered at that time. You

405

forte etiam illi Semproniano senatus consulto me censes
adfuisse, qui ne Romae quidem fui, ut tum de eo ad te
scripsi re recenti.

3   Sed haec hactenus. te, mi Cornifici, etiam atque etiam
rogo ut omnia Lamiae negotia mea putes esse curesque ut
intellegat hanc commendationem maximo sibi usui fuisse.
hoc mihi gratius facere nihil potes.

Cura ut valeas.

434 (XI.16)

Scr. Romae m. Mai. vel Iun. an. 43

M. CICERO D. BRUTO COS. DESIG. S. D.

1   Permagni interest quo tibi haec tempore epistula red-
dita sit, utrum cum sollicitudinis aliquid haberes an cum
ab omni molestia vacuus esses. itaque ei praecepi quem ad
te misi ut tempus observaret epistulae tibi reddendae. nam
quem ad modum coram qui ad nos intempestive adeunt
molesti saepe sunt, sic epistulae offendunt non loco redditae. si autem, ut spero, nihil te perturbat, nihil impedit,
et ille cui mandavi satis scite et commode tempus ad te
cepit adeundi, confido me quod velim facile a te impetraturum.

2   L. Lamia praeturam petit. hoc ego utor uno omnium
plurimum. magna vetustas, magna consuetudo intercedit
quodque plurimum valet, nihil mihi eius est familiaritate
iucundius. magno praeterea beneficio eius magnoque me-

---

² Cf. Letter 357, n.   ¹ Unduly sanguine, one might think,
but this is formulaic; see my Commentary.

might as well suppose that I was present at the drafting of that decree about Sempronius,[2] whereas in fact I was not even in Rome, as I wrote to you at the time just after the event.

But enough of that. Let me ask you again, my dear Cornificius, to look upon all Lamia's affairs as though they were mine, and to make sure that he realizes that this recommendation has been of the greatest service to him. You can do nothing to oblige me more.

Take care of your health.

434 (XI.16)
CICERO TO D. BRUTUS

Rome, May or June 43

From M. Cicero to D. Brutus, Consul-Elect, greetings.

A great deal depends on when this letter is delivered to you—whether at a time when you have something on your mind or when you are quite free from anxiety.[1] I have accordingly instructed the bearer to watch for the right moment to hand you his charge, for a letter delivered unseasonably often annoys us like an inopportune visitor. But if, as I hope, you have nothing to worry and distract you and my messenger chooses a sufficiently tactful and convenient time to make his approach, I am confident that the request I have to put to you will be readily granted.

L. Lamia is standing for the Praetorship. He is the most familiar friend I have. Our intimacy goes back a long way, and we have had a great deal to do with one another; but what counts most is that his friendship gives me as much pleasure as anything in life. Furthermore, I am indebted to

rito sum obligatus. nam Clodianis temporibus, cum equestris ordinis princeps esset proque mea salute acerrime
propugnaret, a Gabinio consule relegatus est; quod ante
id tempus civi Romano Romae contigit nemini. hoc cum
populus Romanus meminit, me ipsum non meminisse tur-
pissimum est.

3   Quapropter persuade tibi, mi Brute, me petere praeturam. quamquam enim Lamia summo splendore, summa
gratia est magnificentissimo munere aedilicio, tamen, quasi ea ita non essent, ego suscepi totum negotium. nunc, si
me tanti facis quanti certe facis, quoniam equitum centurias tenes inque iis[1] regnas, mitte ad Lupum nostrum ut
is nobis eas centurias conficiat. non tenebo te pluribus.
ponam in extremo quod sentio: nihil est, Brute, cum omnia
a te exspectem, quod mihi gratius facere possis.

435 (XI.17)

Scr. Romae eodem fere tempore quo ep. superior
[M.] CICERO [D.] BRUTO S. [D.][1]

1   L. Lamia uno omnium familiarissime utor. magna sunt
eius in me, non dico officia, sed merita eaque sunt populo
Romano notissima. is magnificentissimo munere aedilita-
tis perfunctus petit praeturam, omnesque intellegunt nec

---

[1] in quis *(Iac. Gron.)*   [1] *(SB, Schmieder secutus)*

---

[2] I.e. 'Knights with public horse'; cf. Letter 50, n. 2.
[1] The manuscripts say 'Decimus Brutus'; but this and the preceding letter could not have been written to the same person.

him for a great kindness and service. In Clodius' time, when he was a leading member of the Order of Knights and took a most active part in the campaign for my restoration, he was banished from town by Consul Gabinius, something that had never previously happened to a Roman citizen in Rome. The people of Rome remember this; for *me* not to remember it would be shameful indeed.

Therefore, my dear Brutus, I want you to believe that *I* am standing for the Praetorship. To be sure, Lamia is a most distinguished and influential figure, with a splendid aedilician show to his credit. But I have taken the whole business upon myself, as though none of that were in the case. Now you control the Centuries of Knights[2] and reign supreme in them. If you think as much of me as I know you do, send to our friend Lupus and tell him to make certain of these Centuries for us. I shall not keep you with further words. Let me just put down in conclusion what I feel. Though I expect of you any and every service, there is nothing, dear sir, that you could do to please me more.

435 (XI.17)
CICERO TO M. BRUTUS

Rome, May or June 43

From M. Cicero to M. Brutus[1] greetings.

L. Lamia is my most intimate friend. He has rendered me great services, I will not say as a friend but as a benefactor, and they are very well known to the People of Rome. Having fulfilled his duty as Aedile with a splendid show, he is standing for the Praetorship, and everyone is aware that he lacks neither public respect nor popularity. But the

dignitatem ei deesse nec gratiam. sed is ambitus excitari
videtur ut ego omnia pertimescam totamque petitionem
Lamiae mihi sustinendam putem.

2   In ea re quantum me possis adiuvare facile perspicio,
nec vero quantum mea causa velis dubito. velim igitur, mi
Brute, tibi persuadeas nihil me maiore studio a te petere,
nihil te mihi gratius facere posse quam si omnibus tuis
opibus, omni studio Lamiam in petitione iuveris. quod ut
facias, vehementer te rogo.

competition for the office seems to be becoming so unbridled that I fear anything may happen and feel I must take the whole business of Lamia's candidature upon myself.

How substantially you can help me in this matter I can easily perceive, nor do I doubt your good will towards me. Please believe then, my dear Brutus, that I have nothing to ask of you with greater urgency, and that you can do nothing to please me more than if you assist Lamia in his candidature with all your power and zeal. And I earnestly request you so to do.

APPENDIX

Roman Dates

Until Julius Caesar reformed the calendar the Roman year consisted of 355 days divided into twelve months, all of which bore the Latin forms of their present names except Quintilis (July) and Sextilis (August). Each month had 29 days, except February with 28 and March, May, July, and October with 31. The first, fifth and thirteenth days of each month were called the Kalends *(Kalendae),* Nones *(Nonae),* and Ides *(Idus)* respectively, except that in March, May, July, and October the Nones fell on the seventh and the Ides on the fifteenth. I have kept these names in translation.

The calendar was adjusted by means of intercalation. At the discretion of the College of Pontiffs, usually every other year, an intercalary month of 23 or 22 days was inserted after 24 or 23 February. But in the years immediately before the Civil War the College neglected this procedure, so that by 46 the calendar was well over two months in advance of the sun. Julius Caesar rectified the situation by inserting two intercalary months totalling 67 days between November and December of that year in addition to the traditional one in February. He also gave the months their present numbers of days, thus almost obviat-

ing the need for future intercalations, though in 1582 a further discrepancy had to be met by the institution of a leap year.

Roman Money

The normal unit of reckoning was the sesterce (HS), though the denarius, equal to 4 sesterces, was the silver coin most generally in use. Differences of price structure make any transposition into modern currency misleading. Sometimes sums are expressed in Athenian currency. The drachma was about equal to the denarius, the mina (100 drachmae) to HS400, and the talent (60 minae) to HS2,400. The Asiatic cistophorus was worth about 4 drachmae.

Roman Names

A Roman bore the name of his clan *(gens)*, the *nomen* or *nomen gentilicium,* usually ending in *ius,* preceded by a personal name *(praenomen)* and often followed by a *cognomen,* which might distinguish different families in the same *gens:* e.g., Marcus Tullius Cicero. The *nomen* was always, and the *cognomen* usually, hereditary. Sometimes, as, when a family split into branches, an additional *cognomen* was taken: e.g., Publius Licinius Crassus Dives. Other additional *cognomina* were honorific, sometimes taken from a conquered country as Africanus or Numidicus, or adoptive (see below). Women generally had only the one clan name (e.g., Tullia), which they retained after marriage.

Only a few personal names were in use and they are

414

generally abbreviated as follows: A. = Aulus; Ap(p). = Appius; C. = Gaius; Cn. = Gnaeus; D. = Decimus; K. = Kaeso; L. = Lucius; M. = Marcus; M'. = Manius; N. = Numerius; P. = Publius; Q. = Quintus; Ser. = Servius; Sex. = Sextus; Sp. = Spurius; T. = Titus; Ti. = Tiberius (I omit one or two which do not occur in our text). The use of a *praenomen* by itself in address or reference is generally a sign of close intimacy, whether real or affected, but in the case of a rare or distinctive praenomen, as Appius and Servius, this is not so.

The practice of adoption, of males at any rate, was very common in Rome. According to traditional practice the adopted son took his new father's full name and added his old *nomen gentilicium* with the adjectival termination *-ianus* instead of *-ius:* e.g., C. Octavius, adopted by C. Julius Caesar, became C. Julius Caesar Octavianus. But in Cicero's time the practice had become variable. Sometimes the original name remained in use.

A slave had only one name, and since many slaves came from the East, this was often Greek. If freed, he took his master's *praenomen* and *nomen,* adding his slave name as a *cognomen:* e.g., Tiro, when freed by M. Tullius Cicero, became M. Tullius Tiro. Occasionally the *praenomen* might be somebody else's. Atticus' slave Dionysius became M. Pomponius Dionysius in compliment to Cicero (instead of Titus).

Much the same applied to Greek or other provincials on gaining Roman citizenship. Such a man retained his former name as a *cognomen* and acquired the *praenomen* and *nomen* of the person to whom he owed the grant: e.g., the philosopher Cratippus became M. Tullius Cratippus after Cicero had got Caesar to give him the citizenship.

APPENDIX

For further information on names see my *Two Studies in Roman Nomenclature,* pp. 53–54 (Adoptive Nomenclature) and the introductions to my three Onomastica (to Cicero's Speeches, Letters, and Treatises).

Consuls, 68–43 B.C.

68	L. Caecilius Metellus
	Q. Marcius Rex
67	C. Calpurnius Piso
	M'. Acilius Glabrio
66	M'. Aemilius Lepidus
	L. Volcacius Tullus
65	L. Aurelius Cotta
	L. Manlius Torquatus
64	L. Julius Caesar
	C. Marcius Figulus
63	M. Tullius Cicero
	C. Antonius
62	D. Junius Silanus
	L. Licinius Murena
61	M. Pupius Piso Frugi
	M. Valerius Messalla Niger
60	Q. Caecilius Metellus Celer
	L. Afranius
59	C. Julius Caesar
	M. Calpurnius Bibulus
58	L. Calpurnius Piso Caesoninus
	A. Gabinius
57	P. Cornelius Lentulus Spinther
	Q. Caecilius Metellus Nepos
56	Cn. Cornelius Lentulus Marcellinus
	L. Marcius Philippus

APPENDIX

55 Cn. Pompeius Magnus
    M. Licinius Crassus
54 L. Domitius Ahenobarbus
    Ap. Claudius Pulcher
53 Cn. Domitius Calvinus
    M. Valerius Messalla
52 Cn. Pompeius Magnus (Sole Consul)
    . . . .
    Q. Caecilius Metellus Pius Scipio
51 Ser. Sulpicius Rufus
    M. Claudius Marcellus
50 L. Aemilius Paullus
    C. Claudius Marcellus
49 C. Claudius Marcellus
    L. Cornelius Lentulus Crus
48 C. Julius Caesar
    P. Servilius Isauricus
47 Q. Fufius Calenus
    P. Vatinius
46 C. Julius Caesar
    M. Aemilius Lepidus
45 C. Julius Caesar (Sole Consul)
    . . . .
    Q. Fabius Maximus (suffect)
    C. Trebonius (suffect)
    C. Caninius Rebilus (suffect)
44 C. Julius Caesar
    M. Antonius
    . . . .
    P. Cornelius Dolabella (suffect)
43 C. Vibius Pansa Caetronianus
    A. Hirtius

CONCORDANCE

Vulgate	This edition	Vulgate	This edition
I. 1	12	II. 13	93
I. 2	13	II. 14	89
I. 3	56	II. 15	96
I. 4	14	II. 16	154
I. 5a	15	II. 17	117
I. 5b	16	II. 18	115
I. 6	17	II. 19	116
I. 7	18	III. 1	64
I. 8	19	III. 2	65
I. 9	20	III. 3	66
I. 10	21	III. 4	67
II. 1	45	III. 5	68
II. 2	46	III. 6	69
II. 3	47	III. 7	71
II. 4	48	III. 8	70
II. 5	49	III. 9	72
II. 6	50	III. 10	73
II. 7	107	III. 11	74
II. 8	80	III. 12	75
II. 9	85	III. 13	76
II. 10	86	IV. 1	150
II. 11	90	IV. 2	151
II. 12	95	IV. 3	202

CONCORDANCE

Vulgate	This edition	Vulgate	This edition
IV. 4	203	V. 18	51
IV. 5	248	V. 19	152
IV. 6	249	V. 20	128
IV. 7	230	V. 21	182
IV. 8	229	VI. 1	242
IV. 9	231	VI. 2	245
IV. 10	233	VI. 3	243
IV. 11	232	VI. 4	244
IV. 12	253	VI. 5	239
IV. 13	225	VI. 6	234
IV. 14	240	VI. 7	237
IV. 15	241	VI. 8	235
V. 1	1	VI. 9	236
V. 2	2	VI. 10a	223
V. 3	11	VI. 10b	222
V. 4	10	VI. 11	224
V. 5	5	VI. 12	226
V. 6	4	VI. 13	227
V. 7	3	VI. 14	228
V. 8	25	VI. 15	322
V. 9	255	VI. 16	323
V. 10a	259	VI. 17	324
V. 10c	256	VI. 18	218
V. 10b	258	VI. 19	262
V. 11	257	VI. 20	247
V. 12	22	VI. 21	246
V. 13	201	VI. 22	221
V. 14	251	VII. 1	24
V. 15	252	VII. 2	52
V. 16	187	VII. 3	183
V. 17	23	VII. 4	199

CONCORDANCE

Vulgate	This edition	Vulgate	This edition
VII. 5	26	VIII. 3	79
VII. 6	27	VIII. 4	81
VII. 7	28	VIII. 5	83
VII. 8	29	VIII. 6	88
VII. 9	30	VIII. 7	92
VII. 10	33	VIII. 8	84
VII. 11	34	VIII. 9	82
VII. 12	35	VIII. 10	87
VII. 13	36	VIII. 11	91
VII. 14	38	VIII. 12	98
VII. 15	39	VIII. 13	94
VII. 16	32	VIII. 14	97
VII. 17	31	VIII. 15	149
VII. 18	37	VIII. 16	153
VII. 19	334	VIII. 17	156
VII. 20	333	IX. 1	175
VII. 21	332	IX. 2	177
VII. 22	331	IX. 3	176
VII. 23	209	IX. 4	180
VII. 24	260	IX. 5	179
VII. 25	261	IX. 6	181
VII. 26	210	IX. 7	178
VII. 27	148	IX. 8	254
VII. 28	200	IX. 9	157
VII. 29	264	IX. 10	217
VII. 30	265	IX. 11	250
VII. 31	267	IX. 12	263
VII. 32	113	IX. 13	311
VII. 33	192	IX. 14	326
VIII. 1	77	IX. 15	196
VIII. 2	78	IX. 16	190

CONCORDANCE

CONCORDANCE

CONCORDANCE

CONCORDANCE

GLOSSARY

ACADEMY (*Academia*): A hall (*gymnasium*) and park at Athens sacred to the hero Academus, in which Plato established his philosophical school. Hence Plato's school or system of philosophy, which went through various phases after his time. The terminology became confused, but Cicero recognized the 'Old Academy' of Plato and his immediate successors and the 'New' Academy of Arcesilas and Carneades, which maintained the uncertainty of all dogma and to which he himself professed to belong. In his own times this was modified by his teachers Philo of Larisa and Antiochus of Ascalon, the latter of whom claimed to represent the Old Academy with a system akin to Stoicism. Cicero gave the name 'Academy' to a hall which he built on his estate at Tusculum.

AEDILE (*aedilis*): Third in rank of the regular Roman magistracies. Four at this time were elected annually, two Curule and two Plebeian. They were responsible for city administration and the holding of certain public Games. The chief magistrates in some municipalities were also so called.

ASSEMBLY: I sometimes so translate *populus* or *comitia*, as describing the Roman people convened for electoral or legislative purposes. There were several different sorts

426

varying with the convening magistrate and the business to be done.

ATTIC(ISM): One use of the word was in connection with Roman oratory. In Cicero's time a movement principally represented by Calvus and M. Brutus favoured an austere style like that of the Athenian Lysias.

AUGUR: The priestly College of Augurs were official diviners interpreting signs (mostly from the flight and cries of wild birds or the behaviour of the Sacred Chickens) before major acts of public (and sometimes private) business. The College, like that of Pontiffs, was in practice almost a preserve of the nobility, so that for a 'new man' like Cicero membership was a coveted social distinction.

AUSPICES *(auspicia)*: Divination from birds or other signs was officially necessary as a preliminary to major acts by magistrates, who were said to 'have auspices,' i.e. the power of taking them.

BACCHUS' DAY *(Liberalia)*: The festival of Liber Pater, commonly identified with the Greek god Dionysius or Bacchus, and Libera on 17 March. It was the usual day for a coming of age ceremony.

BOARD OF FOUR: Municipalities (not Roman colonies) were commonly governed by four principal magistrates *(quattuorviri),* divided into two pairs *(duoviri),* and a senate of *decuriones.*

BONA DEA: See GOOD GODDESS.

BOY *(puer)*: Male slaves of any age were so called, as in later times.

CAMPANIAN LAND (DOMAIN, *ager Campanus*): Fertile land in Campania, originally confiscated by Rome in 211

and leased to small tenants. Caesar as Consul passed a bill (the Campanian Law) to distribute it among Pompey's veterans and the Roman poor.

CAMPUS (MARTIUS): The plain adjoining the Tiber on which assemblies of the Centuries were held, often for elections.

CENSOR: Two magistrates usually elected every five years for a tenure of eighteen months. They revised the roll of citizens, with property assessments, also the rolls of Knights and Senators, removing those deemed guilty of misconduct. They further supervised public contracts, including the lease of revenues to the tax farmers, and issued decrees as guardians of public morals.

CENTURIES, ASSEMBLY OF (*comitia centuriata*): Form of assembly in which voting took place by 'Centuries,' i.e. groups unequally composed so as to give preponderance to birth and wealth. It elected Consuls and Praetors, and voted on legislation proposed by them. The first Century to vote (*centuria praerogativa*) traditionally had a determining effect on the rest.

CENTURION: See LEGION.

COHORT: See LEGION.

COMITIAL DAYS: Days in the Roman calendar on which the popular assemblies (*comitia*) could legally be held. The Senate normally did not meet on these days.

COMITIUM: An area north of the Forum where assemblies were held.

COMMISSION, FREE or VOTIVE: See LEGATE.

COMPITALIA: See CROSSWAYS' DAY.

CONSUL: Highest of the annual Roman magistrates. Two were elected, usually in July, to take office on the following 1 January.

GLOSSARY

CONSULAR: An ex-Consul. The Consulars made up a corps of elder statesmen to whom the Senate would normally look for leadership.

CROSSWAYS' DAY *(Compitalia)*: Festival in honour of the Lares Compitales (gods of the crossroads) held annually soon after the Saturnalia on a day appointed by the Praetor.

CURIATE LAW *(lex curiata)*: A law passed by the Curies *(curiae)*, the oldest form of Roman assembly. In Cicero's time it survived only in form, each of the thirty Curies being represented by a lictor, but still had certain legislative functions, notably the passage of laws to confirm the executive authority *(imperium)* of individual magistrates; but the precise nature of these laws is much in doubt.

CURULE CHAIR *(sella curulis)*: Ivory chair, or rather stool, of state used by regular 'curule' magistrates, i.e. Consuls, Praetors, Curule Aediles, and certain others.

DICTATOR: A supreme magistrate with quasi-regal powers appointed to deal with emergencies under the early Republic; his second-in-command, the Master of the Horse, was appointed by himself. The office was revived to legitimize the autocratic regimes of Sulla and Julius Caesar.

EDICT: A public announcement or manifesto issued by a magistrate. The name applied to the codes issued by City Praetors and provincial governors at the beginning of their terms setting out the legal rules which they intended to follow.

EPICUREANISM: A materialistic school of philosophy named after its founder Epicurus, much in vogue among the Roman intelligentsia in Cicero's time.

GLOSSARY

EQUESTRIAN ORDER: See KNIGHTS.

ETESIAN WINDS *(etesiae)*: Northerly winds which blew every year during the dog days.

FASCES: Bundles of rods carried by lictors in front of magistrates as a symbol of authority. Those of victorious generals were wreathed in laurel.

FLAMEN: Priest in charge of the cult of a particular deity. There were fifteen, three (those of Jupiter, Mars, and Quirinus) being superior to the rest.

FORUM: The chief square of Rome, centre of civic life.

FREEDMAN *(libertus)*: A manumitted slave.

GAMES *(ludi)*: Gladiatorial and other shows, some recurring annually and supervised by magistrates, others put on for an occasion by private individuals. Of the former the Roman Games *(ludi Romani)* were held from 5 to 19 September, the Games of Apollo *(ludi Apollinares)* from 5 to 13 July. 'Greek Games' seem to have consisted of performances of Greek plays in the original language.

GOOD GODDESS *(Bona Dea)*: A goddess whose worship was confined to women. Her yearly festival was held in the house of a Consul or Praetor and supervised by his wife.

GOWN *(toga)*: Formal civilian dress of a Roman citizen. The gown of boys and curule magistrates *(toga praetexta)* had a purple hem. At sixteen or seventeen on coming of age a boy was given his White (or Manly) Gown *(toga pura, toga virilis)*.

GREEK GAMES: See GAMES.

GREEKS: In Cicero's time the word was loosely used to include the more or less hellenized inhabitants of Western Asia and Egypt as well as those of Greece proper and the old Greek settlements elsewhere.

HONEST MEN: So I translate Cicero's *boni* (good men, *les gens de bien*), a semipolitical term for people of substance and respectability, supporters of the established order. Their opposites he calls *improbi* (rascals).

IMPERATOR: Commander of a Roman army. But at this period the title was conferred on generals by their soldiers after a victory and retained until they relinquished their imperium.

IMPERIUM: Literally 'command'; the executive authority appertaining to higher magisterial and promagisterial office.

INTERREX, INTERREGNUM: If through death or otherwise the consular office stood vacant and no patrician magistrates holding *imperium* were in office, an Interrex was appointed from among the patrician members of the Senate to exercise consular functions for five days. He was then replaced by another Interrex, and so on until new Consuls could be elected.

KNIGHTS *(equites)*: In effect non-Senators of free birth possessing property over a certain level. They were regarded as forming a class of their own *(ordo equestris)* with special privileges and insignia.

LATIN FESTIVAL *(Feriae Latinae)*: Movable annual festival of the Romano-Latin League held on Mt Alba. Its date was determined from year to year by the Consuls.

LECTURE HALL *(gymnasium)*: The Greek gymnasium was originally a sports ground containing a *palaestra* (which see). But literature, philosophy, and music were also taught in them.

LEGATE *(legatus)*: A provincial governor took several Legates, normally Senators, on his staff as deputies. Caesar in Gaul made them commanders of legions. The duties

431

might, however, be purely nominal. The Senate could also appoint its members to 'free' or 'votive' (i.e. to discharge a vow) *legationes,* thus enabling them to travel abroad with official status. I sometimes translate with 'commission(er).' The word can also be used for any kind of envoy.

LEGION: Roman army unit with a full complement of 6,000 men divided into ten cohorts. Each legion was officered by six Military Tribunes. Each cohort had six Centurions, the highest in rank being called *primi pili* (Chief Centurion). The ensign of a Legion was an eagle, and each cohort had its standard *(signum).*

LÈSE-MAJESTÉ *(maiestas)*: The term *maiestas* covered acts 'in derogation of the majesty of the Roman People,' as of magistrates or governors exceeding the bounds of their authority.

LEX CORNELIA *(de provinciis)*: Law of Sulla regulating provincial administration.

LEX CURIATA: See CURIATE LAW.

LEX GABINIA: A law of 67 or 58 forbidding or restricting loans from Roman citizens to provincials.

LEX JULIA *(de provinciis)*: Consular law of Caesar's on provincial administration.

LEX JUNIA-LICINIA: A law of 62 requiring that copies of proposed legislation be deposited in the Treasury.

LEX POMPEIA: Pompey's law against electoral corruption in 52.

LEX ROSCIA: A law of 67 assigning the first fourteen rows in the theatre to the Knights (the Senate sat below in the Orchestra).

GLOSSARY

LEX SCANTINIA: A law of uncertain date penalizing homosexual acts committed upon persons of free birth.

LIBERALIA: See BACCHUS' DAY.

LICTOR: Official attendant of persons possessing magisterial authority *(imperium),* the number varying with the rank.

LUPERCALIA: Fertility festival on 25 February held in a cave below the Palatine Hill by the Luperci. There were two Colleges of these until 45–44, when Caesar added a third called the *Luperci Iulii.*

MANUMISSION: Process of freeing a slave. This could be done either formally or informally ('between friends'), but in the latter case the master could revoke it at will.

MILE *(mille passus):* The Roman mile was 1,618 yards.

MIME *(mimus):* Type of entertainment with dancing, music, and dialogue which became highly popular in the first century B.C. It was considered more sophisticated and risqué than the Atellan Farce, which it virtually superseded.

MINERVA'S DAY *(Quinquatrus):* Festival of Minerva on 19 March.

NOBILITY: Practically, a noble *(nobilis)* at this period meant a direct descendant of a Consul in the male line. In the early Republic the Roman community was divided into patricians and plebeians, the former holding a virtual monopoly of political power. But after the Consulship was thrown open to plebeians in the fourth century many plebeian families became 'noble,' and the remaining patricians were distinguished chiefly by their ineligibility to hold both Consulships in one year and for

433

the plebeian offices of Tribune and Plebeian Aedile. They also wore special insignia.

NOMENCLATOR: A slave whose duty it was to remind his master of the names of clients and acquaintances whom he happened to meet.

OPS: Roman goddess in whose temple on the Capitol Caesar deposited the state treasure.

OPTIMATES: Literally 'those belonging to the best'—the leading conservatives in the Senate and their supporters throughout the community. Sometimes the term is practically equivalent to the 'honest men' (boni), though more purely political in its implications.

OVATION: A lesser form of Triumph.

PALAESTRA: A space surrounded by colonnades, found in all gymnasia. Literally 'wrestling school' (Greek).

PATRICIANS: See NOBILITY.

PAYMASTER TRIBUNES (tribuni aerarii): At this time probably a class similar to the Knights but with a lower property qualification. Under the lex Aurelia of 70, juries were composed in equal numbers of Senators, Knights, and Paymaster Tribunes.

PLEBEIANS: See NOBILITY.

PONTIFF (pontifex): These formed a priestly College in general charge of Roman religious institutions (including the Calendar), presided over by the Chief Pontiff (pontifex maximus), who was Julius Caesar from 63 until his death.

PRAETOR: Second in rank of the annual magistracies. Eight were elected at this period until Caesar increased the number to twenty. The City Praetor (praetor urbanus) was in charge of the administration of justice between Roman citizens, others presided over the stand-

ing criminal courts. After his year of office a Praetor normally went to govern a province as Propraetor or Proconsul.

PRAETORIAN COHORT *(cohors praetoria)*: A special military unit forming a general's bodyguard.

PREFECT: Officer appointed by a magistrate (usually as provincial governor) for military or civil duties. These might be only nominal, the appointment merely conferring official status and privileges. The Prefect of Engineers *(praefectus fabrum)* acted as adjutant to his chief—no longer any connection with engineers.

PROCONSUL *(pro consule)*: 'Acting Consul,' one who, not holding the office, exercised consular authority outside Rome by senatorial appointment. Similarly Propraetor *(pro praetore)* and Proquaestor *(pro quaestore).*

PROSCRIPTION *(proscriptio)*: A procedure first employed by Sulla, then by the Triumvirs in 43. Lists of names were published, the persons thus 'proscribed' being declared outlaws and their goods confiscated. Their killers were rewarded, their protectors punished.

QUAESTOR: The first stage in the regular 'course of offices,' election to which carried life membership of the Senate. Since Sulla's time twenty were elected annually. The two City Quaestors *(quaestores urbani)* had charge of the Treasury and the Quaestors assigned to provincial governors (usually by lot) were largely concerned with finance.

QUARTAN: A fever recurring every third day; less grave therefore than a tertian, which recurred every other day.

QUIRINUS' DAY (Quirinalia): Festival in honour of Quirinus (the deified Romulus, founder of Rome) on 17 February.

RESOLUTION *(auctoritas)*: A decree of the Senate vetoed by a Tribune was sometimes recorded under this name.

ROSTRA: The speakers' platform in the comitium, so called from the beaks *(rostra)* of captured warships which decorated it.

SATURNALIA: Festival of Saturn beginning on 17 December, marked by merrymaking reminiscent of modern Christmas, to which it contributed some elements.

SECRETARY: I so translate (with a capital letter) Latin *scriba*. The 'scribes' were a corporation of civil servants working in the Treasury and otherwise. City magistrates and provincial governors might be assigned official Secretaries for their personal assistance. Private clerks were called *librarii*.

SENATE: Governing body of the Roman Republic, numbering about 600 (increased to 900 by Caesar) and composed of magistrates and ex-magistrates.

SHEPHERDS' DAY *(Parilia)*: Festival of the god and goddess Pales, protectors of flocks and herds, on 21 April.

SOPHIST: A professional 'wise man,' making money as a teacher and lecturer, often itinerant.

STOICISM: Philosophical school, named from the portico *(stoa)* in which its founder, Zeno of Citium (ca. 300), taught. Cato was its most prominent Roman adherent in Cicero's time.

SUMPTUARY LAW: A series of laws during the Republic attempted to impose restrictions on luxury spending, especially on food. One was enacted by Julius Caesar in 46.

SUPPLICATION *(supplicatio)*: A thanksgiving ceremony decreed by the Senate in honour of a military success, the number of days varying according to the importance

of the victory. It was generally regarded as a preliminary to a Triumph,

TABLETS *(codicilli)*: Wooden tablets coated with wax and fastened together with thread, used for memoranda and short notes.

TAX FARMERS *(publicani)*: Roman taxes, as on grazing land in the provinces or excise, were largely farmed out by the Censors to private companies who bid for the right of collection. The capitalists in Rome as well as their local agents were called *publicani*. In political terms *publicani* and Knights often amount to the same thing.

TELLUS: Earth goddess, whose temple was one of the meeting places of the Senate.

TESTIMONIAL: Renders *laudatio* (eulogy) in one of its senses. It was customary for defendants to ask prominent persons to offer witness to their good character in court either orally or in writing.

TETRARCH: Literally 'ruler over a fourth part.' In Cicero's time many minor eastern princes were called by this title.

TOGA: See GOWN.

TREASURY *(aerarium)*: The Roman state treasury was in the temple of Saturn in the Forum, managed by the City Quaestors with the assistance of Secretaries.

TRIBE *(tribus)*: A division, mainly by locality, of the Roman citizen body. The number had risen over the centuries from three to thirty-five (four of them 'urban,' the rest 'rustic'). Assemblies voting by tribes *(comitia tributa)* elected magistrates below Praetor and could pass legislation proposed by Tribunes.

TRIBUNE: (1) Of the Plebs. A board of ten, originally appointed to protect plebeians from patrician high-hand-

edness. They had wide constitutional powers, the most important being that any one of them could veto any piece of public business, including laws and senatorial decrees. They could also initiate these. They took office on 10 December. (2) Military: See LEGION. (3) See PAY-MASTER TRIBUNES.

TRIUMPH: Victory celebration by a general on his return to Rome. Permission had to be granted by the Senate.

UNIFORM: Magistrates leaving to take command of armies wore the general's red cloak (*paludamentum*) and were said to set out *paludati*.

VALUATION (*aestimatio*): Process by which a debtor's property could be transferred to his creditor in settlement. Caesar made such transfers compulsory on terms favourable to the debtor.

WEAL: The goddess Salus, who had a temple on the Quirinal Hill near Atticus' house.

INDEX

References are to Latin text, by letter and paragraph. A superscript letter r indicates that the order of words or names in the entry is reversed.

INDEX

445

447

INDEX

Dyrrachium (on the west coast of Macedonia, *Durazzo*) 8.7; 9.4

Egnatius Rufus, L. (Roman Knight) 268.1,2; 269; 270; 271; 273.1; 274
Egypt *see* Aegyptus
Eleutherocilices ('Free Cilicians') 110.10
Elis (on the west coast of the Peloponnese) 292.2
Epaminondas (Theban general and statesman) 22.5
Ephesus (on the west coast of Asia Minor, chief town of the province of Asia) 68.5; 73.3; 103.2; 128.9; 129.1; 131.1; 133.2; 134.1; 297.1
    Ephesii 134.1
Epicrates (prominent Athenian) 337.5
Epictetus (part of Phrygia) 73.6
Epicurus (philosopher) 63.3,4; 193.1; 210.1; 216.2. *Cf.* 213.1. *See also* Gargettius
    Epicurius (-reus) 35.1; 63.2; 215.1 (Ἐπικούρειος).
    -rii 114.2. *Cf.* 63.4; 215.1.
    Ἐπικούρειος (adj.) 72.2
Epidaurus (on the east coast of the Peloponnese) 253.1
Epiphanea (in Cilicia) 110.7,8
Epirus (region opposite Corcyra) 8.3; 9.4
    Epiroticae res 284.2
Eporedia (in the foothills of the Pennine Alps) 401.4; 402.2
Eppius, M. (senator) 84.5,6

Eppuleia (wife of T. Ampius) 226.3
Erana (in the Amanus mountains) 110.9
Eros *see* Turius Eros, Q.?
Etruria *(Tuscany)* 234.8; 385.4
    Etrusca disciplina 234.3
Euphrates (river) 87.1; 103.1; 104.1,2
Euripides (tragic dramatist) 147.2; 317.2 (Εὐριπίδης)
Euthydemus (of Mylasa, celebrated orator) 131.1
Eutrapelus *see* Volumnius Eutrapelus
Evander *see* Avianius Evander, C.

Fabatus *see* Roscius Fabatus, L.
(Fabia) (wife of Dolabella) *cf.* 88.1
Fabius (Gallus), Q. (brother of the following) 114.3
Fabius Gallus, M. (friend of Atticus and Cicero, formerly miscalled Fadius) 89; 106.1,2; 114.2,3; 141; 209.1; 260.1; 261.2. Cicero's letters to him: 209; 210; 260; 261
(Fabius Maximus, Q.) (cos. 213) *cf.* 249.1
Fabius Maximus (Sanga?), Q. (cos. suff. 45) 265.1
Fabius Maximus Verrucosus, Q. (Cunctator) 249.1
Fabius Vergilianus, Q. (legate of Ap. Claudius) 66.1,2; 67.1
Fabrateria (Nova) (in Latium) 362.1

452

INDEX

INDEX

Herculanensis, fundus 114.3

Hercules Xenophontius 22.3

Herennius Gallus (actor at Gades) 415.2

Heres *see* Planius Heres, M.

Hermia (freedman of Cicero?) 42.1,2

Herodotus (historian) 22.7

Hesiodus 218.5

Hilarus (freedman of Cn. Otacilius Naso) 304

Hippia(s) (of Calacte) 308

Hippianus *see* Valgius Hippianus, C.

Hippius, Q. 62.1

(Hipponax) (satirical poet) Hipponacteum praeconium 260.1

Hirrus, 'Hillus' *see* Lucilius Hirrus, C.

Hirtius, A. (cos. 43) 181.1; 190.7; 192.1; 193.2; 226.2; 325.1,4–6; 346.2; 350.2; 360.2; 365.2; 378.1,4,5; 383.1; 388.1; 392; 405.5; 409.3–5. *Cf.* 191.1; 352.1–2

Hirtianum ius 191.3.
Hirtinum proelium 409.4

Hispalis *(Seville)* 415.3

IIIspania 70.10; 146.3,4; 153.4; 156.1; 207.2; 209.4; 213.1; 214.3; 234.5; 311.1; 316.3; 428.6

Hispaniae 150.1; 153.3; 157.2; 216.4; 218.2. Hispania citerior 20.13 Hispani 218.2. Hispaniensis casus 154.6

Hispo *see* Terentius Hispo, P.

Homerus 22.7; 74.5; 317.2; 389.2

Horatius (legate of Calvisius Sabinus) 417.7

Hortensius Hortalus, Q. (cos. 69) 12.3; 13.1,2; 16.2; 18.2; 70.9; 78.1; 94.2; 154.3

Hydrus (port in the heel of Italy, south of Brundisium, *Otranto*) 127.2

Hypsaeus *see* Plautius Hypsaeus, P.

Iamblichus (phylarch (emir) of Emesa in Syria) 104.2

Iconium (in Lycaonia, *Konya*) 68.4; 69.6; 70.4,5; 71.4; 103.1; 110.2

Inalpini (inhabitants of the Alps) 342.1

(Insubri) (tribe of Cisalpine Gaul) Insuber (Catius) 215.1

Intimilii (tribe of Liguria) 149.2

Isara (tributary of the Rhône, *Isère*) 390.3; 391.2; 395.2,4; 414.3; 418.1

(Isauria) (region in southern Aaia Minor) Isauri 105.1

(Isocrates) (Athenian rhetorician and publicist) Isocratia ratio oratoria 20.23

Issus (in the southeast corner of Cilicia) 86.3

Italia 2.1,8; 8.3,7; 20.13,16; 32.3; 50.1; 66.1; 87.1; 119.2; 125.2; 127.2; 143.3; 149.1;

455

INDEX

INDEX

Lucullus *see* Terentius Varro Lucullus, M.

Lupercal (grotto at the foot of the Palatine) 333.1

Lupus (friend or agent of D. Brutus) 343; 353.1; 354.1; 394.1; 420.1; 434.3

Lupus *see* Rutilius Lupus, P.

Lusitania (region of southwestern Spain) 409.3

Lutatius Catulus, Q. (cos. 78) 196.3

Lycaonia (region in central Asia Minor) 104.2; 105.1; 110.2 Lycao(n) 73.10

Lycia (region on the south coast of Asia Minor between Caria and Pamphylia) 405.1; 406.2,5

Lynceus 177.2

Lysippus (sculptor) 22.7

Lyso (of Lilybaeum) 305. His father and granfather *ibid.*

Lyso (of Patrae) 123.1,2; 124.1; 127.3,4; 285.1–3; 290.1–3. His son 285.2

Maccius Plautus, T. (author of comedies) 190.4

Macedonia 6.3; 28?.3,4; 406.1 Macedonicae, legiones 347.2

Macula *see* Pompeius? Macula

Maecius Tarpa, Sp. (chairman of the Poets' Guild?) 24.1

Maenius Gemellus, C. (client of Cicero) 285.2

Magius Cilo, P.? (friend and

murderer of M. Marcellus) 253.2

Magnus *see* Pompeius Magnus

Maleae (promontory at the southeast end of the Peloponnese, *Malia*) 253.1

Mamercius, Q. (Roman Knight of Arpinum) 278.1

Manilius (jurist) 29.2; 33.2

Manilius, M'. (cos. 149) 331

Manlius, T. (in business in Thespiae) 288.1,2

Manlius Sosis, L. 301.1. His brother *ibid.*

Manlius Torquatus, A. (pr. 70?) 242.2. Cicero's letters to him: 242–45

Manlius (Torquatus?) Acidinus 253.2

Mantinea (in Arcadia, scene of battle between Spartans and Thebans) 22.5

Marcellinus, Marcellini *see* Cornelius (-lii) Lentulus (-li) Marcellinus (-li)

Marcellus, Marcelli *see* Claudius (-dii) Marcellus (-li); Mindius Marcellus, M.

Marcilius, M.? (Cicero's interpreter) 132

Marcilius, M. (son of the foregoing) 132

Marcius Crispus, Q. (procos. 44–43) 366.1; 387.3

Marcius? Figulus, L. (naval commander under Dolabella) 419.3

Marcius Philippus, L. (cos. 56)

459

INDEX

INDEX

Peloponnesus 200.1

Perga (-ge) (on the coast of Pamphylia) 405.8; 406.7

Pescennius (friend of Cicero) 6.6

Pessinus (in Galatia) 95.2

Petreius, M. (pr. 63?) 146.4

Petrinum (mountain and district near Sinuessa) 262.1

Phaedria (character in Terence) 20.19

Phaedrus (Epicurean) 63.2,4,5

(Phalerum) (Attic deme)
Phalereus *see* Demetrius Phalereus

Phamea 190.8. 260.2

Phania (freedman of Ap. Claudius) 64.1,2; 68.3; 69.1,2; 93.2. *Cf.* 70.5

Pharnaces (king of Bosporus) 174.2

Philargyrus (freedman or slave of A. Torquatus) 242.6

Philemo *see* Aemilius Philemo

Phileros (courier) 196.1

Philhetaerus *see* Clodius Philhetaerus

Philippus (of Lacedaemon) 295.1

Philippus *see* Marcius Philippus

Philo (Academic philosopher) 63.2; 254.1

Philo (freedman of Caelius Rufus) 84.10; 95.2

Philo *see* Clodius Philo, C.

Philocles (of Alabanda) 131.2

Philoctetes (in Accius' play) 192.1

Philomelium (in Phrygia) 70.5,6; 110.2; 268.1

Philotimus (freedman of Terentia) 72.1; 79.2; 144.2; 170. *Cf.* 151.1

Philotimus (identity uncertain) 151.1

Philoxenus (of Calacte) 308

Philoxenus *see* Avianius Philoxenus, M.

(Phocis) (region to the north of Boeotia)
Phocicum bellum 22.2

(Phrygia) (region in west-central Asia Minor)
Phryx 73.10

Pilius Celer, Q. (brother? of Atticus' wife) 84.2,3

Pinarius, T. 430

Pindenissum (hill town in Cilicia) 86.3; 110.10

Pinnius, T. 135

Pinnius, T.? (son of the foregoing) 135

Piraeus (port of Athens) 248.4; 253.1,2

Pisaurum (on the coast south of Ariminum *Pesaro*) 146.2

Piso *see* Calpurnius Piso

Pius *see* Caecilius Metellus Pius Scipio, Q.

Plaetorius, M. (friend of Lentulus Spinther) 19.1

Plancius, Cn. (quaest. 58) 8.3; 127.2; 247.1. Cicero's letters to him: 240, 241

Plancus *see* Munatius Plancus; Plautius Plancus, L.

INDEX

Quinquatrus 95.1; 373.1
Quintus *see* Cornificius (373.5),
Tullius Cicero, Q.

Rabirius Postumus, C. *see*
Curtius Postumus, C.
Racilius, L. (tr. pl. 56) 18.2. *Cf.*
20.15
Ravenna *(Ravenna)* 20.9; 77.4
Regium *(Reggio,* at the toe of
Italy) 334; 373.3
Regium Lepidi (west of Mutina,
Reggio Emilia) 365.2; 380.2
    Regienses 320.4
Regulus *see* Livineius Regulus
Rex (Marcius or Rupilius?) 312.
    Cicero's letter to him: 312
Rhodanus (Rhône river) 379.3;
    382.2; 396.1
Rhodo 115.1
Rhodos *(Rhodes)* 117.1; 183.5;
    230.4; 325.3; 349.8; 406.2,5
    Rhodii 405.2,3; 406.2,3
Roma or urbs *passim*
    Romanus, civis (-ni, cives)
    259.1; 301.1; 307.2; 406.1;
    408.1; 415.3; 434.2. -nus,
    eques (-ni, equites) 61; 82.4;
    136; 268.1; 271; 278 1, 281.1;
    302.1; 309; 372.1; 432. -ni,
    ludi 84.1. *See also* Circenses
    ludi. -nus, mos 26.3; 32.3ʳ
    37.3. -nus, populus 5.2;
    14.2,3; 20.20; 101.1; 102.1;
    104.2,3,5; 105.2,5,7; 110.5;
    117.4; 148.2; 234.9; 248.4;
    318.2; 344.2; 346.2; 353.2;
    354.2; 364.2; 365.3; 370.2;

377.4; 397.1,3; 409.5; 416.2;
422.1; 433.1; 434.2; 435.1.
imperium populusque
Romanus 406.2. senatus
populusque Romanus 25.2;
70.3; 110.13; 318.2,3; 353.3;
360.1; 361.2; 370.1; 406.2;
422.1
    -nae res 89. -nus, rusticus
337.7. -ni sales 196.2
Roscius Fabatus, L. (pr. 49)
409.4
Roscius Gallus, Q. (actor in
comedy) 189.1
Rubellinus, C. (one of Q.
Turius' heirs) 431.1
Rubria (mother of C. Carbo)
188.3
Rufio (slave or freedman of
Trebatius) 333.1
Rufrenus, T.? (tr. pl. 43) 391.4
(Rufreni)
Rufus (friend of Papirius
Paetus) 362.1
Rufus cognomen to the follow-
ing: Caelius, Egnatius,
Mescinius, Sextilius,
Titurnius, Titius
Rullus *see* Servilius Rullus, P.
Rupa (Curio's agent in charge?)
47.1
Rupilius (Rex?), P. (chairman of
the Bithynian Company)
139.2
Rutilius *(or* (Sempronius)
Rutilus?) Cicero's letter to
him: 321
Rutilius Lupus, P. (tr. pl. 56)
12.3; 13.2

467

INDEX

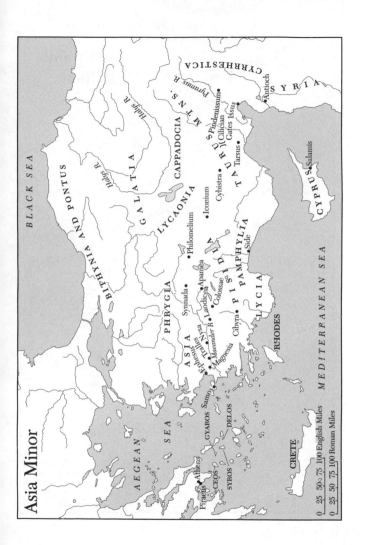

Asia Minor

BLACK SEA

BITHYNIA AND PONTUS

Sangarius R.

Halys R.

GALATIA

CAPPADOCIA

LYCAONIA

Iconium

PHRYGIA

Philomelium

Synnada

Apamea

Laodicea

Colossae

PISIDIA

Maeander R.

Tralles

Nysa

Magnesia

Cibyra

PAMPHYLIA

Side

LYCIA

ASIA

Ephesus

RHODES

Samos

GYAROS

CEOS

SYROS

DELOS

Athens

Piraeus

AEGEAN SEA

MEDITERRANEAN SEA

CRETE

CYPRUS

Salamis

TAURUS MTS.

Pindenissum

Cilician Gates

Issus

Cybistra

Tarsus

Pyramus R.

Antioch

SYRIA

CYRRHESTICA

0 25 50 75 100 English Miles
0 25 50 75 100 Roman Miles

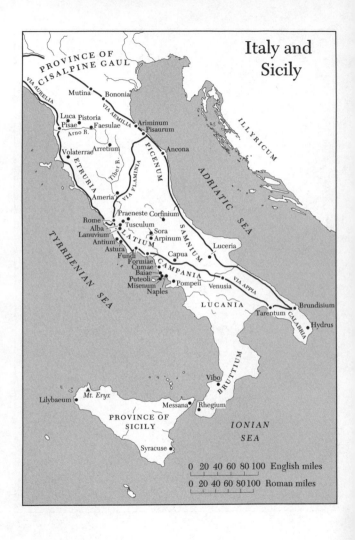

Italy and Sicily

PROVINCE OF CISALPINE GAUL

VIA AURELIA

VIA AEMILIA

Mutina • Bononia

Luca Pistoria
Pisae • Faesulae
Arno R.

Ariminum
Pisaurum

Volaterrae
Arretium

ETRURIA

Tiber R.

VIA FLAMINIA

PICENUM

Ancona

ILLYRICUM

ADRIATIC SEA

Ameria

Praeneste Corfinium

Rome • Tusculum
Alba
Lanuvium • Sora
Antium • Arpinum
Astura
Fundi
Formiae
Cumae
Baiae
Puteoli
Misenum
Naples

SAMNIUM

LATIUM

Capua

CAMPANIA

Pompeii

Luceria

VIA APPIA

Venusia

Brundisium

Tarentum

CALABRIA

Hydrus

TYRRHENIAN SEA

LUCANIA

BRUTTIUM

Vibo

Lilybaeum • Mt. Eryx

Messana

Rhegium

PROVINCE OF SICILY

IONIAN SEA

Syracuse •

0 20 40 60 80 100 English miles

0 20 40 60 80 100 Roman miles

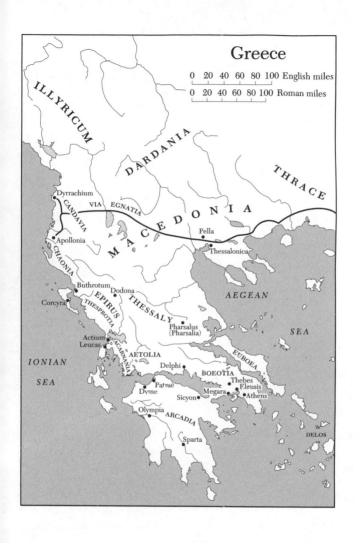

Greece

0 20 40 60 80 100 English miles

0 20 40 60 80 100 Roman miles

ILLYRICUM

DARDANIA

THRACE

MACEDONIA

Dyrrachium

VIA EGNATIA

CANDAVIA

Pella

Apollonia

Thessalonica

CHAONIA

Buthrotum

Dodona

AEGEAN

Corcyra

THESPROTIA

EPIRUS

THESSALY

Actium

Pharsalus

Leucas

(Pharsalia)

ACARNANIA

SEA

AETOLIA

EUBOEA

Delphi

IONIAN

BOEOTIA

Thebes

SEA

Patrae

Eleusis

Dyme

Megara

Athens

Sicyon

Olympia

ARCADIA

DELOS

Sparta

*Composed in ZephGreek and ZephText by
Technologies 'N Typography, Merrimac, Massachusetts.
Printed in Great Britain by St Edmundsbury Press Ltd,
Bury St Edmunds, Suffolk, on acid-free paper.
Bound by Hunter & Foulis Ltd, Edinburgh, Scotland.*